P9-AGA-191

"In *Improbable Planet*, Ross holds readers' hands, leading them in a readable yet gently technical format through a compelling layer-upon-layer argument for the distinctiveness of the planet on which we live and of the preparation for inimitable life on Earth. The text is replete with references from primary scientific articles in some of the most well-respected journals, underscoring the highest academic rigor taken in substantiating the factual claims. Only the shamefully flippant could dismiss this book as being a faith-filled presentation rather than the scholarly work it represents."

**James M. Tour**, T. T. and W. F. Chao Professor of Chemistry,
Rice University; *R&D* magazine's 2013 Scientist of the Year

"This book, *Improbable Planet*, brings forth from the reader a triumphant shout of thanksgiving to a God who is the Author of our creation. In the process, Hugh Ross brilliantly silences those who would claim that this Earth, this solar system, this galaxy, and this universe are nothing but a mere accident. *Improbable Planet* is technical yet poetic; thoroughly scientific yet faith-inspiring. I commend it to anyone who seriously contemplates the wonder of this planet we call Earth."

**Pat Robertson**, founder/chairman, The Christian
Broadcasting Network, Inc.

"Hugh Ross takes us on a riveting tour of the scientific story, from the beginning of the cosmos to present humankind. He shows, from the perspective of cosmology, planetary science, geology, ecology, and biology, how that story pushes us toward the conclusion that purpose has driven the whole story, with the different pieces intertwined and each supporting the production of an ideal habitat for human beings right here and right now. But that isn't the final goal of the story: rather, we were brought here to live eternally with our Maker. Not only will this commend Christian faith to scientifically minded inquirers, but it will also strengthen the confidence of believers that we inhabit and participate in a meaningful and purposeful story."

**C. John "Jack" Collins**, professor of Old Testament,
Covenant Theological Seminary

"*Improbable Planet* provides sound biblical and scientific support for a Creator. With thorough notations and research, Dr. Hugh Ross takes us on a journey through time and space to bring us firmly back to our own planet, formed by one Creator. For those who need a scientific explanation of our universe and the life-forms within it, you will be satisfied. For those who already believe that God's divine hand created the world and all life within, you will be validated. Hugh Ross writes to stretch our intellect and to strengthen our faith. *Improbable Planet* does the improbable— demonstrates that the language of science does not threaten but instead augments the prose of evangelism."

**Ed Young**, senior pastor, Second Baptist Church, Houston, TX

"Hugh Ross is a gift. He belongs to that rarefied and exceedingly small group of people who combine brilliance of mind, an originality of thought that rivals the most creative thinkers, and an encyclopedic knowledge of both the Bible and science. *Improbable Planet* is the latest expression of these traits. You do not need to know either science or the Bible to understand the book, but the more you know about either, the more impressive you will find the achievement. Anyone would immensely benefit from reading *Improbable Planet*."

**Dennis Prager**, nationally syndicated radio talk show host and columnist, *New York Times* bestselling author, and founder of PragerUniversity.com

"When topics like intelligent design and fine-tuning are being explained, Hugh Ross is one of the beloved and most widely read scientific authors. Adding to Ross's reputation, this book will not disappoint readers. Whether the topic is the mass of the universe, the Milky Way Galaxy, the failures of abiogenesis, or the Cambrian explosion, much of this text reads like the explanations behind the gorgeous photos of space that we often witness. I predict a wide audience!"

**Gary R. Habermas**, Distinguished Research Professor of Apologetics and Philosophy, Liberty University

"Dr. Ross has done it again! With his typical clarity, insight, and precision, Ross shows how recent scientific findings undermine naturalism while simultaneously providing evidence that there is a plan, purpose, and design in the universe. Whether you are a skeptic or a believer, you will be challenged and equipped immensely by reading *Improbable Planet*. I highly recommend it."

Sean McDowell, PhD, professor, Biola University; bestselling author of over 15 books, including *A New Kind of Apologist*

"In *Improbable Planet*, Hugh Ross presents the most detailed analysis yet of the Goldilocks 'just right' circumstances that make Earth home to all of its inhabitants. The book builds an enthralling tale of the conditions that allow and promote life to exist and thrive here."

Gerald B. Cleaver, professor and head, Early Universe Cosmology and Strings Division, Baylor University

"*Improbable Planet* is a remarkably researched and detailed account of the geological, chemical, and biological history of Earth. Readers will encounter a fascinating and informative book, even apart from any theological or philosophical implications. An unimaginable series of finely timed and tuned events were required in order for the primordial Earth to develop into a planet capable of supporting higher life forms and allowing an advanced civilization to thrive. The improbability of our planet becoming the paradise that it is provides strong evidence that there is a divine plan and providential design behind it all and that humans and our planetary home have a deep significance in the universe."

Michael G. Strauss, David Ross Boyd Professor, University of Oklahoma

"As one who has spoken to millions of despairing atheists in Russia and Ukraine, I am persuaded that the case for the Creator as proposed by Ross is well nigh irrefutable. Hugh's observation that we find ourselves in a collection of 200 billion stars, in a universe of some 200 billion galaxies, in just the right place, at just the right time, and with just the right view, makes one think that perhaps Someone designed it all. Here is a fact-filled book that will stir the debate about origins while intellectually challenging popular atheistic concepts."

John Carter, president, The Carter Report, Moorpark, CA

"Hugh Ross's proven scientific credentials and his enduring commitment to biblical Christianity qualify him to speak authoritatively in the often raucous encounter between science and theology. The quality of Hugh Ross's work in *Improbable Planet* is characterized in his stated efforts to respond to Carl Sagan's assertion that 'the cosmos is all there is or ever was or ever will be.' Using scientific evidence, Ross skillfully validates the biblical affirmation that this universe serves as a launching pad for the new creation to come. He powerfully reveals the deep biblical foundations that undergird his extensive scientific explanations, offering a model of thoroughness that should characterize biblical Christianity's interface with science."

**Byron D. Klaus,** former president, Assemblies
of God Theological Seminary

# IMPROBABLE
# PLANET

# IMPROBABLE
# PLANET

## HOW EARTH BECAME
## HUMANITY'S HOME

# HUGH ROSS

BakerBooks
a division of Baker Publishing Group
Grand Rapids, Michigan

Published by Baker Books
a division of Baker Publishing Group
P.O. Box 6287, Grand Rapids, MI 49516-6287
www.bakerbooks.com

Printed in the United States of America

Library of Congress Cataloging-in-Publication Data is on file at the Library of Congress, Washington, DC.

ISBN 9780801016899 (cloth)
ISBN 9780801072963 (ITPE)

16  17  18  19  20  21  22      7  6  5  4  3  2  1

# Contents

9

# Contents

# Acknowledgments

During the five years I spent reviewing the literature and organizing my thoughts for this book, my Sunday morning Paradoxes class became my sounding board. The class members' questions, challenges, and critiques played a significant role in shaping the content. So thanks to everyone who patiently and persistently participated in those interactions.

The next person to help me organize my thoughts, arrange them into chapters, and put them into words was my partner in life and ministry, Kathy. As usual, she protected my writing time, encouraged me to keep going, and then took the lead in editing the manuscript. She faced the nearly impossible job of balancing my demand for scientific accuracy with the readers' desire for accessibility. Thanks, Kathy, for never giving up on this task—or on me.

After this initial work, five more editors who are part of my team at Reasons to Believe stepped up to help. Special thanks to Joe Aguirre, Sandra Dimas, Linda Kloth, Maureen Moser, and Amanda Warner for checking and rechecking all the citations and quotations in the book, helping me work in the revisions and additions suggested by early reviewers, performing detailed copyedits, and preparing the index. The many hours you invested made an enormous difference in the quality of this work. I cannot thank you enough.

As these editors continued their labor, a stellar group of scholars including and in addition to my colleagues at RTB took time to review the science and offer their recommendations. I'm especially grateful to astronomer

## Acknowledgments

Kyle Cudworth, biochemist Russ Carlson, and geologists Ken Wolgemuth and Steve Keyes. Your many helpful suggestions and revisions improved the book's content without exceeding reasonable limitations on word count.

Others who deserve special mention and appreciation include my assistant, Diana Carrée, and the members of RTB's advancement and ministry care teams. Your support, encouragement, and extra effort allowed Kathy and me to focus intensely for weeks on writing and editing. Time and again your service goes far beyond the call of duty. I'm blessed to work with men and women who share my passion for providing new reasons to believe in Jesus Christ, our Creator and Savior.

Finally, let me go back to where this writing project began—in conversations with my agent, Steve Laube, and Baker Publishing Group's executive editor Bob Hosack. What started as a discussion of the fossil record grew much deeper and wider as we went along. Thank you for allowing me to expand the scope of the project I had initially proposed. Your enthusiasm has been, and remains, invaluable.

# 1

# Why Ask "Why"?

A few years ago I wrote a book called *Why the Universe Is the Way It Is* to show what the characteristics of the universe—its age, mass, dimensions, physical laws, and other physical features—tell us about humanity's ultimate purpose and destiny.[1] I wrote it also as an appeal to those who reject the Creator on the basis that they, as mere humans, can conceive of a better universe than ours to reconsider their claim in light of new discoveries. My aim in that book was to demonstrate how our seemingly "imperfect" universe fits perfectly with what I describe as a two-creation model of reality. Rather than upholding Carl Sagan's assertion that "the cosmos is all that is or ever was or ever will be,"[2] evidence supports the biblical assertion that this universe serves as a launchpad for the new creation to come—a reality more perfect than any of us can think of or imagine, one that fulfills all our greatest hopes and deepest longings.

In many respects the book in your hands is a sequel to that book—a *necessary* sequel, given popular notions about Earth as a not-so-special, often hostile, and, in a worst-case scenario, possibly replaceable home for humanity. Of all the things in life we tend to take for granted, our terrestrial

13

residence and its resources might be one of the biggest. We don't seem to be amazed and astonished by Earth's beauty and treasures, its capacity to support more than 7 billion people and even more billions of other creatures.

Most people I meet, including scientists, acknowledge that Earth has undergone some changes since it first coalesced from the disk of gas and dust surrounding our star, the Sun, but few can even imagine how radically different it is today. Many suggest that Earth's life-sustaining features are just "amazing coincidences" that somehow fell into place in a way that suits human needs and, at the same time, determines what life-forms exist.

Evidence and logic compel me to challenge such a notion. Ongoing research tells us that Earth has been shaped not only by an intricately orchestrated interplay of physical forces and conditions, but also by its vast abundance and diversity of life-forms. By means that no depth and breadth of scientific research can explain, life arose early in Earth's history under anything but the benign conditions it would seem to require and somehow persisted through multiple mass extinction events, always appearing or reappearing at just-right times and in just-right forms to meet the needs and demands of the revised environment.

The more thoroughly researchers investigate the history of our planet, the more astonishing the story of our existence becomes. The number and complexity of the astronomical, geological, chemical, and biological features recognized as *essential* to human existence have expanded explosively within the past decade. The importance of this new information cannot be overstated. An understanding of what is required to make possible a large human population and advanced civilization has raised profound questions about life, especially about our purpose and destiny. In other words, discovering at this level of detail why the history of Earth looks the way it does impacts all discussion of why you and I are here. Are we simply the result of a colossal matrix of innumerable, narrow coincidences, against all odds, or is there a more reasonable explanation? And if the world *is* the handiwork of a divine Creator, why is it so full of misery and danger for so many of its inhabitants?

The reason most reviews of Earth's history fail to arrest our attention and rivet our thoughts about humanity's purpose and destiny may well reside in the cursory manner whereby the subject is typically addressed.

We all know—or at least think we know—what Earth's history looks like. A bunch of dust surrounding the newly formed Sun clumped together by gravity to form a seemingly random set of planets. One of those planets, the one we call Earth, was the "Goldilocks planet," a just-right place with just-right conditions and ingredients for a simple life-form to pop into existence from a conglomeration of chemicals and somehow manage to stay in existence. We learned in school that over a very long time and despite some occasional setbacks, Earth's environment allowed for and produced progressively more diverse and complex life. We learned that this extended process eventually gave rise to human beings, endowed with the resources and capacities to launch, develop, and perhaps sustain advanced civilization.

What most of us do not know, however, is how radically Earth has changed since it first formed into a more or less solid ball. What's more, even those at the cutting edge of research are just now gaining a glimpse at how many and what kinds of physical steps transformed that lifeless ball into our fully animated orb, our home.

One reason we don't know is that this research and its findings are so new. Another is that the puzzle pieces that would help us bring the picture into focus come from a diversity of scientific disciplines: cosmology, astronomy, geophysics, atmospheric physics, geology, physical chemistry, biochemistry, and the whole spectrum of the biological sciences. A third reason, and perhaps the most significant of all, arises from what my friend Kenneth Samples would refer to as the zeitgeist, the spirit of the times. Through repeated misuses and abuses, scientific findings have lost much of their power to impact people's view of reality and, thus, their thoughts about life's biggest questions. While such questions are easy to postpone, they cannot be ignored. No matter how hard and how often we push them to the background, life has a way of propelling them to the forefront, often (but not always) in the face of life-altering and globally impactful events. So why wait? Let's look together at the data scientists now have in hand and carefully consider what they tell us about how Earth, humanity, and civilization—and you and I—came to be. The story that emerges might just impact how you choose to live here and now.

# 2

# The Way the World *Is*

We live on an amazing planet, a world like no other we know. The world that we know and enjoy is the result of a very long history of astronomical, physical, geological, chemical, and biological events. Without that long, complex history we would not have our present-day world, the world that *is*.

### Preserved Record of the Past

Because of the way the world is, we have a fairly comprehensive record of how the planet got to be in its present state. Geological records throughout the world reveal Earth's transition from a planet with only water on its surface to a realm where landmasses and oceans coexist. Thanks to these records, geologists possess a detailed understanding of the growth history of Earth's islands and continental landmasses.

The Milky Way Galaxy, the Sun, the Moon, and the configuration of the solar system's planets and asteroid and comet belts reveal how Earth obtained its unique stockpile of elements and minerals that enable Earth today to sustain such an enormous biomass and biodiversity. The fossil record, isotope records, geological layers, sediment cores, ice cores, and biodeposit (biological decay products embedded in Earth's crust) inventories provide biologists and ecologists with a chronicle of Earth's life.

Earth's preserved record of past physical and biological events reveals an unanticipated synergy. While scientists expected that Earth's physical history would play a role in determining life's history, it was a surprise for them to recently discover that for the physical history of Earth to be the way it is, certain kinds and quantities of life must exist in just-right locations at just-right times.

The sheer abundance and diversity of life on Earth implies that a record of Earth's past geochemistry and life has been preserved not only here but also on other solar system bodies. Asteroids, comets, and meteorites have bombarded Earth throughout its history. These collisions have resulted in over a million tons of Earth material, including the remains of embedded microorganisms, being deposited on the surfaces of the Moon, Mars, Venus, and other solar system bodies.[1]

## Persistent Life

A remarkable feature of our world is the permanence of its life. Thanks to how long life has endured, global civilization is presently sustainable (as succeeding chapters in this book will show).

Fossils of Earth's life date back to 3.47 billion years ago.[2] Carbon-13 to carbon-12 isotope ratio measurements (see ch. 8) indicate that life was present on our planet as far back as 3.83 billion years ago.[3]

Once life first appeared on Earth it persisted. While there is no geological period of life during which extinctions did not occur, and while occasional mass extinction events have wiped out more than half of all existing species, life nonetheless continued. There is no apparent time during the past 3.5 billion years when Earth became sterile.[4] How and why Earth never experienced a permanent sterilization event throughout the past 3.5 billion years forms the thesis for much of this book.

## Abundance and Diversity

In spite of all the stresses and catastrophes it encountered throughout the past 3.8 billion years, life on Earth nonetheless has remained extremely, even maximally, abundant and diverse. This book will explore how and why that is. The biodeposit wealth within Earth's crust alone testifies of the enormous past abundance of life. Similarly, the high oxygen and low carbon dioxide content in Earth's atmosphere implies that photosynthetic activity must have proceeded with little or no interruption at virtually the maximum level the physical laws would permit. The fossil record testifies of exceedingly rapid recoveries from extinction events. Whoever or whatever is responsible for Earth's life seems intent on keeping the planet as full of life as is physically possible.

The fossil record clearly exhibits a trend toward increasing diversity. Only recently have ecologists determined—with any degree of precision—the total number of species of life. That number is about 8.7 million eukaryotes: 6.5 million land species and 2.2 million marine species.[5] Not included are prokaryotes (bacteria and archaea), unicellular species whose cells lack a nucleus. Estimates of the number of prokaryotic species range from 100,000 to 10 million.[6]

Considering Earth's small surface area, 8.7 million eukaryotic species is an incredibly high number. As a team of six astrobiologists asked, "Of special relevance to astrobiology and central to evolutionary biology, we ask why there are so many species on Earth?"[7] Their question will be addressed in later chapters.

The fossil record is most complete for animals. It documents that animals first appeared shortly after 600 million years ago. From there until the present, the number of animal species existing per unit of time has increased. The strongest trend observed is for large-bodied animals.

Where the fossil record is less complete, paleontologists see the same trend. Whether they observe plants, fungi, lichens, eukaryotic unicellular life, or prokaryotic unicellular life, paleontologists note that species diversity increases with respect to time.

**Simple to Complex**

Previous to 600 million years ago it was impossible for the physical and chemical environment of Earth at that time to support animals' existence. As later chapters will reveal, the physical and chemical conditions on Earth changed dramatically over the past 4 billion years. One of the enigmas of life's history is that the complexity and diversity of life has continuously increased in direct response to the changing physics and chemistry of Earth's surface, progressively permitting the existence of more complex and diverse life.

There are no time lags. The moment conditions allow for a greater complexity and diversity of life, that complexity and diversity immediately appear. Furthermore, they appear up to maximal limits permitted by the improved physical and chemical conditions. These patterns of immediacy and maximal complexity and diversity raise the "why" question—a vital query this book will address.

## Gradualism vs. Quantum Jumps

One defining feature of Earth's life is its episodic history. The progression from simple to complex, low diversity to high diversity, tiny body sizes to large body sizes is neither linear nor gradual.

For the first 2.8 billion years of life's history the only life-forms observed were either unicellular or colonies of unicellular life. Differentiated multicellular organisms did not arise until 1 billion years ago and animals not until 600 million years ago.

Charles Darwin presumed that the development and transformation of life throughout Earth's history was gradual, smooth, and continuous.[8] However, in landmark articles published in 1972 and 1977, paleontologists Niles Eldredge and Stephen Jay Gould pointed out that the fossil record is typified by species remaining in extended stasis (little or no net evolutionary change) interrupted by quantum jumps where species disappear suddenly and then are followed quickly by sudden appearances of very different species.[9] Even before the publication of Eldredge and Gould's papers, other paleontologists, such as George Gaylord Simpson, had noted an even more radical feature of the fossil record. It is not only at the species level where quantum jumps are observed but also at the level of families, orders, and classes of organisms" (see table 2.1, "Classification of Life").[10]

## Table 2.1: Classification of Life

This scientific taxonomy has its origin in Carl Linnaeus's research. Linnaeus grouped species according to shared physical characteristics. In the twentieth century his groupings have been revised to correspond with the Darwinian assumption of common descent by natural means.

| Category | Example 1 | Example 2 | Example 3 |
| --- | --- | --- | --- |
| | Monarch butterfly | Lion | Human being |
| Domain | Eukaryota | Eukaryota | Eukaryota |
| Kingdom | Animalia | Animalia | Animalia |
| Phylum | Arthropoda | Chordata | Chordata |
| Class | Insecta | Mammalia | Mammalia |
| Order | Lepidoptera | Carnivora | Primates |
| Family | Nymphalidae | Felidae | Hominidae |
| Genus | Danaus | Panthera | Homo |
| Species | *Danaus plexippus* | *Panthera leo* | *Homo sapiens sapiens* |

## Three Creations of Life

As noted, Earth provides an enduring home for life. Because of the way Earth was and now is, it affords habitats for three radically different kinds, or categories, of life: (1) physical; (2) physical and mind-possessing; and (3) physical, mind-possessing, and spiritual.

However, proponents of the abiogenesis hypothesis challenge this perception of three distinct forms of life. Abiogenesis refers to the premise that some set of natural processes was responsible for life arising from nonliving matter and for primitive life evolving into advanced life. In other words, life differs by degree, not by kind.

This naturalistic perspective on life's origin and history has impacted how astronomers view the "anthropic principle." The original definition of the anthropic (from *anthropos*—Greek for "man") principle states that humanity's existence places severe constraints on the physical constants, structure and history of the universe, the Milky Way Galaxy, the solar system, Earth and Earth's life. However, astronomer Marcelo Gleiser points out that what is now referred to as the anthropic principle in the astronomical research literature almost always amounts to nothing more than the "preconditions for primitive life."[11] Thus, the anthropic principle has become the prebiotic principle. It presumes that all life differs from the most primitive life only by degree and not by kind.

Primitive life, that is, unicellular bacterial life, is but the simplest form of life on Earth. There are three other general divisions (under category 1 above) of purely physical life: (1) differentiated multicellular organisms (for example, fungi); (2) plants; and (3) animals. In addition to purely physical life, Earth today sustains two kinds of life that possess distinctly *nonphysical* attributes.

One of these kinds is a group of animals that possesses a mind (category 2 above), a mind that is capable of experiencing and expressing emotions, exercising intellectual analysis, and making decisions in response to that analysis and the animal's emotional state. All mind-possessing animals share in common the attribute of parents providing sacrificial care for their offspring. Animals in this category include all mammals and birds and a few of the more advanced reptilian species such as the crocodile and the alligator.

Another kind of life-form possessing nonphysical attributes (category 3 above) is the species *Homo sapiens sapiens*. Human beings not only possess a mind, they also are endowed with a spirit. This spiritual component enables humans to engage in philosophy and theology and to address questions of ultimate meaning and purpose not only about themselves but also of the rest of Earth's life and the entirety of the universe.

The different kinds of purely physical life-forms and those possessing both physical and nonphysical attributes explains the observed hierarchy in Earth's physical and biological features. Unicellular life can thrive without the existence of more complex life. However, multicellular organisms cannot exist without unicellular organisms. Multicellular life also requires a more highly fine-tuned physical environment than unicellular life. Likewise, mind-possessing life needs the support of mindless life and requires far more fine-tuned physical habitats. Spirit-possessing life cannot survive without all the other different kinds of life simultaneously thriving on Earth, and it demands an extremely fine-tuned physical environment. This hierarchy of dependence suggests a teleology—that the origins and history of life on Earth have a destiny and purpose, culminating in *Homo sapiens sapiens*.

In addition to generating habitats for life, another reason the world is the way it is appears to be so that all the different kinds of life can coexist at high population levels. Existence of the three distinct kinds of life—purely physical; physical and mindful; and physical, mindful, and spiritual—poses a challenge for all models attempting to explain how our world came to be the way it is. Earth needed to prepare for not just one, but three, origins of life.

## Rare Galaxy, Rare Earth

The recognition that Earth today possesses abundant and diverse species of multiple levels of advanced life and that the existence of such life requires a very long history of much simpler life has spawned what is known in the scientific literature as the "rare Earth" hypothesis.[12] Even scientists who believe the origin of a bacterium is an easy step and that natural processes efficiently evolve life acknowledge that it takes an extraordinary planet for all these supposedly easy steps to occur.[13]

The panoply of advanced life on Earth also requires a universe with an extraordinary history for there to be any possibility for the kind of spiral galaxy in which such an exceptional planet can exist. Furthermore, that planet must reside in a planetary system that experiences a highly specified birth and journey within its extraordinary galaxy. The next chapter tells the story of the cosmic and galactic preparation that made possible our rare Earth.

# 3

# Essential Construction Materials

Any home-building project requires considerable work *before* construction begins. One of the initial concerns has to do with available resources. For the home to meet the needs of its occupants, essential construction materials—the right ones for the type of home you want—in sufficient quantities must be available. If you're planning an adobe brick home, for example, you need to be sure you can assemble enough bricks to construct the size and shape of structure you want. The availability of these bricks, of course, depends on the availability of sand, clay, and water, plus some kind of fibrous material all mixed together in appropriate proportions, and baked in appropriate shapes and sizes by someone with know-how.

The same practical matter applies to construction of our home, Earth. Not just any universe will provide the appropriate construction materials. A potential home for life, even in its simplest form, requires the availability of sufficient quantities of certain elements—the most fundamental building materials.

## Just-Right Mass

To understand why our home needs a particular kind of solar system seems simple enough. We need the Sun's energy and the right kind and amount of gas and dust to make some planets. But who can help wondering why we need a universe so massive, one with some 50 billion trillion stars—all of which comprise just one percent of its total stuff?[1]

Famed physicist Stephen Hawking raised this question years ago in his popular book *A Brief History of Time*. He suggested that this vast number of stars and galaxies seems a waste.[2] However, ongoing research has given us good reasons—all relevant to life's existence—for the massiveness of the cosmos. We need it for essential construction materials.

The initial mass density of matter's building blocks—protons and neutrons (called baryons, collectively)—critically impacted what happened in the first few minutes of the universe's existence. That's when hydrogen, the lightest element, fused into the next heavier elements, helium and lithium. The amount of helium and lithium produced at that time then determined how much planet- and life-building material (the elements essential for life) could be produced later on within the nuclear furnaces of stars.

If the universe contained a slightly lower mass density of protons and neutrons, then nuclear fusion in stellar furnaces would have yielded no elements as heavy as carbon or heavier; if a slightly greater mass density, then star burning would have yielded only elements as heavy as iron or heavier. Either way, the universe would have lacked the elements most critical for our planet and its life—carbon, nitrogen, oxygen, phosphorus, and more. For life to be possible, the universe must be no more or less massive than it is.

Mass density is critical to yet another feature of the universe, the relative spacing of galaxies throughout its history. Together with a mysterious "something" called dark energy (the term for expansion energy embedded in the three-dimensional surface of the universe, where all the objects in the universe reside), mass density controls the cosmic expansion rate. Dark energy operates on the universe's space surface like an anti-elastic band. The more the cosmic surface expands, the more energy it gains to accelerate the cosmic expansion rate. In other words, the more extensive the spatial surface, the more powerfully dark energy propels its expansion.

Gravity operates in the opposite manner. Gravity draws objects closer together. The closer objects are to one another and the more massive the objects, the more powerfully gravity attracts them toward one another. Thus, when the universe was younger and the cosmic space surface smaller, mass bodies in the universe were closer together, causing gravity to more powerfully brake, or slow down, the cosmic expansion rate.

Both dark energy and the cosmic mass density must be exquisitely fine-tuned for life to have any possibility of existing. If the cosmic mass density were even slightly smaller, the universe would expand so rapidly that gravity would be unable to collapse any gas pockets to form galaxies, stars, or planets. If the cosmic mass density were even slightly greater, gravity would work too effectively. All the stars in the universe would be much larger than the Sun and would burn up too quickly for any planets orbiting them to sustain any kind of advanced life. In fact, even if the density were just the tiniest bit greater, the universe's gas would quickly compress into nothing more than black holes and neutron stars, where matter is so compacted that neither molecules nor atoms can possibly exist.

Given the laws of physics by which the universe operates, its massiveness proves essential to both our home's and our own existence. (As for why our universe's laws of physics are what they are, my book *Why the Universe Is the Way It Is* is devoted to answering that question.)


## Just-Right Age

In addition to questioning the supposed wasted mass in the universe, some people also question why there's so much seemingly wasted time. If you've ever had to wait for deliveries or for the permits to start construction, you certainly know the feeling that time is being lost unnecessarily. If weeks or days seem a long delay, imagine a wait of 9 billion years! That's how long the universe existed before construction of our home planet could get under way.

This lengthy wait would be better characterized as an active preparation period—anything *but* a waste. As with the mass of the universe, so also with its age: research reveals two good reasons for the timing of Earth's formation.

The first reason has to do with formation of a sufficient abundance and diversity of heavy elements. Similar to the formation of adobe bricks, these elements—which you may recall from the periodic table—require an extensive chain of stellar burning events. In their nuclear burning process, stars a few times more massive than the Sun generate and eventually expel elements ranging in mass from helium to iron.

Stars many times more massive than the Sun end their nuclear burning with supernova eruptions. Such explosions generate all the known elements heavier than iron, which include such life-essentials as copper, zinc, selenium, and molybdenum. Astronomical research reveals that several generations of giant stars must form, burn up their fuel, and then explode in order to build up the abundance of heavy elements needed to make our planetary home and its life a possibility. Each of these steps takes hundreds of millions of years.

A second reason for the long wait is the formation of critically important radioisotopes (or radioactive isotopes). It takes 9 billion years of cosmic history for enough supernovae to explode and produce the required quantities of radioisotopes. Since short-lived radioisotopes decay rapidly, they need to be replenished constantly by ongoing supernova eruptions. Meanwhile, many successive generations of supernovae must occur to build up the required inventories of such long-lived radioisotopes as uranium-238 and thorium-232, which have half-life decay times of 4.47 and 14.05 billion years, respectively.

Both short-lived and long-lived radioisotopes prepare Earth for habitability. The short-lived radioisotopes generate the heat that blasts away the primordial planet's light gases and water that otherwise would have left Earth with an atmosphere far too thick and an ocean far too deep for life (at least any kind of advanced life) to be possible.

Certain long-lived radioisotopes, such as uranium and thorium, play a critical role in establishing Earth's strong and enduring magnetic field as well as its strong and ongoing plate tectonic activity, both of which are also essential for advanced life. Long-lived radioisotopes salted into Earth's core provide the enduring heat source that sets up and sustains the dynamo that produces our strong, stable magnetic field. The magnetic field, in turn, protects life from deadly cosmic and solar radiation and prevents Earth's atmosphere from being sputtered away by solar particles.

Long-lived radioisotopes in the core and mantle also drive Earth's plate tectonics—the movement of various large and small pieces of our planetary crust. Plate tectonic activity generates continents, which together with the oceans, recycle nutrients and steadily remove potentially destructive greenhouse gases from the atmosphere (see chs. 9–12).

Where do all these radioisotopes come from? As with the heavy elements identified above, all are produced by 9 billion years' worth of giant star formation, burning, and explosion. But the mere existence of these materials cannot explain the existence of our home and its inhabitants. Additional factors, some call them amazing events or coincidences, played critical parts, as we will see in a tour of Earth's neighborhood in the next chapter.

# 4

# The Right Neighborhood

The search for a desirable site, one that matches the needs and wants of a homebuilder and the home's future occupants, takes top priority once the decision to go ahead with construction finalizes. A multitude of factors goes into the process of identifying the best possible location—an available (and affordable) spot in a particular neighborhood in a particular county in a particular state in a particular country. Depending on the number, ages, and other characteristics of the home's future residents, various sites will be more or less suitable than others, and some can easily be ruled out—or *in*.

What several decades of research has revealed about Earth's location within the vastness of the cosmos can be summed up in this statement: the ideal place for any kind of life as we know it turns out to be a solar system like ours, within a galaxy like the Milky Way, within a supercluster of galaxies like the Virgo supercluster, within a super-supercluster like the Laniakea super-supercluster. In other words, we happen to live in the best, perhaps the one and only, neighborhood that allows not only for physical life's existence but also for its enduring survival.

## Making Room

At the cosmic creation event the entire universe began to emerge from an infinitesimally small volume. To state the obvious point, the universe is not static. It is dynamic. It has been continually expanding from that moment onward.

At one point, the universe became large enough that stars and galaxies began to form. However, when the universe was very young, these galaxies were jammed so tightly together that they routinely ripped spiral arms—sites of strong star formation—off one another (due to the pull of gravity). After several billion years of cosmic expansion, galaxy clusters and the galaxies within them spread far enough apart that this ripping process became much less frequent.

A typical galaxy cluster contains several thousand galaxies, separated from one another by only a few galaxy diameters. A typical cluster also contains at least one supergiant galaxy, often several, the presence of which substantially impacts the dynamics of hundreds, if not thousands, of the other galaxies in the vicinity. (Supergiant galaxies range from 10 to 1,000 times the mass of our Milky Way.)

As the universe continued to expand and galaxy clusters spread farther apart from one another, galactic interactions within the clusters still caused considerable chaos. This chaos sometimes resulted in galaxies' ejection from their clusters. Today, astronomers observe many of these free-floating galaxies in the spaces between clusters.

One of these relatively peaceful solo galaxies might seem, at first glance, a suitable environment for advanced life, but this first impression is misleading. For advanced life to be possible, a several-billion-year history of simple life must precede it (see chs. 9–14). Such a long history of life requires a spiral galaxy with stable, symmetrical spiral arms (see "Why a Spiral Galaxy?" on page 31). To sustain such a spiral structure, a spiral galaxy must gravitationally consume gas-rich dwarf galaxies at a frequent and regular rate. The reason is that a certain level of ongoing star formation is needed to maintain the spiral structure. Without the additional gas provided by the accreted dwarf galaxies, the appropriate level of star formation cannot continue for a long enough time.

A problem for a free-floating galaxy, then, is that in the voids between galaxy clusters, the density of dwarf galaxies falls below the minimum needed to sustain the necessary spiral structure. A home in a free-floating galaxy would be about as livable as an igloo in the middle of the Sahara or a bamboo hut near the South Pole.

One problem for a galaxy residing in a typical galaxy cluster is that it experiences frequent collisions, mergers, and close flybys with other galaxies. These events can be devastating for potential life because they disturb stars' orbits, moving stars into different orbits about the host galaxy's center. Such a move would expose any potentially habitable planet orbiting a disturbed star to deadly radiation or to encounters with other stars and molecular clouds that would pull it out of its safe orbit.

A second neighborhood problem for a spiral galaxy in a typical galaxy cluster comes from "ram pressure stripping,"[1] a phenomenon caused by close encounters with other large galaxies within the cluster.[2] This stripping causes the galaxy to lose so much of its gas that it cannot maintain the structure and symmetry of its spiral arms for the length of time needed for advanced life to become a possibility.

A third problem stems from the typical cluster's tendency to capture external galaxies. As the captured galaxies fall toward the cluster's core, they drag many or most of the cluster members with them.[3] This infall causes close encounters or, worse yet, merging events that either distort, disrupt, or destroy a spiral galaxy's structure.

For a long history of life to be possible, life's host galaxy must reside within a grouping of galaxies that includes no supergiant galaxies and remains distant from any dense cluster. The group must contain a sufficiently high availability of dwarf galaxies to ensure that this one special spiral galaxy can accrete enough gas (from the dwarf galaxies) to sustain its spiral structure for many billions of years. The number and density of dwarf galaxies must not be so high, however, as to generate any significant disturbance or warping in the host galaxy's spiral arms. Also, the group must be sufficiently dispersed that large and medium-sized galaxies cause no disruption to the symmetry, size, or shape of the host galaxy.

All these requirements for an enduring history of life are met in the Milky Way Galaxy's location. Its group, the not-so-colorfully labeled Local

Group, contains no supergiant galaxies and just two large galaxies: our own Milky Way Galaxy (MWG) and the Andromeda Galaxy. This group just happens to include an estimated few hundred dwarf galaxies (only the nearest of the smallest dwarf galaxies can be seen through today's largest telescopes), a just-right number for maintaining the MWG's spiral structure for about 10 billion years without generating any significant disruption of its symmetry, spiral arm separation, or spiral arm sizes, and without causing any dangerous warping of its spiral disk.

The Local Group is located in the outer fringe of the Virgo supercluster of galaxies, which is located in the outer fringe of the Laniakea super-supercluster of galaxies. That location is sufficiently distant from both cores that the Local Group runs little or no risk of disruption from large

### Why a Spiral Galaxy?

Only a *spiral* galaxy can support life; elliptical galaxies and irregular galaxies cannot. Elliptical galaxies (which are either ellipsoidal or spheroidal in shape) compare with a dilapidated neighborhood. They contain mostly ancient stars and limited resources (as in gas). Because star formation ceases relatively early in elliptical galaxies, they produce an insufficient abundance and diversity of the heavy elements life needs. Furthermore, stars in elliptical galaxies are so crowded together that long-term, stable planetary orbits are impossible. Stars in the outer fringes of elliptical galaxies may not suffer crowding from adjacent stars, but they will lack the abundance and diversity of heavy elements needed for such stars to generate life-supporting rocky planets.

Irregular galaxies lack distinct regular shapes. They are chaotic in appearance without either spiral arms or a nuclear bulge. Large irregular galaxies possess active nuclei, which spew deadly radiation. Small irregular galaxies lack the quantities of heavy elements that life requires. All irregular galaxies manifest chaotic stellar orbits, which can disrupt planetary orbits or bring bright young ultraviolet-emitting stars into the vicinity of a life-sustaining planet.

Only in a spiral galaxy is a long history of life possible. A spiral galaxy of the just-right size and the just-right structure can yield adequate heavy elements for life as well as a possible location where a planetary system can reside for billions of years without being exposed to deadly radiation and without gravitational disruptions from adjacent stars and molecular clouds.

infalling galaxies.[4] And yet, it is not so distant from the cores that it cannot accrete a few passing dwarf galaxies.

The Local Group represents a rarity.[5] As far as astronomers are able to see, the Local Group is the only grouping of galaxies wherein a host galaxy can sustain a planet on which a long history of diverse, complex, and abundant life is possible.

## Narrowing In

To meet the needs of advanced life, not any old spiral galaxy will do. First, new stars must form there at a rate that can sustain the galaxy's spiral structure and symmetry. If the rate is too slow or unsteady, the galaxy will lack the low-density regions where a planetary system can survive, free from the disruption caused by gravitational interactions with other stars and molecular clouds. Star formation must also be sufficiently aggressive to produce the essential kinds and quantities of heavy elements any potential planets and life-forms will need.

Second, the spiral galaxy must be neither too big nor too small. A galaxy more massive than the MWG will form a huge, supermassive black hole at its nucleus. Such a black hole accretes enough mass to ignite potent relativistic jets of deadly radiation. These larger galaxies also force (by their gravitational power) mergers with multiple smaller galaxies. These merger events tend to chaotically disrupt, or even destroy, the spiral structure of the merging galaxies.

A galaxy either larger or smaller than the MWG presents life support with another set of problems primarily associated with the galaxy's co-rotation radius. The co-rotation radius is the precise distance from the galactic center at which stars revolve around the center at the same rate as the galactic arms. (The rates typically are not the same because Newtonian mechanics determines the revolution rate of stars, whereas long-lived density waves determine the rotation rate of the spiral arms.) In other words, it's that one place where the stars and the arms are rotating around the galactic core at the same speed. At the co-rotation distance, a star's velocity relative to the spiral arm's velocity is zero. Only planetary systems located at or very near this co-rotation radius avoid the disruption of frequent spiral arm crossings—another critical requirement for a long history of life.

**Figure 4.1a.** The Andromeda Galaxy. Note the warping of the galaxy's outer arms and the inner ring of star-forming nebulae offset from the galaxy's center.

For galaxies much larger than the MWG, the co-rotation radius is long—too long, in fact, for life's sake. Because the abundance of life-essential heavy elements steadily declines with distance from the galactic core, a long co-rotation radius means the abundance of heavy elements at such a distance is inadequate to meet the needs of advanced life.

In a galaxy smaller than the MWG, the co-rotation radius is too short for life's sake. Any planetary systems at such a short radius will be closer to the deadly radiation emanating from the galactic core. They would also be closer to adjacent spiral arms and closer to supergiant stars and giant molecular clouds within those arms.

## Stabilizing the Locale

A team of French astronomers discovered that the MWG is an "exceptionally quiet" spiral galaxy.[6] The team pointed out that while the Andromeda Galaxy has been called the MWG's twin, the two galaxies are distinctly different. Although the Andromeda and MWG share the same overall mass, Andromeda's stellar mass and angular momentum are significantly greater.

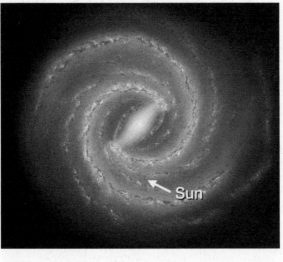

Credit: NASA/JPL-Caltech/R. Hurt (SSC-Caltech)

**Figure 4.1b.** The Milky Way Galaxy. Astronomers produced the lower image of the MWG by carefully piecing together maps of different regions of the MWG produced at radio, infrared, optical, and ultraviolet wavelengths. Unlike the Andromeda Galaxy, the MWG has highly symmetrical spiral arms and no big warp.

The MWG's lesser star mass and angular momentum have now been identified as important—and unexpected—factors in making possible a long history of life. The French team noted that the vast majority of galaxies resemble the Andromeda Galaxy. Most MWG-sized spiral galaxies have undergone major merger events with other galaxies over the past 10 billion years. A huge warp in its spiral arms indicates that Andromeda has, indeed, undergone such mergers. It also has an offset ring of star-forming nebulae that formed when a galaxy passed through Andromeda's center about 210 million years ago.[7]

The only galaxies the MWG has absorbed during the past 10 billion years are small to medium dwarf galaxies. Consequently, the MWG has retained its highly symmetrical spiral arms—no very large star-forming nebulae and no big warp (see fig. 4.1b).

The MWG possesses yet another unique stability feature. Spiral galaxies tend to break down as they age. As a young galaxy grows older, its elegant spiral structure gradually frays into myriad substructures—spurs, feathers, and filaments—branching off from the main arms. These substructures can interfere with the needs of advanced life in a significant way.

Bright stars and dense molecular clouds are plentiful in the substructures of aged galaxies. Such stars and clouds destabilize the orbits of planets or whole planetary systems anywhere near them. They also shower nearby planets with intense radiation. However, in spiral galaxies young enough to be unfrayed, life-essential heavy elements exist in insufficient abundance. The appropriate abundances become available only when a galaxy reaches the not-so-youthful age of 9 or 10 billion years.[8]

The answer to this challenge resides in a sufficiently aged spiral galaxy with minimal fraying and a just-right planet in a region least impacted by the fraying. Such a location is exactly where our solar system finds itself.

Recent discoveries shed light on just how amazing this coincidence may be.[9] Research shows that the fraying process is intricately complex, affected by multiple galactic conditions. To keep the fraying within the acceptable range for advanced life, the galaxy's magnetic field must be relatively weak, yet strong enough to prevent the spiral structure's collapse. Its disk must be dense enough but not too dense. The quantity of gas in the spiral arms as well as the differential compression of gas flowing through them must be relatively low, yet high enough to sustain the spiral structure.

A team of researchers at the University of Maryland has shown that near the co-rotation distance, substructures part company, leaving a small gap similar to the part in a person's hair. So, once again, the best place for an advanced-life-supportable planet is near the co-rotation distance.[10] And that, of course, describes the location of our solar system.

In the *Star Wars* movies, advanced civilizations exist in "a galaxy far, far away." However, as astronomers have developed the capability to observe spiral galaxies in adequate detail,[11] they have yet to identify one with features that would allow for, let alone sustain,[12] the needs of advanced life.

## Initial Site

The MWG's exceptional features pave the way for the existence of an exceptional solar system within it. As it turns out, our solar system is special in ways that prove critical for advanced life. For example, it is particularly volatile-poor and refractory-rich.[13] Paradoxically, our little grouping of planets possesses a dearth of gases and liquids and yet a wealth of metals, light and heavy, including heavy radioisotopes.

This unique inventory of elements stands in sharp contrast to that of the few "Goldilocks planets" and planetary systems among the 2,000+

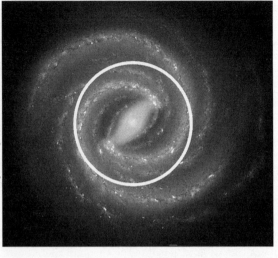

Background image credit: NASA/JPL-Caltech/R. Hurt (SSC-Caltech)

**Figure 4.2.** Milky Way Galaxy's Co-Rotation Radius. A little less than halfway out from the center of the optically visible portion of our galaxy, stars revolve around the galaxy's center at the same rate that the spiral arm pattern rotates. Stars closer to the center will revolve faster, and stars more distant will revolve slower. The farther a star is from the co-rotation distance, the more frequently it will cross one of the galaxy's spiral arms.

that astronomers have discovered thus far. Goldilocks planets resemble Earth in that they possess both carbon and liquid water—two of the basic requirements for life. That's where the similarity ends. Earth holds nearly 1,200 times less carbon-based atmospheric gas and about 500 times less liquid water than planets of similar size and surface temperature.[14] Earth's paucity of liquid water (less than 0.03 percent of its total mass) allows continents to form, and the combination of continents, rivers, lakes, and seas provides for multiple habitats and efficient nutrient recycling for advanced life. Earth's thin atmosphere permits the existence of creatures with lungs.

Astronomers now understand that the solar system's unusual mix of elements and radioisotopes results from its unusual place of origin. Apparently, its construction began in a vast cluster of at least 10,000 stars located well inside the MWG's co-rotation radius. Only in such a location would the emerging solar nebula and its newly forming planets be exposed to the requisite number, kind, and proximity of supernova eruptions—the only possible source of their heavy elements and suite of radiometric isotopes.[15]

At the MWG's co-rotation distance (about 26,000 light-years from the galactic center, see fig. 4.2), a phenomenon called mean motion resonances disrupts star formation. This disruption limits both the density of stars and the abundance of metals, especially heavier metals, in this location.[16]

**Figure 4.3. Metal Abundance Relative to Distance from the Galactic Center**

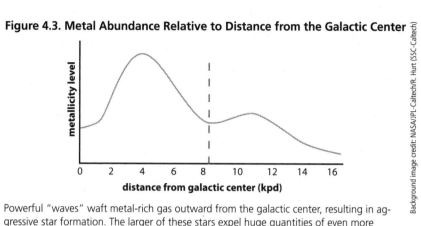

distance from galactic center (kpd)

Background image credit: NASA/JPL-Caltech/R. Hurt (SSC-Caltech)

Powerful "waves" waft metal-rich gas outward from the galactic center, resulting in ag-gressive star formation. The larger of these stars expel huge quantities of even more metal-rich gas into the galactic medium. Beyond 4 kiloparsecs (13,000 light-years) from the galactic center, the star formation rate and abundance of metals steadily decline, reaching a minimum at the co-rotation distance (dotted line). Beyond 11 kiloparsecs (36,000 light-years), the star formation rate and metal abundance steadily decline again.

The drawn curve is based on data taken from Yu. N. Mishurov, Jacques R. D. Lépine, and I. A. Acharova, "Corotation: Its Influence on the Chemical Abundance Pattern of the Gal-axy," *Astrophysical Journal Letters* 571 (June 2002): L113–L115.

Given Earth's great abundance of such metals—phosphorus, fluorine, alu-minum, titanium, uranium, and thorium, for example—astrophysicists recognize that our planet and its solar system companions could not have formed anywhere near our galaxy's co-rotation radius. Rather, they must have formed closer to the galactic center, where the abundance of elements heavier than helium (known as "metals" to astronomers and physicists) is near peak value (see fig. 4.3).[17]

Only at a location much closer to the galactic core than Earth's current location would a tight cluster of 10,000 or more stars be possible. And only when closer to the galactic center would the supernova activity be sufficient to enrich the solar system with its full panoply of heavy elements. This exposure to supernova activity did not merely provide essential heavy elements, however. It also altered the quantity of light elements. From this finding comes a complex scenario for the origin of our solar system with its unique suite of planets and their unusual elemental composition.

The Sun and its emerging system of planets apparently formed in just-right proximity to several supergiant stars that exploded as supernovae. These explosions occurred not so close as to destroy or seriously disrupt the planets but close enough (in distance and timing) to provide the infant planetary system with an essential profusion of heavy elements—and to drive away a vast quantity of light elements.

Because different supernova eruptions produce different suites of heavy elements, the Sun's disk of protoplanetary material must have been exposed to multiple supernova eruptions almost simultaneously. The primordial Earth's inventory of elements indicates its exposure to at least four distinct kinds of supernova eruptions, including an especially rare one.[18] These supernovae also bathed the entire emerging planetary system in huge quantities of aluminum-26, for example.

The extreme fine-tuning in this scenario prompted astronomers Richard Parker and James Dale to test an alternate explanation.[19] This second scenario proposes that massive stars formed first, erupted as supernovae, and sent expanding shock waves that triggered the formation of the solar system. Their computer simulations, however, showed that the second scenario required "very contrived situations"[20] and that the "triggered star formation event is as improbable, if not more so, than the direct pollution of the protosolar disc."[21]

In 2009, two British astronomers pointed out[22] that early exposure to an extreme quantity of aluminum-26 explains why the solar system's planets are so volatile-poor compared to planets beyond the solar system.[23] Intense heat released from the radioactive decay of aluminum-26 drove off most of the forming solar system's volatiles (gases and liquids), leaving the solar system volatile-poor but refractory-rich (refractory metals are heat- and wear-resistant heavy elements). Planets smaller and closer to the Sun were most dramatically impacted. The solar system's early exposure to aluminum-26 also helps explain why Earth's crust is so abundant in aluminum (the nonradioactive aluminum isotope). While aluminum comprises less than 0.01 percent of the universe's ordinary matter, it makes up 8.1 percent of Earth's crust.

Earlier mixing of clumpy supernova ejecta into the molecular cloud from which the Sun emerged might also have played a significant role in producing Earth's inventory of elements.[24] Another contributor was the exposure of the Sun's protoplanetary disk to various asymptotic giant branch stars (low- to medium-mass stars near the end of their helium-burning phase) and white dwarf binary stars (gravitationally connected pairs of low- to medium-mass burnt-out stars) at just the right distance and timing.

This complex orchestration of exposure to stellar burning on different scales and in multiple phases provides the best and, so far, the only viable explanation for Earth's particular quantities of all 94 elements in the periodic table. (Plutonium and neptunium, though present on early Earth, have since completely decayed away.)

Yet another factor in determining the elemental makeup of the solar system is the intensity of far ultraviolet (FUV) radiation in the place of its origin. In the tightly packed cluster of 10,000 or more stars where our Sun and planets began to take shape, FUV radiation would have been extremely intense. It came predominantly from young massive stars, and the greater the number and proximity of such stars to our young Sun and its surrounding disk, the greater their exposure to FUV radiation.

A team of American astronomers has demonstrated that the intensity of FUV radiation hitting our circumstellar disk as it condensed into planets determined how our solar system shaped up. Because FUV radiation burns off lighter gases, it impacted the kinds, masses, and distances of the solar system's gas giant planets as well as the mass and spread of the Kuiper Belt objects beyond Neptune.[25] If the FUV radiation had been any stronger, Uranus, Neptune, and the Kuiper Belt would never have formed and Saturn would have been smaller. On the other hand, if the FUV radiation had been any weaker, Saturn, Uranus, Neptune, and the Kuiper Belt would have been much more massive. Either scenario would have negatively impacted the possibility for advanced life's future existence on Earth.

## A Timely Relocation

The Sun and its accompanying suite of young planets, asteroids, and comets could not stay for long in their place of origin. This nascent system had to leave this highly energetic star cluster in order to become suitable for life support. However, not just any kind and direction of departure would do.

To stay intact, the solar system had to be ejected outward in the opposite direction from the galactic center, along a trajectory that avoided any points that could spell disaster for life's future possibility. Its trajectory carried it safely past giant stars, X-ray and gamma-ray sources, and giant molecular clouds and brought its radial velocity (outward movement within the MWG) to a halt just before it reached the co-rotation distance.

If it had continued farther, landing *right at* the co-rotation distance, the mean motion resonances there would have pulled it apart. But where it did stop, *just inside* the co-rotation radius, the forming solar system experienced only a few spiral arm encounters and few gravitational encounters with other stars. In fact, a team of Brazilian astronomers found that a galactic ring of both minimum stellar density and minimum gas density exists right at the radius where our solar system landed.[26]

The future needs of advanced life required that the solar system originate in one of the most dangerous (to life) locations in the MWG and then quickly move into the MWG's safest (for life) location. The solar system's origin and development was anything but ordinary.

## Staying within the Plane

All stars in the MWG, including the Sun, move slowly up and down relative to the plane of the galaxy's disk as they orbit the galactic center. The range of up and down movement is called the z-axis motion. For a long history of life—especially a history that includes *advanced* life—the solar system's z-axis motion must remain very small. A large z-axis motion means dangerous levels of radiation exposure.

The MWG's stellar disk is about 1,000 light-years thick, which means that the population of disk stars extends from about 500 light-years above the disk's plane to about 500 light-years below it. A typical star in a disk of this size will bounce up and down from near the top of the disk to near the bottom, from 400+ light-years above the galactic plane to 400+ light-years below over several million years. As it moves up and down, this star's exposure to radiation varies significantly because the gas and dust that shield it are denser near the plane and become sparser in proportion to distance above and below.

The intense radiation this gas and dust help to block emanates from supernova eruptions, as well as from the galactic nucleus. If an earthlike planet were orbiting this typical star, its radiation exposure at the top and bottom of this bounce cycle would destroy any complex life it might carry. Its ozone shield would be stripped away, allowing deadly levels of ultraviolet radiation to reach the surface unimpeded. Such radiation would ultimately drive the planet's temperature outside the range that carbon-based life (the only biochemically conceivable form of physical life) can survive.

Unlike the typical star orbiting in the MWG, however, the Sun remains relatively close to the galactic plane, bouncing no more than 228 light-years above or below it. Thus, life on Earth remains well shielded for most of the solar system's existence. Currently, the solar system resides very near the galactic plane, the location where protection from radiation is maximal. In fact, we humans find ourselves on Earth at the time of our solar system's greatest radiation protection.

The period of the solar system's z-axis cycle (the time between its high point and low point relative to the galactic plane) is about 33 million years. This value suggests a possible correlation with the mass extinction cycle observed in the fossil record. Over the past 600 million years, mass extinctions have occurred approximately every 27 million years. A research team led by physicist John Matese showed that the shifting gravitational tide generated by the z-axis cycle could periodically dislodge comets in the Oort cloud (an immense spherical cloud surrounding our solar system, extending about 3 light-years from the Sun) and send them hurtling into the inner solar system, with deadly consequences.[27] Geologist Michael Rampino noted that the solar system's z-axis cycle could periodically expose Earth to dense clumps of exotic dark matter.[28] These exposures might heat Earth's core through the annihilation of exotic dark matter particles, which could explain the observed 30-million-year periodicity in terrestrial geological activity and, at least in part, a similar cycle of biological extinctions.

**The Bonus View**

The solar system's move to a safer location for advanced life also happened to carry it to the best imaginable site for a view to the wonders of the universe. Everywhere else in the MWG, either conditions make advanced life impossible or the night sky is filled with bright objects that would severely limit astronomical observations.[29] Because of our solar system's

41

location, observers on Earth can explore and map the detailed structure of the universe and determine its detailed history back to the very earliest moments of its existence.

These observations and explorations provide a framework within which we can consider the implications of such an amazing multiplex of coincidences. While we have much to learn and understand, a strong suggestion of intentionality and purpose has clearly emerged. As physicist Freeman Dyson wrote in his book *Disturbing the Universe*, "The more I examine the universe and study the details of its architecture, the more evidence I find that the universe in some sense must have known we were coming."[30]

This perception of intention can be tested further as we consider the early history, the foundational era, of our now securely placed solar system. The next chapter examines what occurred as the solar system emerged that helped prepare a construction site for the eventual arrival and survival of future inhabitants.

# 5

# Site Preparations

With the question of location now settled, construction can move into full swing. However, the lot itself may need significant preparation before the foundation is laid and framing begins. At this point, the site is far from ready for inhabitants. In fact, a builder typically keeps plants, pets, and people away from the scene until grading, boulder removal, and any other hazardous tasks have been completed.

*Hazardous* seems the right word to describe the first 740 million years of our solar system's history, once it arrived in its relatively safe spot just inside the Milky Way Galaxy's co-rotation radius. Astronomers call this next era the Hadean (in reference to Hades). Two main factors contributed to the hellish conditions during that time: (1) asteroid and comet bombardment so frequent and intense as to sometimes melt the surface of the rocky planets—Mercury, Venus, Earth, and Mars; and (2) frequent violent solar flares and solar bursts of intense X-ray and ultraviolet radiation.

Though horrific in some respects, the Hadean era predated life and actually served to enhance the possibility for future life. During this extended epoch, several amazing developments, with precise timing and just-right parameters, helped prepare the surface of the third rock from the Sun for later habitation. These developments produced the conditions and resources not only for so-called simple life-forms but also for the more complex creatures of later eras. Step one involved setting up a secure perimeter around the eventual home site.

## Gas Giant Guardians

Of the nearly 2,000 planets outside our solar system astronomers have discovered and measured to date, the majority are gas giants. As their label implies, such planets are relatively huge (from 10 times Earth's mass to 13 times Jupiter's mass, which is 317.83 Earth masses). Though we have much more to learn about these planets, scientists observe that they differ significantly in orbital and physical features from our solar system planets, including our own gas giants, and their positions and pathways strategically impact the characteristics of their planetary systems.

Ongoing research has led astronomers to conclude that a planet sufficiently like Earth to be able to sustain advanced life requires a very particular suite of accompanying gas giant planets, a suite that formed in a very particular way. In fact, the more planets astronomers study both inside and outside our solar system and the more models they build in an effort to understand planetary system formation, the more evident the uniqueness of Earth's solar system becomes.

As a team of American and Canadian astronomers discovered, the existence of rocky planets depends on the presence and features of nearby gas giants. By their mass and proximity, these gas giants dynamically excite any newly forming rocky planet "embryos" (the building blocks of fully formed rocky planets).[1] The more excited these planetary embryos become, the fewer rocky planets will form, the more massive they'll be, and the closer they will orbit around the central star. For a planet capable of supporting advanced life to be possible, some level of dynamical excitement is essential. However, this excitement must be at a precise, low level.

At the same time, the existence of a suite of relatively distant gas giant planets is essential to protect any rocky planets from taking too many destructive hits from asteroids and comets. Such a suite of planets acts like a gravitational shield for any potentially habitable planet. Their gravitational pull either deflects comets and asteroids away from the habitable planet or draws them in so that the gas giants absorb most of the hits themselves.[2] If the gas giant planets are either too small or too distant, the shielding will be inadequate. On the other hand, if they are too large or too close, their gravitational potential will disrupt the smaller planets' orbits.

It is crucial for the existence of advanced life that the gas giant nearest the Sun provides most of the gravitational shielding, and the one next nearest the Sun plays the second greatest shielding role. To fulfill their protective task, these gas giant planets must remain in place for the long haul. However, the typical pattern observed outside our solar system is that these gas giants migrate inward toward their star. Some 793 of the 937 gas giant planets listed in the exoplanet catalog (as of March 21, 2015) orbit their stars closely, within 300 million miles or less.[3]

A team of astronomers from Germany, Japan, and the United States recently demonstrated how Jupiter and Saturn came to be and how they remain where they are.[4] Using computer simulations they showed that by the time Jupiter had formed completely, the remaining protoplanetary disk had lost considerable mass. The disk's remaining mass was equal to or slightly less than the mass of Jupiter alone. So within the disk, Jupiter's formation created a significant gap, and this gap induced the rapid formation of Saturn. Then Saturn's speedy formation—before the protoplanetary disk became totally depleted—allowed Saturn to acquire its dense core and thick envelope of gas. This precise sequence of events shaped the solar system's entire suite of gas giant planets.

These gas giant planets—Jupiter, Saturn, Uranus, and Neptune—with their respective masses, distances from the Sun, and orbital configurations, not only served as the inner planets' protective "fence" but also influenced Earth's mass, distance from the Sun, and orbital features, all of which turned out to be just right to allow for the possibility and survivability of (later) advanced life.

## The Grand Tack

As exacting as formation of the solar system's suite of gas giant planets must have been for future life's sake, formation of the four terrestrial planets that comprise the inner solar system seems even more challenging to explain. As previously mentioned, when astronomers observe planetary systems beyond the solar system, our system looks distinctly different, and in more ways than just its gas-giant-and-rocky-planet configuration.

One of the differences appears in the population of asteroids. These other systems show evidence for either no asteroids (the vast majority)[5] or truly enormous asteroid belts (a tiny minority).[6] Planetary formation models indicate that at the time of its emergence, the solar system possessed an inner asteroid belt at least a thousand times more massive than the one it possesses today. Asteroids populating the primordial belt manifested nearly zero orbital eccentricities and inclinations. Today's remaining asteroids possess orbits that are significantly eccentric and inclined.

Planetary formation models reveal that inward migration of gas giant planets would completely eradicate that system's inner asteroid belt. They also show that where little or no migration of the gas giant planets occurs, the system's primordial inner asteroid belt remains virtually intact. Neither scenario accounts for the reality of our solar system. Nor does either explain the characteristics of Mars. Virtually all solar system formation models had predicted that Mars should be at least 50 percent more massive than Earth.

A nonexistent asteroid belt would severely inhibit the delivery of life-essential chemicals and minerals to Earth. A huge asteroid belt would pelt Earth with frequent catastrophic colliders.[7] A more massive Mars could steer many more comet and asteroid colliders toward Earth. A more massive Mars could also, by its brightness, significantly limit astronomical observations.

All these modeling problems were resolved by a team of French and American astronomers.[8] Their model agreed with earlier models that Jupiter was the first planet to form. But from that point onward it proposed an intricate dance of planets leading to the solar system we see. After Jupiter had fully formed, enough gas remained in its vicinity to stimulate its inward migration. Then, when Saturn approached its final mass, it began to migrate inward, too, but at a faster rate. Both planets continued their inward migration until they got caught in a mean motion orbital resonance (with Jupiter orbiting the Sun either three times for every two orbits of Saturn or two times for every single orbit of Saturn, depending on the mass of the leftover gas in the disk).[9] Once caught in this orbital resonance, the two planets *reversed* their migration direction.

This model became known as the "Grand Tack" because this change of direction in the planets' migration resembles the pathway of a sailboat tacking into the wind. It occurred during the final million years of the solar system's condensation from a gaseous nebula. If it occurred at 1.5 times Earth's current distance from the Sun, then this reversal effectively "explains the current structure of the Solar System at an unprecedented level."[10] Such a reversal would have

1. truncated the solar system's disk of planetesimals (protoplanetary bodies ranging in size from a few kilometers to a few thousand kilometers in diameter) at Earth's current distance from the Sun, thus explaining why Mars is nine times less massive than Earth;

2. depleted, then partially repopulated, the asteroid belt, with inner belt bodies forming just at or a few times beyond Earth's current orbital distance from the Sun and outer belt bodies originating between and beyond the gas giant planets;

3. accounted for the compositional differences across the asteroid belts; predicted the gas giant planets' initial orbital positions, which explain, in turn, the Late Heavy Bombardment event (see ch. 6);

4. explained the timing and the mass of the later Moon-forming collision event (see pages 48–58);[11] and

5. accounted for the total mass of the "late veneer" (see pages 58–60).[12]

The Grand Tack scenario received further corroboration from a study by astronomers at the University of Bordeaux (France). Their research showed that, independent of the mass-growth history of Jupiter and Saturn, a two-phase migration would be expected during the final phase of our solar system's emergence from a gaseous nebula.[13]

The unusual conditions that led to the Grand Tack also helped astronomers understand the difference between our planetary system and what they've observed thus far about extrasolar planetary systems. As of March 21, 2015, 796 planets the mass of Saturn or greater had been discovered and measured with some precision. Of these planets, 618 orbit their host stars more closely than Jupiter orbits the Sun.[14] One reason so many gas giant planets orbit their stars closely is that no reversal of inward migration occurs if the gas giant planet nearest to its host star is not the most massive in the planetary system.[15]

For Jupiter and Saturn to approach the Sun as closely—no more and no less—as they did, and then to migrate outward as far as they did (no more and no less) requires certain precise conditions, including a specific density of solar nebula gas at the time and location of Jupiter's and then Saturn's formation. Also, the initial masses of Jupiter and Saturn and the planets' initial locations relative to the Sun must be no greater or lesser than they were. The Grand Tack, in turn, set up the precise conditions for occurrence of the Moon-forming collision event and the late veneer, as well as other life-relevant phenomena described in later chapters.

All this fine-tuning prompted two American astrophysicists to develop computer simulations to investigate how the inward and outward migrations of Jupiter, Saturn, Uranus, and Neptune would affect the orbits of Mercury, Venus, Earth, and Mars.[16] The two astronomers found an 85 percent probability that the inward and subsequent outward migration of Jupiter and Saturn into their present orbits would cause at least one of the rocky planets to either be ejected from the solar system or fall into the Sun and less than 1 percent probability of achieving the present-day orbital features of all eight of the Sun's planets.

The Grand Tack team, however, has already included in their model the ejection of a small gas giant planet from the solar system (see ch. 6). This adjustment to the Grand Tack model provided a superior explanation for Mars' current mass and orbit. The possibility also exists that the original solar system possessed five rocky planets, one of which was either ejected from the solar system or had fallen into the Sun. So far, the Grand Tack model, fine-tuned as it is, remains the only existing model that explains all the known features of the solar system's planets and belts of asteroids and comets (see ch. 6).

## Moon-Forming Event

Although early events in our solar system's formation stripped away an abundance of gases and liquids and added an abundance of light metals, these levels remained substantially unsuitable for life. Earth retained far too much water and far too thick an atmosphere to allow for advanced life and too little of various heavy metals and long-lived radioisotopes, particularly those needed to drive plate tectonics and generate a magnetic field. If ever this planet were to become the dwelling of plants, animals, and people, something had to change—dramatically. What event or sequence of events could accomplish this transformation?

As researchers puzzled over this question, they began to see a possible connection with another mystery that had intrigued astronomers for centuries: How did Earth get its one huge satellite, the Moon? Compared to the mass of its planet, the Moon is fifty times larger than any other moon in the solar system (see fig. 5.1), and our Moon orbits more closely than any large satellite yet discovered.

Dynamical models developed during the 1960s and 1970s utterly failed to account for the Moon's existence. They showed it to be too large, too close to Earth, and (with Earth) too close to the Sun to have formed within the Sun's protoplanetary disk. Yet all collision or capture scenarios yielded the destruction of Earth or the formation of an Earth-Moon system radically different from the one we observe. In their frustration some researchers went so far as to comment that the Moon must be some kind of illusion—or, perhaps, a miracle.

Ongoing research has produced a scenario in which the Moon's existence is, indeed, real and violates no known laws of physics. However, the conditions under which the Moon formed seem so unlikely, from a naturalistic worldview, as to defy credibility. Current models show that a just-right impactor struck Earth with just-right timing,

Credit: NASA

**Figure 5.1.** *Voyager 1's* 1977 Image of the Earth-Moon System

angle, and velocity to allow for the Moon's formation (see fig. 5.2). Astronomers call the impactor Theia.

Alastair G. W. Cameron and William R. Ward, the first astrophysicists to develop a collision scenario for Moon formation, proposed a slow, grazing impact of proto-Earth by a Mars-sized collider.[17] According to their model, the force of the impact vaporized the outer parts of both bodies. The heavy metals (iron, uranium, thorium, etc.) in the collider's core fell into the molten Earth and sank into its core. Most of the remainder of the shattered collider eventually coalesced (under gravity's influence) to form the Moon.

A team of Japanese astronomers discovered that for the impact to have generated a debris disk from which a lunar-sized ball could form, that debris disk could not have been dominated by superheated gases, which would include metallic minerals heated to a vaporized state.[18] Such gases would generate spiral shocks leading to the destruction of any circumterrestrial disk (debris disk surrounding Earth) within just a few days. Early

Credit: NASA/JPL-Caltech

**Figure 5.2.** Artist's Rendition of the Moon-Forming Impact Event

Earth's already low volatile levels helped limit the quantity of such gases, but even without significant quantities of volatiles, a high-energy impact would have produced a gas-dominated disk. High impact energy would have vaporized the rocky material of Earth, the impactor, or both.

Given this limited impact energy, researchers concluded that the primordial Earth must have been smaller than its current size at the time of the impact, and the impactor must have been no more than about 20 percent of Earth's current mass. The collision impact angle must have been no more or less than about 45°, and the impactor velocity relative to Earth must have been no more than 12 kilometers per second. If any of these conditions had been significantly different, the impact energy would have been too great. The impact would have yielded some result other than the Earth-Moon system we observe.

In 2000, Ward and fellow astrophysicist Robin Canup found a connection that further affirmed the collision scenario outlined by the Japanese research team. They noted that the substantial inclination of the Moon's orbit, relative to Earth's equator, can be explained only if the Moon emerged from an impact-generated debris disk.[19] In 2001, Canup and another researcher, Erik Asphaug, used a method known as smooth particle hydrodynamics to produce a computer-generated model for Moon formation that correctly predicted even more observed features of the Earth-Moon system, such as the Moon's low iron abundance[20] and the mass and angular momentum of both the Moon and Earth.[21] This model confirmed that the Moon formed when the earth was nearly finished accumulating material from the Sun's protoplanetary disk, roughly 50 to 100 million years after Earth initially coalesced.

Based on a 2004 study, Canup proposed that the collision angle must have been 45°, the impactor's mass between 0.11 and 0.14 Earth masses (for comparison's sake, Mars = 0.11 Earth masses), and the impactor velocity, relative to Earth's velocity, less than 4 kilometers per second (as compared with typical preatmospheric meteor velocities, relative to Earth, at 50 to 100 kilometers per second).[22] In a 2008 study, Canup developed a still more refined and comprehensive model for the Moon's formation. This model took into account the rotation rate and the direction of rotation of both the impactor and the "toddler" Earth.[23] It showed that the current

Earth-Moon system's angular momentum could best be accounted for if the value for the impactor's mass was nearly twice the mass of Mars as it struck the retrograde-rotating proto-Earth.

In 2012, a team of planetary scientists removed any reasonable doubt about a giant impact origin for the Moon. They measured zinc isotope ratios and zinc abundance levels in lunar magmatic rocks.[24] Their analysis showed that large-scale evaporation of zinc occurred in the aftermath of the Moon-forming event. Additional confirmation came from a study revealing a difference between the Earth and Moon in their relative oxygen-17 composition.[25]

Ongoing research has yielded considerable debate over the details of the Moon-forming collision event. This debate has intensified as scientists recognize two realities: first, how significant a role this event, or sequence of events, played in shaping the features and conditions of Earth that made possible the existence of advanced life; second, how utterly improbable and highly fine-tuned this event, or sequence of events, turns out to be. Readers interested in an overview of the ongoing research and the points of debate will find them in the paragraphs to follow. For those who'd prefer to see the bottom line, skip ahead to page 56.

## Debate over Moon Formation

One study showed that the primordial Earth must have possessed a liquid-water ocean hundreds of times deeper than Earth's current oceans.[26] Only such a huge quantity of liquid water explains why Earth today has fifty times less argon-36 in its atmosphere than does Venus. Such plentiful water at the Moon-forming collision site generated a cloud of superheated steam, ejecting virtually all Earth's primordial water and atmosphere into interplanetary space.[27] The low shock impedance (ratio of applied impact force to the velocity of resulting vibration at the impact site) removed the just-right amounts of water and atmosphere, but also ensured that the just-right amounts of the heavier elements, especially iron, uranium, and thorium, were transferred from the collider into Earth's core and mantle. In order for the shock impedance to be sufficiently low, but not too low, to make all this happen, the collider, as already confirmed by

Canup's models, had to strike Earth at a low-impact angle and a very low velocity.

The challenge comes in developing a solar system formation model that would produce such a precise low-impact angle, low-velocity collision. For his doctoral thesis, astronomer Eugenio Rivera ran 191 computer simulations of a solar system with five inner planets wherein the fifth planet (Theia) orbited between Venus and Mars.[28] Four of the simulations produced a collision between Earth and Theia that resulted in the current orbital configurations for Mercury, Venus, Earth, and Mars. The question remained, then, as to which of the four provides the best fit with other details.

Several studies reveal that both the Earth and the Moon possess similar oxygen,[29] titanium,[30] chromium,[31] tungsten,[32] and silicon[33] isotope compositions. This isotope identity implies that Theia and the proto-Earth formed at about the same distance from the Sun. Such proximity also would explain the low-impact angle and the low-collision velocity. However, it raises a question: How could a body as large as Theia have formed in an orbit so similar to Earth's without colliding very early on with Earth? All the Moon-forming models require both Theia and the proto-Earth to have developed iron cores, and this development requires several tens of millions of years.

This conundrum led mathematician Edward Belbruno and astrophysicist J. Richard Gott to suggest that the collider actually shared Earth's orbit about the Sun.[34] Newtonian mechanics allows for the possibility of a shared orbit, at either the L4 or L5 Lagrange points (see fig. 5.3). A smaller planet situated 60° back or ahead along Earth's orbital path can remain there in a stable orbital configuration, providing the Sun is at least 25 times more massive than Earth. Given that the Sun is actually 333,400 times more massive, the stability condition is easily met. However, for a population of planetesimals at Earth's distance from the Sun to form both a proto-Earth and a body as large as Theia at one of Earth's L4 or L5 Lagrange points, though not impossible, proves highly unlikely.[35]

The long-term stability condition is guaranteed, however, only if just three massive bodies were involved. The presence of other planets in the solar system, particularly the presence of Jupiter and/or nearby planetesimals, means that, given sufficient time, the smaller planet sharing Earth's

## Figure 5.3. The Lagrange Points

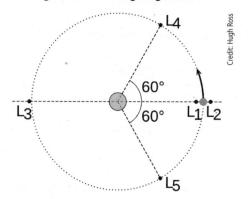

Newtonian mechanics allows for five special points in the vicinity of two orbiting objects where a third, smaller object can orbit at a fixed point from the more massive ones. Only L4 and L5 are stable over long time periods.

orbit would have been wriggled away (by the gravitational influence of these other bodies) from its Lagrange point. This circumstance yields a high probability that the smaller planet (Theia) would creep slowly toward Earth and eventually a high possibility that it would collide with Earth at a low-velocity and a low-impact angle.

The cover article for the December 5, 2013, issue of *Nature* reported Canup's concern that "current theories on the formation of the Moon owe too much to cosmic coincidences."[36] Indeed, the essential "coincidences" and challenges continue to pile up. For example, Canup referred to research showing that the Moon and Earth (in its outer layers) share similar isotope ratios and similar chemical composition. Canup's models cannot explain this fact *unless* certain highly specific conditions were met: (1) the total mass of the collider and the primordial Earth were four percent larger than the present-day Earth's mass; (2) the ratio of the collider's mass to the total mass lay between 0.40 and 0.45; and (3) a highly specific orbital resonance with the Sun were to remove the just-right amount of angular momentum from the resultant Earth-Moon system.[37]

Astronomers Matija Ćuk and Sarah Stewart looked for another way to explain the similar isotope ratios and composition. In their model, an impactor about the mass of Mars collided with a fast-spinning (rotation rate = 2.3–2.7 hours) primordial Earth.[38] The fast spin generated a Moon-forming debris disk made up primarily of mantle material from the primordial Earth, yielding the similar isotope ratios and chemical composition. As with Canup's earlier model, this one requires a fine-tuned orbital resonance between the Moon and the Sun.

In the same 2013 issue of *Nature* that cited Canup's concerns, an article by Stewart raised a provocative question about the likelihood of so many coincidences. She first noted that for the giant impact models to successfully explain the Moon's formation, "lunar material is derived either from a range of depths in the proto-Earth's mantle . . . or equally from the entire mantles of two colliding half-Earths."[39] Stewart asked, "With the nested levels of dependency in a multi-stage model, is the probability of the required sequence of events vanishingly small?"[40] Canup suggested that perhaps a small-collider (Mars-sized) model can be retained without all the added fine-tuning of the Ćuk-Stewart model *if* the collider's initial chemical composition were more Earth-like rather than Mars-like. However, extra fine-tuning may be needed to explain this required composition.

Earth scientist Tim Elliott commented, in that same issue of *Nature*, that the complexity and fine-tuning in lunar origin models appear to be accumulating at an exponential rate. The impact on lunar origin researchers, Elliott noted, is that "the sequence of conditions that currently seems necessary in these revised versions of lunar formation have led to philosophical disquiet."[41]

Findings published in the April 3, 2014, issue of *Nature* only add to this "disquiet." A team of astronomers at the Observatoire de la Côte d'Azur in Nice, France, conducted more than 250 detailed computer simulations of the Moon-forming event in an effort to make a better determination of its timing.[42] These simulations took into account not only the similar chemical and isotope-ratio compositions of the Earth and Moon, but also the abundances of highly siderophile (iron-loving) elements (HSEs) in Earth's crust and upper mantle layers. (HSEs include cobalt, nickel, manganese, gold, and all the platinum group elements.)

If the Moon-forming event occurred early in Earth's formative years, then the amount of material accreted by Earth after that event—in a layer called the late veneer—would be much greater than what we see. The low abundance of HSEs found in Earth's crust and upper mantle layers indicate the Moon-forming event occurred 95±32 million years after the formation of Earth.[43] This date matches the oldest lunar crust ages. It also matches a date determined from studying main-belt asteroids (asteroids with orbits predominantly between the orbits of Mars and Jupiter). Debris left over from the Moon-forming event collided with main-belt asteroids. Because the debris heated those asteroids much more than collisions among the main-belt asteroids, astronomers have used the impact-heating signatures in main-belt asteroids to date the Moon-forming event. That date = 96±10 million years after Earth's formation.[44] This relatively late date would more easily explain the similar chemical and isotope-ratio compositions of the Earth and Moon.

## Implications of the Moon-Forming Event

Although scientific models will undergo further refinement and debate in coming years, the Moon's formation nevertheless represents an intricately layered sequence of coincidences that happened to prepare Earth for life—advanced life, especially. Here is a brief list of what the collision accomplished:

1. The collision replaced Earth's thick atmosphere, providing in its place an atmosphere with optimal (for life) chemical composition, appropriate (for life) heat-trapping capacity, appropriate transparency for efficient photosynthesis, and precise air pressure for making possible the eventual operation of lungs.[45]

2. Earth's mass and density were augmented, enabling Earth to retain (via its gravity) a large, but not too large, quantity of water vapor for billions of years.

3. The amount of iron in Earth's core increased, bringing it closer to the level needed to provide Earth with a strong, enduring magnetic field (the remainder came later) to shield Earth's future life from deadly cosmic rays and solar X-rays and to prevent the sputtering away of Earth's atmosphere.

4. The collision delivered iron and other critical elements to Earth's core and mantle in just-right ratios to produce long-lasting, continent-building plate tectonics at levels just right for life.

5. The quantity of iron delivered via the collision to Earth's crust was just right for supporting an abundance of ocean-dwelling phytoplankton that, in turn, supports the entire oceanic food chain and also provides oxygen for advanced terrestrial life.[46]

6. Earth's interior was salted with an abundance of long-lasting radio-isotopes, the heat from which drives most of Earth's tectonic activity and volcanism.[47]

7. Earth's crust and upper mantle layers were peppered with just-right quantities of HSEs—not so much as to prove poisonous to (later) life but enough to sustain myriad plants and animals, as well as to allow for the eventual launch and maintenance of global high-technology civilization.[48]

8. The collision produced a moon with sufficient mass to stabilize Earth's rotation axis tilt, protecting the planet from rapid and extreme climatic variations.[49]

9. The resulting Moon also gradually slowed Earth's rotation rate to a life-sustaining level (see "The Moon's Marvelous Mass" on page 58).

The importance (for future Earth inhabitants) of our Moon's existence and precise characteristics cannot be overstated. Even its exact diameter and distance from Earth prove beneficial. During one very brief epoch of Earth's history, which happens to coincide with human existence, perfect solar eclipses (eclipses during which the apparent disk of the Moon in the sky is exactly the same size as the apparent disk of the Sun) occur. Through measurements of these eclipses, scientists have made many important discoveries about the solar system, the universe, and the laws of physics.[50]

## Finishing Touches

The Moon-forming event stripped the early Earth of all its water and virtually all its atmosphere, but not for long. Earth regained essential volatiles by accretion from the solar system's remaining planetesimals (small objects

### The Moon's Marvelous Mass

Thanks to the Moon's extremely large mass relative to its host planet and to its close orbit, Earth alone among all the Sun's rocky planets possesses a stable rotation axis tilt. The angle, stability, and longevity of Earth's rotation axis tilt are among several fine-tuned lunar features making advanced life possible on Earth.[51] These findings led geophysicist David Waltham to consider the Moon as a tool for testing the power and scope of the anthropic principle—the tenet that the universe and its various components manifest fine-tuned characteristics that make possible the existence of human beings. If the anthropic principle is a valid description of physical reality, Waltham reasoned, then scientists should discover additional lunar characteristics that prove beneficial to humanity's existence.[52]

Waltham's investigation revealed that the Moon is nearly twice as massive as is necessary to stabilize Earth's rotation axis. The Moon, in fact, proves almost too massive. Increase it by a mere 2 percent and the Moon would pull Earth's rotational tilt out of stability. Waltham wondered whether some anthropic reason might be found for this excessive-to-the-point-of-risky lunar mass.

Soon he recognized that the Moon's mass creates the tidal friction that gradually puts the brakes on Earth's rotation rate. A Moon less massive would take longer than 4.5 billion years to slow Earth's rotation rate from just a few hours to 24 hours per day. To extend this slowing effect over more than 4.5 billion years would mean exposing Earth to a brighter, less stable Sun—one too luminous and too unstable for advanced life. A more rapid rotation rate during the current era of solar burning would also prove problematic. More rapid rotation means a higher surface temperature (see ch. 6), greater temperature extremes over the planetary surface, and less evenly distributed rainfall.

remaining in the solar system's disk). The total mass of these planetesimals at this time was about one percent of the Earth's present mass.[53]

Uranium-to-lead and iodine-to-xenon chronologies show that delivery of volatiles from these remaining planetesimals to Earth peaked about 50–100 million years after the Moon-forming event.[54] Astronomers call this delivery the late veneer, or the late accretion.

The late veneer crucially aided Earth's potential for long-term life support in at least six ways. First, it lessened the high eccentricity, high inclination orbits of Venus, Earth, and Mars, which were established during the giant impact phase of early solar system history—the phase that culminated in the Moon-forming event. Dynamical interaction between the residual planetesimals and the terrestrial planets served to dampen the planets' orbital eccentricities and inclinations, bringing them to their nearly circular coplanar levels we now see.[55]

If the orbits of Venus, Earth, and Mars had not been dampened to near zero eccentricity and inclination values, conditions on Earth would never have become stable enough for advanced life. Mercury's orbit was little dampened by the late veneer, but its high eccentricity and inclination present no trouble because Mercury is so small (one-nineteenth Earth's mass) and so close to the Sun that its gravitational perturbations of Earth's orbit are negligible.

Second, the late veneer added an additional quantity of highly siderophile elements (HSEs) to Earth's crust and upper mantle. Adequate quantities of these HSEs play an essential role for the possibility of high-technology civilization. And yet an overabundance of HSEs, because of their toxicity and radiation, would have seriously limited the profusion and survivability of advanced life if it were to exist.

Third, the late veneer delivered both water and an atmosphere to Earth. Both the just-right quantity of water and the just-right combination of atmospheric gases must be available for life to have a chance. Too few or too many atmospheric gases would either trap too much or too little of the Sun's heat to make life possible on Earth's surface. Too much water would eliminate the possibility of continents and nutrient recycling. Too little water would cripple both the water cycle and plate tectonic activity.

Water and atmospheric gas delivery by the late veneer represents a delicate operation. On any given planet in the solar system, the net amount of water and atmospheric gas accumulated from the late veneer depended upon a competition between impact delivery of new supplies and their impact ejection into interplanetary space.[56] For a body as large as Earth and with its high surface gravity, this competition strongly favored the net accumulation of both water and atmospheric gases. Size and surface gravity explain why Earth gained substantial quantities of water and atmospheric gases while Mars gained only a little, by comparison.

Fourth, the late veneer hit Earth's crust with sufficient force to deliver a small amount of water to Earth's mantle. This water delivery triggered the onset of mantle convection, which in turn activated plate tectonics. Plate tectonics, as mentioned above, produced landmasses and provided for nutrient recycling.

Fifth, the late veneer augmented Earth's mass, just slightly but enough to ensure that Earth could sustain enduring plate tectonic activity and lose very little of the water vapor in its atmosphere. As chapters 7–9 explain, the magnitude and longevity of tectonic activity depend very sensitively on a planet's mass. A planet's mass also plays a major role in determining its escape velocity (the velocity at which a particle, rock, rocket, etc., escapes the planet's gravitational pull). Earth's mass is large enough, but just barely, to prevent the gravitational loss of any of its water vapor to interplanetary space.

Finally, most of the late veneer accretion came from carbonaceous asteroids.[57] Such asteroids and meteorites contained the biogenic compounds that could potentially serve as the building blocks for prebiotic molecules (see chs. 6 and 8).

For these six features of the late veneer to bring about such life-serving effects required a number of additional coincidences. One, the total mass of the late veneer must take on a specified value—no more or less than about one percent of Earth's present mass. Two, the average size and size distribution of the objects making up the late veneer must be neither too large nor too small. Three, the late veneer's timing relative to the Moon-forming event and the origin of life on Earth must have been precise, neither too early nor too late. And four, the average composition and composition distribution of the late veneer accretion had to provide the essential elements and compounds in appropriate abundances.

## Almost Ready for Habitation

The site is now sufficiently protected, cleared, and supplied for the next phase of home construction. Earth has already benefited from blessings disguised as "disasters"—the jarring move from its solar system's origin site, hellish bombardment, a Moon-forming impact, and additional pelting by asteroids, comets, and meteoroids. However, still more preparation is necessary before the site is ready for life. The next chapter examines the remaining steps of preparation known to have occurred in the half billion years just prior to life's arrival.

# 6

## Not Quite Ready

Even after a building site has been located, surveyed, and cleared for construction to begin, new obstacles almost always arise. Every construction project I've observed or been part of, large scale or small, has encountered delays. Sometimes the delays become permanent. Much to my sons' dismay, our city's plan to create a skateboard park on a vacant lot just a few blocks from our home came to a screeching halt when an environmental study revealed hazardous materials underground.

In the case of Earth, even with our solar system and the Earth-Moon system taking shape, certain hazards remained. More preparation was needed to give life a chance. Another half billion years of transformation to the Sun, our neighboring planets, other nearby objects, and Earth's own surface had to occur before the foundation—the most primitive life-forms—could be laid. During this next era, a number of events, some interdependent and some intricately connected, not only prepared Earth's surface for unicellular life but also cleared away obstacles that would have prevented the future arrival and survival of more advanced, ultimately human, life.

## Invisible Hazards

During the first 700 million years of our planetary system's history, solar energy output varied dramatically. During this time, the Sun's X-ray and ultraviolet radiation exceeded current levels by orders of magnitude (see fig. 6.1).[1] This variable and intense radiation ruled out the possibility for life's existence on any solar system body, including Earth, at this time. Even more significantly, the Sun lost 15–20 percent of its mass during this era.[2] This loss of mass resulted in the Sun's dimming by about a factor of two (see fig. 6.2), enough to cause more than an 80 percent loss of its luminosity (light emission). This was a level too low for life. (The degree of dimming occurred because the luminosity of any nuclear burning star increases or decreases in proportion to the fourth power of its mass.)

### Figure 6.1. Solar Flare Activity throughout Solar History

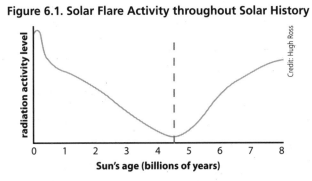

The Sun's flaring activity and X-ray and ultraviolet radiation were at far higher levels (vertical scale of the above graph is logarithmic) during the first billion years of solar history than they are at present (the dotted line). We are living during the Sun's most benign epoch.

Other subtle hazards abounded during this early era of solar system history. The gas giant planets experienced changing distances from the Sun and some chaos in their orbits. Asteroids, comets, and planetesimals (objects larger than asteroids but smaller than planets) were larger, more numerous, and closer to the Sun than they are today. These objects on average orbited more chaotically than they do today (see ch. 5). Consequently, the rate and intensity with which they bombarded the planets during the 700 million years after the solar system's origin precluded the enduring existence of even the simplest life-form.

## Figure 6.2. The Sun's Luminosity during Earth's History

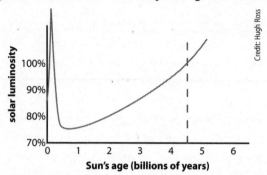

At its birth the Sun brightened quickly as it accumulated mass. During its youth, however, the Sun lost 15 percent or more of its mass, enough to cause more than an 80 percent loss of its luminosity (light emission). As it aged, its nuclear furnace converted more and more hydrogen into helium, increasing the Sun's core density. This increasing core density results in more efficient nuclear burning, and this increasingly efficient burning causes the Sun's brightness once again to rise, gradually. The Sun's brightening continues to this day and will one day generate so much heat energy as to make Earth uninhabitable. The dotted line indicates the current era.

### Taming the Tug-of-War

The youthful solar system's enormous population of asteroids, comets, and planetesimals resided primarily at the orbital distances of Jupiter, Saturn, Uranus, and Neptune. All these objects interacted gravitationally with the gas giant planets in a way that caused the planets to drift outward gradually, away from the Sun, and ultimately to develop orbits free of mean motion resonances. (If two planets orbit the same star, and the ratio of their orbital periods equals two small integers—for example, if planet A makes exactly two orbits for every three orbits of planet B—their combined gravitational influence, or mean motion resonance, produces gravitational disturbances throughout the planetary system.)

Researchers' efforts to model how our planetary system came to be as it is indicate that the gas giant planets formed along quasi-circular, quasi-coplanar orbits that, if unchanged, certainly would have led to the development of mean motion resonances. Four planetary scientists at the Observatoire de la Côte d'Azur in Nice, France—Alessandro Morbidelli, Kleomenis Tsiganis, Harold Levison, and Rodney Gomes—explained how our system avoided these resonances. Their research produced what has come to be known as the Nice (pronounced *niece*) model.

This model reveals what some might describe as an intricate planetary dance. In the outer part of the solar system, Jupiter and Saturn approached, attained, and then escaped a 1:2 orbital resonance. The way they interacted actually prevented the establishment of permanent mean motion resonances.[3] (In the 1:2 resonance, Jupiter made exactly two orbits of the Sun for every single orbit of Saturn.)

The 1:2 Jupiter-Saturn orbital resonance arose when the densest portion of the asteroid-comet-planetesimal cloud orbiting beyond Jupiter (this is not the main belt of asteroids residing between Mars and Jupiter) came closer to Saturn than to Jupiter. This configuration, along with the fact that Saturn's mass = 0.299 of Jupiter's mass, caused Saturn to migrate outward from the Sun at a faster rate than Jupiter did. As a result, Jupiter went from orbiting the Sun *fewer* than two times for every one of Saturn's circuits, to orbiting *exactly* two times for every Saturn circuit, to orbiting slightly *more* than two times for every Saturn circuit.

According to the Nice model, this precisely choreographed and timed 1:2 orbital resonance event between Jupiter and Saturn produced "all the important characteristics of the giant planets' orbits, namely their final semimajor axes [distances from the Sun], eccentricities, and mutual inclinations."[4] In a later paper the Nice team showed that this 1:2 orbital resonance event also produced both the orbital distribution and total mass of the 4,000+ asteroids, known as the Trojan asteroids, that share Jupiter's orbit.[5] The Trojan asteroids cluster around Jupiter's two (stable) Lagrange points (see fig. 5.3), 60° ahead and 60° behind Jupiter in its orbit.

The Nice team went on to show how the 1:2 orbital resonance event between Jupiter and Saturn also yielded the long-elusive answer to what caused the Late Heavy Bombardment (LHB).[6] During a relatively brief episode 700 million years after formation of the solar system planets, tens of thousands of asteroids and comets pummeled Mars, Earth, the Moon, Venus, and Mercury. The LHB brought to Earth, alone, an average of some 200 tons of bombardment material per square yard, distributed over Earth's entire surface.[7]

## A Beneficial Blast

The first tangible evidence for the LHB and its timing came from lunar rocks collected by Apollo missions 15, 16, and 17.[8] Radiometric dating of rocks that had been melted by impacts placed the timing of these impacts between 3.8 and 4.0 billion years ago. Astronomers then measured erosion patterns observed in the Moon's craters. (The Moon is continually bombarded by micrometeorites, which, together with the Moon's thin atmosphere of mostly argon gas, gradually erode its craters over the course of a few billion years.) The erosion measurements indicated that nearly 90 percent of the Moon's craters formed about 3.9 billion years ago.

When astronomers later measured the erosion patterns of both Mercury's and Mars' craters,[9] these measurements, along with other clues, confirmed that the entire inner solar system suffered an intense bombardment of asteroids and comets in the span of no more than a hundred million years between 3.95 and 3.80 billion years ago and peaked between 3.90 and 3.85 billion years ago.[10]

Additional evidence for the LHB came from a study of lunar craters in and near the Nectaris basin (located between the Sea of Tranquility and the Sea of Fecundity). A team of astronomers and geophysicists determined that the projectiles responsible for forming these craters (in the Nectaris region) had struck the lunar surface at twice the velocity of those that created the oldest craters on the lunar terrain.[11] The team concluded, "This dramatic velocity increase is consistent with the existence of a lunar cataclysm."[12]

In seeking answers to what caused this cataclysmic bombardment, the Nice team found that when the 1:2 orbital resonance between Jupiter and Saturn occurred, it destabilized the orbits of Uranus and Neptune.[13] This destabilization, in turn, disrupted the enormous cloud of planetesimals, asteroids, and comets orbiting in the vicinity of the four gas giants, triggering the rapid launch of hundreds of thousands of projectiles into the inner solar system. Their research also established that the disruption strongly perturbed the main-belt asteroids between Jupiter and Mars. The combined effect of these two perturbations superbly explains the LHB.

The Nice team went on to determine that the 1:2 orbital resonance event explains virtually *all* the observed features of the Kuiper Belt—and

Neptune's orbit, as well.[14] The Kuiper Belt (see fig. 6.3) refers to a region of the solar system that extends from the orbit of Neptune, at 3 billion miles from the Sun, out to slightly more than 5 billion miles. Within this zone, where Pluto orbits, astronomers have discovered three additional dwarf planets, or plutoids—Eris, Haumea, and Makemake—and over a thousand asteroids and comets. What they have found so far leads them to conclude that some 70,000 or more objects larger than 100 kilometers (62 miles) in diameter still reside in the Kuiper Belt. Based on this number, astronomers estimate that the total mass of the Kuiper Belt exceeds that of the main belt by about one hundred times.

## Figure 6.3. Kuiper Belt and Jupiter's Trojan Asteroids

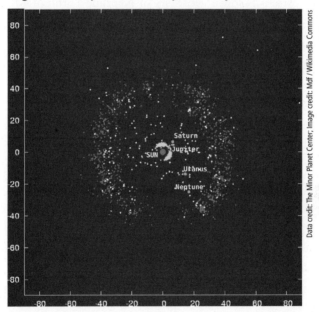

The Kuiper Belt includes two populations of objects: a main population (dark grey) and a scattered population (white). The two flared zones (light grey) emanating from Jupiter show where the Trojan asteroids reside.

These modeling studies showed that the solar system's primordial disk of planetesimals extended roughly 3 billion miles out from the Sun, with most of the objects clustered near what is now Saturn's orbit. The outer edge of this disk of planetesimals marks where Neptune's outward migration came to a sudden halt 3 billion miles out from the Sun. The region we know as the Kuiper Belt was initially empty. Then, the 1:2 orbital resonance event between Jupiter and Saturn thrust what remained of the huge cloud of planetesimals, asteroids, and comets outward, where it came to reside between the orbits of Uranus and Neptune. This movement also amplified (for a time) the eccentricity of Neptune's orbit, raising it to a value as high as 0.3 (the eccentricity of a circle = 0, of a parabola = 1, of an ellipse = between 0 and 1). Interaction between the cloud and Neptune explains nine of the observed characteristics of the outer solar system today:

1. The distance of Neptune's orbit from the Sun (2.8 billion miles)
2. The extremely low eccentricity of Neptune's orbit (e = 0.011)
3. The coexistence of both a resonant and nonresonant population of Kuiper Belt objects
4. The eccentricity and inclination distribution of the plutoids and plutinos (trans-Neptunian objects in a 2:3 mean motion resonance with Neptune)
5. The outer edge of the Kuiper Belt at the 1:2 mean motion resonance with Neptune
6. The correlations between inclination and physical properties of classical Kuiper Belt objects
7. The existence of an extended, scattered disk of objects within the Kuiper Belt
8. The bimodal (two distinct categories of) inclination distribution of classical Kuiper Belt objects
9. The peculiarly low eccentricity of inner Kuiper Belt objects

The team definitively showed that the current Kuiper Belt is the leftover remnant of the enormous planetesimal-asteroid-comet cloud that originally centered roughly on Saturn's orbit.[15] The fact that the Kuiper Belt, though large and massive, is only about one percent the size of the original cloud testifies to the magnitude of the Jupiter-Saturn resonance event.

Over the course of six years, the Nice research team demonstrated what a remarkable range of solar system features are explained by the 1:2 orbital resonance event between Jupiter and Saturn. Other research teams have also added to the list of features explained by this resonance event:

1. The characteristics of Saturn's rings and moons[16]
2. The elimination of the Extended-belt (E-belt) asteroids (part of the primordial main belt that orbited close to the Martian orbit)[17]
3. The heavy element enrichment of the gas giants' atmospheres[18]
4. The presence of primordial trans-Neptunian objects in the main belt[19]
5. The orbital characteristics of the Eos family of asteroids (a group of nearly 300 main belt asteroids that apparently resulted from the breakup of a parent body)[20]
6. The elevated abundances of highly siderophile (iron-loving) elements (rhenium, osmium, iridium, ruthenium, platinum, and palladium) in the mantles of Earth, the Moon, and Mars[21]

In relation to Earth, the LHB did more than just load up our planet with more of the highly siderophile elements (HSEs). It altered the tilt of Earth's rotation axis by as much as 10°.[22] It infused Earth's core with extra sulfur, oxygen, iron, uranium, and thorium[23] and removed much of Earth's chlorine and other halogens.[24] In other words, it reconfigured Earth's atmosphere, crust, mantle, outer core, and inner core so as to enable Earth's surface to eventually support advanced life.

Virtually every known feature of both the 1:2 orbital resonance event and the LHB played a crucial role in preparing Earth for possible existence of advanced life. Meanwhile, astronomers have discovered yet another amazing story from the solar system's youth.

## Jumping Jupiter

More than 650 million years before the LHB and many millions of years before the Moon-forming event, Jupiter, Saturn, Uranus, and Neptune began migrating. Angular momentum (rotational analog of linear momentum) transfers between the gas giants and the scattered planetesimals (those pre-planetary bodies remaining after dissipation of the nebular disk) launched their migrations. However, the standard migration models could not account for the formation of the solar system's terrestrial planets (Mercury, Venus, Earth, and Mars) as they are currently configured.[25]

These standard models predicted that Mars should be many times more massive than it is. They also predicted different distributions and characteristics of the solar system's belts of asteroids and comets. A piece of the puzzle was missing.

Although the "Grand Tack" scenario (proposed by the same team that formulated the Nice model) resolved nearly all the terrestrial planet formation problems (see pages 45–48), it did not explain the observed configurations of the solar system's gas giant planets and belts of asteroids and comets. To resolve these conundrums the Nice team proposed a "jumping Jupiter" model.

According to this scenario, either Uranus or Neptune experienced a close encounter with Saturn and was, consequently, moved inward.[26] The inward migration resulted, then, in a close encounter with Jupiter wherein Uranus (or Neptune) was strongly pushed back outward. This second close encounter led to a rapid increase in the separation between Jupiter's and Saturn's orbits.[27]

This scenario successfully explained the current orbits of Jupiter, Saturn, and one of either Uranus or Neptune. However, it also predicted that either Uranus or Neptune would have been ejected from the solar system.[28] Clearly, a model adjustment was needed to account for this inaccurate prediction.

One explanation for the solar system's retention of both Uranus and Neptune could come from the possible existence of a transplanetary disk of planetesimals with a total mass greater than 50 Earth masses. If this enormously massive belt of planetesimals had existed some 5 to 15 times Earth's current distance from the Sun, it could account for the positions of the solar system's gas giant planets, but it would have reduced their orbital eccentricities far below observed values.[29]

Another explanation for retention of Uranus and Neptune posits that 4 billion years ago the solar system possessed five giant planets—two gas giants (Jupiter and Saturn) and three ice giants (Uranus, Neptune, and another Neptune-sized planet). In this scenario, Jupiter ejected one of the three ice giants into interstellar space.[30] If the ejection timescale was relatively brief, this model would account for all the known features of the Kuiper Belt, with its asteroids and comets.[31] Furthermore, if the close encounters between Jupiter and the ice giants were few in number and brief, the model would account for all the observed features of Jupiter's four large moons.[32]

The third ice giant planet may not have been completely ejected from the solar system. A clustering of orbits of distant Kuiper Belt objects may indicate the presence of a planet more than ten times Earth's mass orbiting the Sun at a distance of about 65 billion miles (about 23 times the distance that Neptune orbits the Sun).[33]

By including five initial giant planets in their solar system formation model, the Nice team was able to account not only for our current solar system planets' configuration but also that of the multiple asteroid belts.[34] The outward migration of Neptune would have restructured the Kuiper Belt and pushed it outward to a zone between 3 and 5 billion miles from the Sun.[35] In a very elegant manner, the jumping Jupiter phenomenon explains the resonances that swept through most of the main belt and depleted the inner part of the belt.[36]

Together with the Jupiter-Saturn 1:2 resonance event, this scenario explains the missing Extended-belt (E-belt) asteroids that other models predict should exist in large numbers between the current inner boundary of the main belt and the orbit of Mars (1.7–2.1 times the distance of Earth from the Sun).[37] The latest version of the jumping Jupiter model also answers the question of how Jupiter captured its Trojan asteroids.[38] Additionally, it explains the total mass of the Trojan asteroids, their orbital distribution, and potentially the observed asymmetry in the number of leading and trailing Trojans (not all observations confirm this asymmetry).[39]

## A Wonderment

While the possibility exists for a planet such as Jupiter to "jump" in the manner that generated our solar system's current configuration, the likelihood of such an occurrence remains, nonetheless, remote.[40] In fact, the entirety of the LHB, its details and its effects, has caused researchers to pause and ponder. One member of the Nice team joined with several other planetary physicists to calculate the probability of an LHB event in an extrasolar planetary system. They constructed models of what that planetary system's asteroid-comet belts would have looked like prior to an LHB. Comparing their results with observed debris disks of different ages surrounding Sun-like stars, the researchers demonstrated that LHB events around stars similar to the Sun must, indeed, be rare.[41]

Planetary system models developed by a pair of Greek astronomers showed that orbital resonances among gas giant planets would be expected to excite (or energetically enhance) the inclinations of all planetary orbits within a planetary system.[42] Thus, the low-angle tilt of all the planets' orbits (in any system), relative to the stellar system plane, would be unexpected. This conclusion has been confirmed by analysis of extrasolar planet statistics.[43] And in considering how a planetary system could end up with planets exhibiting the mass, composition, and orbits of Uranus and Neptune, another team of astronomers described it as an extreme challenge.[44] In their words, "very specific conditions are required."[45]

## Help from the Belts

The story of our solar system formation would be incomplete without a more detailed description of the various asteroid belts referenced above. The main belt of asteroids and comets, familiar to most people, orbits between Mars and Jupiter, and is just one of five belts associated with our solar system. The Centaurs orbit between Jupiter and Neptune. The scattered disk extends from just outside the orbit of Uranus (about 2 billion miles from the Sun) out to 20 billion miles from the Sun. The Kuiper Belt resides just outside the orbit of Neptune, between 4 and 6 billion miles out from the Sun. The fifth belt, the Oort cloud, stretches from about 10 billion to 2 trillion miles out from the Sun.

Asteroids and comets in each belt possess physical and/or orbital properties that distinguish them from asteroids and comets in the other four belts. As described above, there is some overlap in the spatial distribution of the belts.

To understand the importance of these belts and the objects within them, consider the importance of roadways and waterlines. No real estate developer begins home construction without ensuring these basics are in place. They represent vital access and supply lines, not only for construction purposes, but also for the needs of the home's future residents.

Building a home where asteroid and comet belts are too massive or too nearby would be like starting construction in the middle of a major freeway or aqueduct. These belts would deliver too many devastating collisions and far too much water. On the other hand, building where asteroid and comet belts are insufficiently massive or too far away would be like building a home on the dark side of the Moon. The supplies of water, carbonaceous compounds, and heavy metals that advanced life and civilization depend upon would be far too limited.

Terrestrial planets, such as Mercury, Venus, and Earth, form in a dry region of the protoplanetary disk.[46] For water to exist on such a planet, it must be delivered. For the most part it comes via comets (which can be as much as 85 percent water) and asteroids (which can be more than 10 percent water). If too much water is delivered, even very aggressive plate tectonic processes would fail to produce enough silicates to generate exposed (above sea level) continental landmasses. If too little water, oceans will be too small to sustain an adequate water cycle or to recycle life-essential nutrients. During its early history, Earth was molten, and its gravity pulled heavy elements into the core, leaving the surface depleted of these elements. Again, it took asteroids and comets to deliver the essentials. They peppered Earth's crust with iron, copper, nickel, silver, gold, platinum, and other elements.

Recent research[47] indicates that the existence, location, mass, and influence of our system's asteroid and comet belts represent a departure from the norm. This research referred to experiments and computer simulation studies showing that asteroids form adjacent to a planetary system's snow line.[48] (The snow line refers to the distance from a central star at which water and other volatiles, such as ammonia and methane, freeze into solid grains. Rocky planets form far inside the snow line, and gas giants form beyond it.) In our solar system, the snow line is 40–50 million miles inside the orbit of Jupiter.[49]

Confirmation that asteroids indeed form at the snow line comes from observations of warm dust (the signature of asteroid belts) orbiting 20 solar-type stars.[50] The warm dust orbiting these 20 stars consistently shows up at their snow lines.

The formation of an asteroid belt is dependent upon the existence of a giant planet orbiting beyond the snow line (where giant planets form). The gravity a giant planet exerts prevents planet formation just inside of its orbit. The planetesimals existing there do not coalesce. Instead, they grind against one another to form an asteroid belt.

Theoretical models show, however, that the vast majority of giant planets, once formed, continue to interact with planetesimals and undergo substantial inward migration. Indeed, observations of giant planets outside our solar system reveal that more than 94 percent orbit their stars *inside* the snow line.[51] This inward migration typically obliterates a planetary system's asteroid and comet belts, scattering and then ejecting the asteroids and comets from the system. (A small percentage would fall into the star and the star's gas giant planets.)

One team of researchers demonstrated that in only 1–2 percent of planetary systems will the most massive planet linger somewhere near the orbital distance of Jupiter.[52] This rarity may explain why warm dust (the signature of the presence of asteroids and comets) has been observed around so few stars.[53]

Investigation by NASA astronomers Rebecca Martin and Mario Livio pointed out, however, that a small amount of gas giant migration is necessary.[54] Otherwise the belts of asteroids and comets remain much too large. The just-right amount of migration will thin them out, removing a large fraction of these objects. If such migration does not occur, asteroid and comet impacts on the terrestrial planets will be numerous, far too many to allow for the existence of advanced life.

For a giant planet to remain at or near the place it began, it must form at the moment when the gas in the interplanetary disk becomes completely depleted. As Martin and Livio explained, "There appears to be a very narrow 'window of opportunity' of time during which the giant planet should form, in order for the correct amount of migration to take place—potentially making our Solar system even more special."[55]

Even without reference to our asteroid and comet belts, Earth's planetary system appears exceptional. The list of rarities, all of which serve the eventual needs of long-enduring life, up to and including advanced civilization, starts with the system's origin cluster and goes on to include its ejection from that cluster, the Grand Tack sequence, the Moon-forming event, the late veneer, the LHB, the fifth planet's timing, and jumping Jupiter. The existence and locations of our planetary system's five asteroid and comet belts simply add to the already long list of features that must be in place *before* life can originate on Earth and possess any possibility of survival for a few billion years. The "coincidences" compound with each new discovery.

## Fresh Confirmation

A remarkable sequence of events over the course of a billion years somehow worked together to place the solar system's eight planets (not to mention its other objects) in their current orbital positions. The observation that these positions provide optimally for the existence and survival of advanced life on Earth adds considerable weight to what scientists and philosophers refer to as the anthropic principle, or the law of human existence. Some loathe it while others embrace it for the enormity of its implications. In brief, the anthropic principle states that all the features of the universe appear fine-tuned for the benefit of human life.

The apparent "specialness" of our solar system carries weighty implications well worth additional testing. And modeling research continues, as it should. For example, two Brazilian astronomers produced dynamical maps of the regions beyond the precise orbital positions of Jupiter, Saturn, Uranus, and Neptune as they are currently configured. These regions abound in mean motion resonances.[56] In fact, destructive mean motion resonances are nearly ubiquitous. As it is, Uranus is close to a 7:1 resonance with Jupiter, a 2:1 resonance with Neptune, and a 3:1 resonance with Saturn. Meanwhile Jupiter and Saturn are very close to 5:2 resonance. If any of these gas giant planets' orbital positions were to shift even slightly, that shift would generate instabilities in the orbit of one or more of the solar system's eight planets. Such instabilities would shatter the possibility of a long history of life on Earth, a history leading to human life and civilization.

Three Canadian astronomers further demonstrated that the Earth-Moon system plays a vital role in stabilizing the dynamics of the inner solar system.[57] In particular, the Earth-Moon system suppresses a resonance in the orbit of Venus that would result from the orbital pattern of Jupiter, Saturn, Uranus, and Neptune. (The orbital pattern of the gas giants has been stable for at least the past billion years.) Without the presence and configuration of the Earth-Moon system, the orbits of both Venus and Mercury would destabilize and eventually generate destructive chaos in the inner solar system.

Another research team performed a long-term integration study of the solar system's planetary orbits. They found that the orbits of the four gas giant planets and the five inner solar system bodies (including the Moon) produce the just-right orbital variations and just-right resonances to generate the just-right timing and frequency of asteroid and comet collisions with Earth to provide for the needs of advanced life.[58]

At the same time, however, they showed that orbital chaos in the inner solar system—at a level that would be disturbing for advanced life—is actually the rule, rather than the exception. Remarkably, they noted, "Despite being chaotic, orbital evolution in the inner solar system appears to have been quite uneventful for the past 50 Myr."[59] This current and temporary period of exceptionally benign inner solar system orbital dynamics coincides perfectly with the timing of Earth's most advanced life-forms.

### Getting the Place Ready

The difference between preparing to pitch a tent for a few nights and preparing to build the Wilshire Grand Center in Los Angeles or 432 Park Avenue in New York reflects the difference in what is at stake. Failure to notice a bit of a slope or some rocks and roots or a nearby swelling stream may lead to an uncomfortable night's sleep when camping. However, even the slightest miscalculation in preparation for construction of one of these towers could cost lives.

While the meticulous and lengthy preparation of the solar system to make Earth ready for even the simplest life-form has come to light, many or most origin-of-life researchers appear unaware of it. The "habitability" indices they've developed seem to suggest to them that the origin and survival of life are relatively trivial steps. From this assumption, they reason that life must be present on millions, if not billions, of planets in the Milky Way Galaxy alone. They go on to extrapolate, based on these supposedly easy steps, that the development of advanced life from simple life also must be relatively simple and straightforward.

Such analysis implies that life, up to and including human life, just happened and, thus, possesses no inherent meaning or significance. Meanwhile, the community of astronomers, astrophysicists, and others continues to raise questions about the viability of these habitability indices. Just how straightforward is the origin of life? These questions and others relevant to life's origin are addressed in the next chapter.

# 7

# Ready for the Foundation

The more residents a structure will house and the more environmental variables it must endure, the deeper and more complex its foundation must be. For the Wilshire Grand Center, with its 900 hotel rooms and 400,000 square feet of office space rising 73 stories above earthquake-prone land and into the pathway of Santa Ana winds, the foundation required immense care and precision. The *Los Angeles Times* reported that some 2,120 truckloads of wet concrete had to be poured into an 18-foot-deep hole nearly two-thirds the size of a football field *without interruption* in less than 30 hours.[1] Then 90,000 feet of polypropylene hoses had to circulate 40,000 gallons of water chilled to 45° for the next two weeks to ensure that the slab would remain intact—otherwise uncontrolled heat would crack the concrete's crystal structure and turn it to gravel.[2]

Similarly, the foundation of the structure that would one day support human life and technologically advanced civilization took shape in Earth's deep past—and came together quickly. A wealth of evidence tells us that life arose on Earth as soon as solid rocks and liquid water first began to exist with some stability on the planet's surface.[3] What's more, isotope evidence indicates that when life first emerged on Earth, it appeared as a complex ecosystem of diverse unicellular species in high abundance.[4] The implications of this extremely early, diverse, and abundant presence of life has generated intense debate. Did it come from biogenesis, as the creation from another living being, or from abiogenesis, as the outcome of strictly natural processes at work in nonliving matter?

Confident that abiogenesis requires only solid rocks and liquid water, NASA scientists spearheaded the active search for extraterrestrial life with their follow-the-water strategy. This confidence also explains astronomer Steven Vogt's bold assertions. When his research team claimed to have discovered the extrasolar planet Gliese 581g, Vogt told reporters, "My own personal feeling is that the chances of life on this planet are 100 percent."[5] In a press release he added, "The fact that we were able to detect this planet so quickly and so nearby [only 20 light-years from Earth] tells us that planets like this must be really common."[6]

Amir Aczel, an internationally known mathematician and author of the bestselling book *Probability 1: The Book That Proves There Is Life in Outer Space*, claims that the enormously large number of planets in the universe essentially guarantees that life exists on many planets beyond the solar system. He did concede, though, that the probability for abiogenesis on any given planet *could be small*.[7] Recently, two astrobiology research teams announced that by their calculations, the number of habitable planets in the Milky Way Galaxy (MWG) stands at 40 billion[8] or 45.5 billion,[9] respectively.

Acknowledging that these numbers may prove overly optimistic, many astrobiologists have focused their efforts on finding Earth analogs, or "twins." Of the over 2,000 extrasolar planets studied and measured to date, none proves truly identical.[10] As astronomers Daniel Foreman-Mackey, David Hogg, and Timothy Morton noted, "Hundreds of planets have been found around Sun-like stars that are either Earth-sized but on shorter periods, or else on year-long orbits but somewhat larger."[11] Although these differences may seem trivial, they carry enormous consequences for life's possibility.

### Liquid Water and Solid Rocks = Life?

Vogt's confidence that the planet Gliese 581g contained life arose from his assumption that Gliese 581g has liquid water on its surface. Vogt's team measured the planet's mass to be 3.1 to 4.3 times that of Earth[12] and found that Gliese 581g closely orbits a dim red dwarf star (twice as closely as Mercury orbits the Sun). This orbital distance suggests that the planet's average surface temperature (*if* it possesses an Earth-like atmosphere) ranges between -12°C (10°F) and -31°C (-24°F).

While such a low average temperature may seem inhospitable for life, Gliese 581g, like the Moon, is tidally locked. In other words, one side of the planet perpetually faces its host star. One hemisphere is permanently illuminated, and the other, permanently dark. The lit side stays hot while the dark side stays hundreds of degrees below freezing. However, Gliese 581g would certainly possess a twilight zone, a longitude between shadow and bright light. Vogt imagined that emerging life-forms would have a wide range of temperatures to choose from, depending on their longitude, no matter how much greenhouse warming the Gliese 581g atmosphere may induce. Some longitude or other would always fall within the right temperature range for liquid water to exist.

Ongoing research has chipped away at Vogt's and others' initial optimism. First, any pools of water, even if the sole requirement for life's origin and survival, would be transitory, at best. As it turns out, the other planets orbiting the same star (Gliese 581), gravitationally perturb Gliese 581g with such frequency that the twilight longitude must vary over relatively short time scales.

Second, even if Gliese 581g began with some water at or near its surface, the host star's radiation would most likely have sputtered it away into interplanetary space. Third, red dwarf stars emit strong ultraviolet (UV) flares. This level of UV radiation would prevent both the origin and the survival of life.

Not only are other astronomy research teams skeptical about Gliese 581g as a possible life site, they now doubt that Gliese 581g even *exists*.[13] Their measurements show that rather than the system containing six planets, two of which could possibly possess some liquid water, Gliese 581 actually contains just four planets, none of which possesses any liquid water.[14]

This one case does not mean, however, that planets with liquid water must be rare. After molecular hydrogen ($H_2$ and $H_3$), water is the most abundant molecule in the universe. Researchers should expect to find multiple planets containing water, even an abundance of water. But does the combination of water and rocks realistically and inevitably lead to the spontaneous generation of life from nonlife? Scientists who specialize in origin-of-life research would answer a resounding no to this question—not based on their lack of insight to the mystery, but rather based on their in-depth and meticulous probing of it.[15]

## Habitable Zones

Astronomers and astrobiologists refer to that region about a star where some conceivable sort of life could possibly exist as the circumstellar habitable zone. Here a potential "carrier" planet or moon (see appendix A for an explanation of why surface life is not possible on a moon) might exist, and where life could reside for a reasonable length of time. The extent of this zone depends entirely on assumptions about what characteristics and resources life requires for its existence. Some scientists as well as laypeople tend to see just one or two properties and supplies (such as a certain radiation level and quantity of liquid water) as sufficient for habitability. However, this picture comes into sharper focus as research reveals how many *more* features and supplies—each representing a distinct zone—life requires.

These multiple zones, then, must converge to some extent and for some duration to make life conceivable. Only in this much narrower region where all the habitable zones overlap, do all life's necessities come together. Of course, the region of overlap for advanced life will be much smaller yet. The following list describes what ongoing studies have revealed, to date, about the kinds and sizes of eight distinct habitable zones.

### 1. Liquid Water Habitable Zone

The liquid water habitable zone is that region about a star wherein liquid water can exist on a planetary surface. For water to remain, of course, requires an appropriate level of atmospheric pressure. (Where pressure is low, such as on Mars, a drop of water would evaporate in a second.) The liquid water habitable zone may also be called the temperature habitable zone. At least some part of a planetary surface must range between 0–100°C (32–212°F)—assuming a surface air pressure similar to Earth's—to retain liquid water.

Whether or not any part of a planet's surface stays at a temperature that permits the existence of liquid water depends on three factors: (1) the host star's luminosity, or total energy output; (2) the planet's atmospheric pressure; and (3) the quantity of heat-trapping gas in the planet's atmosphere. Early studies led by geoscientist James Kasting indicated that at the Sun's current luminosity level, the liquid water habitable zone lies between 95 and 137 percent of the Earth's distance from the Sun.[16]

Kasting's team showed that a planet orbiting closer than 95 percent Earth's distance from the Sun would experience a runaway evaporation. Increased heat from the Sun would evaporate more of the water, and because water vapor is a greenhouse gas, this added water vapor would trap more heat, which would cause more water to evaporate and, thus, trap still more heat, and so on until no liquid water remained. A planet at or beyond 137 percent Earth's distance from the Sun would experience the opposite, a runaway freeze-up. Less heat from the Sun would mean more snowfall and more frozen surface water, both of which would reflect heat, causing even more snow to fall and more water to freeze, and so on, until no liquid water remained.

Cloud cover or atmospheric haze could possibly mitigate the cooling effects of reflection from snow and ice. Or, if the planet's albedo (surface reflectivity) is more like that of the Moon, which reflects only 7 percent of incident radiation at visible wavelengths, than that of the Earth, which reflects 30–35 percent of incident radiation, then less of the Sun's heat would be reflected away. These additional factors push the possibility of liquid water (on a planet) out to 167 percent of Earth's distance from the Sun.

More recent studies of newly derived water vapor and carbon dioxide absorption coefficients show the inner limit of the liquid water habitable zone at 99 percent of Earth's distance from the Sun.[17] This narrowing of the zone so troubled extraterrestrial life enthusiasts as to spur development of a new model for the liquid water habitable zone. This model invokes planets that are much drier than Earth, and with surface rocks significantly more reflective than Earth's. Researchers showed that if these desert worlds were to possess thin atmospheres with humidity levels no greater than 1 percent and a rotation axis tilt near 0° and a distance from their star roughly equal to the orbital distance of Venus, then a runaway water vapor greenhouse effect could possibly be avoided.[18] These models further require that the tiny amounts of liquid water be restricted to the host planet's high latitudes. One extreme model showed that if no water transport between one region and any other were to occur, runaway water vapor evaporation could be avoided even for planets as close to their star as Mercury is to the Sun (just 39 percent of Earth's distance from the Sun).[19]

Extraterrestrial life enthusiasts have also proposed an extension to the outer boundary of the liquid water habitable zone. Models show that water worlds (planets with water covering their entire surface) would have much higher surface temperatures than planets with at least some dry land.[20] Geothermal hot spots could potentially heat pools of water to life-sustaining temperatures on planets more distant from their host star than 167 percent of Earth's distance from the Sun.[21] These enthusiasts claim the outer limit can be pushed out to 225 percent Earth's distance from the Sun, well beyond Mars' distance. A major challenge, however, comes from the fact that carbon dioxide would freeze at such a distance. So, its potential greenhouse warming effect would be lost.

The notion of an extremely wide habitable zone gives rise to bold assertions, such as the claim that 40+ billion Milky Way planets could potentially be "home" to life. But these terms need clarification. If one defines "life habitable zone" as a region where the most primitive conceivable unicellular life-form could survive for a very brief time, it may be a bit wider than Kasting's early calculations indicated—but only *if* life requires only a certain minimal amount of liquid water and not much more and *if* it really does arise spontaneously from nonlife under such conditions.

For a long history of life, one that includes the possibility of advanced life, the liquid water habitable zone by itself would be much narrower than the narrowest limits described above. Advanced life requires more than merely a stable supply of liquid water. As ongoing research tells us (see chs. 13–15), it requires a habitat in which frozen water, liquid water, and water vapor exist simultaneously over long time periods. It also requires a habitat in which water transitions efficiently from one of its states to the other two.

What's more, water represents only one of life's requisites. Other essentials exist in their distinct zones, which may or may not overlap.

### 2. Ultraviolet Habitable Zone

The ultraviolet habitable zone is that region about a star where incident UV radiation arriving on a planet's surface is neither too strong nor too weak to provide for life's needs. UV radiation is a double-edged sword. Without it several essential biochemical reactions and the synthesis of many life-essential biochemical compounds (such as DNA repair and vitamin D manufacturing) cannot occur. Too much of it, however, will damage or destroy land-based life. Both the quantity and the wavelength of incident UV radiation must fall within a certain range for life to survive, and an even narrower range for life to flourish.

The acceptable range of UV radiation seems especially narrow for human beings. Skin exposure to UV radiation serves as the primary source of vitamin D production in human bodies. Vitamin D helps grow strong bones, prevents many kinds of cancer, and maintains the immune response system. UV radiation exposure stimulates the pineal gland, which helps elevate positive moods. It can also help alleviate skin conditions such as psoriasis and eczema. However, only slightly more UV radiation exposure than the minimum levels required for these health benefits would raise the incidence of skin cancer and damage our eyesight. Still more would generate life-threatening melanoma and blindness.

Although the UV zone may prove relatively wide for the sake of more primitive life-forms, it may not be wide enough even then to overlap with the liquid water habitable zone. For host stars with effective temperatures less than 4,600 kelvin (K)—that's the number of Celsius degrees above absolute zero—the outer edge of the UV habitable zone falls closer to the star than the inner edge of the liquid water habitable zone.[22] For host stars with effective temperatures greater than 7,100 K, the inner edge of the UV habitable zone sits farther from the host star than the outer edge of the liquid water habitable zone.[23] For older stars that have completed their hydrogen-burning phase, the UV habitable zone appears about ten times more distant from the host star than the liquid water habitable zone.[24] As a basis for comparison, the Sun has an effective temperature of 5,778 K.

The fact that the liquid water and UV habitable zones must overlap for the sake of life eliminates most planetary systems as possible candidates for hosting life. This requirement effectively rules out all the M-dwarf and most of the K-dwarf stars, as well as all the O-, B-, and A-type stars. All that remain are F-type stars much younger than the Sun, G-type stars no older than the Sun, and a small fraction of the K-type stars. As described in chapter 5, only stars at a certain distance from the galactic core can be considered candidates for life support. In the MWG, some 75 percent of all stars residing at this appropriate-for-life distance are older than the Sun.[25] Once these and other noncandidate stars are ruled out, only 3 percent of all stars in our galaxy remain as possible hosts for planets on which primitive life could briefly survive.

### 3. Photosynthetic Habitable Zone

The photosynthetic habitable zone refers to the range of distances from a host star within which a planet could possibly possess the necessary conditions for photosynthesis to occur. While some life-forms can exist in the absence of photosynthesis, such life exhibits metabolic rates from hundreds to millions of times lower than those of photosynthetic life.[26] In other words, without photosynthesis, large-bodied warm-blooded animals would not be possible.

Photosynthetic life requires much more demanding constraints on the quantity, stability, and spectral light range available on a planet's surface. Limited photosynthetic activity is possible for a planet where the UV and liquid water habitable zones overlap. However, for the scope of photosynthetic activity advanced life requires to endure and thrive, these seven factors must fall within highly specific ranges:

1. Light intensity
2. Ambient temperature
3. Carbon dioxide concentration
4. Seasonal variation and stability

5. Mineral availability

6. Liquid water quantity

7. Atmospheric humidity (for land-based life)

To maintain these features within appropriate ranges presents an even greater challenge due to ongoing changes in surface conditions. Over the past 3.9 billion years, Earth has undergone some dramatic variations in solar luminosity and spectral response, and these variations impacted all seven conditions for photosynthesis. Detailed models of the early history of the Sun and Earth (between 4.0 and 3.0 billion years ago) show that surface radiation levels were at least thousands of times higher in the 2,000–3,000 angstrom (Å) wavelength range than current levels in this range.[27] (One angstrom is equal to 0.1 nanometer.) This finding tells us that life-forms on Earth previous to 3 billion years ago had to endure far greater solar X-ray and UV radiation than do life-forms today.

Figure 6.1 shows the incident UV radiation history for Earth's surface. This history explains, in part, why only unicellular life-forms and colonies of these life-forms existed on Earth for the first 3 billion years following life's origin. Appropriate conditions for both large terrestrial advanced plants and animals have been present for only the past 250 million years. (Large terrestrial plants did *begin* to appear during the Devonian period 420–359 million years ago; even forests appeared by the late Devonian.) Because incident UV radiation seriously degrades photosynthetic efficiency, the level of crop cultivation necessary to sustain billions of people and a technologically developed civilization became possible (on the basis of photosynthetic capacity) only relatively recently in Earth's history.

### 4. Ozone Habitable Zone

The ozone habitable zone describes that range of distances from a star where an ozone shield can potentially form. When stellar radiation impinges upon an oxygen-rich atmosphere, it produces a quantity of ozone in that planet's atmospheric layers. This ozone, in turn, affects the amount of radiation reaching the planetary surface.

Ozone, a molecule composed of three oxygen atoms, forms in a planet's stratosphere as short wavelength UV radiation and, to a lesser degree, stellar X-ray radiation react with dioxygen ($O_2$). Meanwhile, its reaction with atomic oxygen in the stratosphere destroys ozone ($O_3 + O \rightarrow 2O_2$). The quantity of ozone in the stratosphere at any given time depends on the status of this balancing act.

Currently, ozone in Earth's stratosphere absorbs 97–99 percent of the Sun's short wavelength (2,000–3,150 Å), life-damaging UV radiation while allowing much of the longer wavelength (3,150+ Å), beneficial radiation to pass through to Earth's surface. What makes this life-favoring scenario possible is the combination of three main factors: (1) the necessary quantity of oxygen in Earth's atmosphere; (2) the just-right intensity of UV radiation impinging on Earth's stratosphere; and (3) the relatively low variability of this UV radiation bath.

For the level of stellar UV emission to be sufficiently stable for life's sake, the host star's mass must be virtually identical to the Sun's. Stars more massive than the Sun exhibit more extreme variation in UV emission. So do stars less massive than the Sun. The host star's age also must be virtually the same as the Sun's (see fig. 6.1) and for the same reason—limited variability. Given that the quantity of oxygen in a planet's atmosphere must also fall within a limited range, especially for advanced life, only a narrow range of distances from a host star allows for a planet's stratospheric ozone to remain at appropriate levels for life.

For life protection purposes, the ozone quantity in a planet's troposphere (the atmospheric layer extending from the surface up to a certain distance, in Earth's case, from sea level to six miles up) must amount to about 10 percent of that in the stratosphere. Too much ozone in the troposphere would hinder respiration for large-bodied animals while also reducing crop yields and wiping out many plant species. Insufficient tropospheric ozone would lead to an ever-increasing buildup of biochemical "smog" particles emitted by tree-like vegetation. These factors place additional constraints on a host star's UV radiation intensity and stability, and on the host planet's distance from the star, especially given that ozone production in a planet's troposphere receives a boost from lightning.

### 5. Rotation-Rate Habitable Zone

A planet's rotation rate impacts the reflectivity of its clouds and, thus, how much of the host star's light penetrates to the planetary surface. Three-dimensional atmospheric circulation models show that rapidly rotating planets compared to slowly rotating planets would generate much narrower bands of clouds at low latitudes (given the same atmospheric magnitude and composition).[28] These narrower tropical cloud belts would reflect much less of the host star's light and, consequently, allow the planet's surface to reach much higher average temperatures.

A planet's rotation rate actually affects the positions and sizes and potential overlap of multiple habitable zones. The faster the rotation rate, the more distant from the host star the water, UV, photosynthetic, and ozone habitable zones would be. Rotation rate would also impact (in different ways) the breadth of all these habitable zones.

### 6. Obliquity Habitable Zone

The tilt of a planet's rotation axis relative to its orbital axis (i.e., its obliquity) plays a significant part in determining the planet's surface temperature. Climate simulation studies demonstrate that the higher the obliquity, the warmer a planet's surface.[29] Specifically, high obliquity warms the oceans and cools the continents.

Just as a planet's rotation rate impacts the positions of several habitable zones, so does the planet's obliquity. Greater obliquity pushes certain habitable zones—water, UV, photosynthetic, and ozone—outward from the host star. The planet's obliquity also affects the breadth of these habitable zones in different ways.

### 7. Tidal Habitable Zone

The tidal habitable zone refers to the distance range from a host star where the planet is near enough for life-essential radiation but far enough to prevent tidal locking. Due to gravity, a star exerts a stronger pull on the near side of its surrounding planets than on the far side. Tidal force describes the difference between the near-side tug and the far-side tug, a difference that carries great significance. The tidal force a star exerts on a planet is inversely proportional to the fourth power of the distance between them. Thus, shrinking the distance by one half increases the tidal force by 16 times.

If a planet orbits too close to its star, it becomes tidally locked (as the Moon is tidally locked with Earth), which means one hemisphere faces permanently toward its star. As a result of tidal locking, one face of the planet would receive an unrelenting flow of stellar radiation while the opposite side would receive none. On a tidally locked planet, then, the only conceivable place where life could exist would be in the twilight zone—that narrow region between permanent light and permanent darkness. If such a planet happened to reside in the liquid water habitable zone and possess an atmosphere, water would move via atmospheric transport from the day side to the night side, where it would become permanently trapped as ice.[30] So, no liquid water would exist anywhere on its surface. For life to exist on a tidally locked planet, it would have to be unicellular, exhibit extremely low metabolic rates, and reside below the surface.

Tidal locking takes time to develop. A planet's initial rotation rate gradually slows to equal its rate of revolution. The rate at which a planet becomes tidally locked to its star is inversely proportional to the sixth power of its distance from the star. For example, if Earth were to orbit ever so slightly nearer to the Sun, it would experience so much rotational slowing as to approach tidal locking and its consequences. As it is, Earth's rotation has slowed from a rate of 3–4 hours per day at the time of the Moon-forming event to about 21 hours per day 488 million years ago (as evidenced by coral reef banding)[31] to the current 24-hour-day rate—a rate that happens to match the needs of human life and civilization in profound ways. The Sun's tidal contribution to this rotation rate decrease is about half the Moon's. Given the mass of the Moon, the just-right level of tidal braking requires a Sun neither more nor less massive than it is and neither more nor less distant than it is.

A star's tidal force also erodes its planets' rotation axis tilt. If a planet orbits too close to its star, tidal force would drive its rotation axis tilt to less than 5° and, consequently, prevent the occurrence of seasons there. The lack of seasons would radically shrink the planet's habitable area. Food crops would be rare to impossible while any existent pathogens would potentially thrive. Intelligent life likely would be constrained to small populations with few means to advance beyond Stone Age technology.

The star's mass also comes into play in erosion of a nearby planet's rotation axis tilt. To avoid such erosion and maintain the necessary tilt over a period of a billion years—while also remaining in both the water habitable and UV habitable zones—the mass of the star around which the planet orbits must fall within a precise range. The bottom end of that range is 0.9 times the mass of the Sun.[32] This value represents the limit for a young planetary system. For a planet to maintain stable seasons and provide a secure foundation for later intelligent life, the mass of the host star must be no less than that of the Sun.

For stars more massive than the Sun, the habitable zones move out to greater distances. Such distances eliminate the possibility of catastrophic tidal effects, but these more massive stars burn up more rapidly and with more radical luminosity variations during their existence. They also emit more UV radiation. A star more massive than the Sun would possess a UV habitable zone only when that star is much younger than the Sun. Such a star could conceivably host a planet on which unicellular life would be able to survive for a relatively brief time, but not a planet on which life persists and becomes the foundation for more advanced life.

The Sun's mass proves just right for life on other counts, beyond applying tidal forces to ensure Earth's just-right rotation rate at the just-right time for the benefit of human life. The complex interaction of both solar and lunar tidal effects permits Earth to sustain an enormous biomass and biodiversity at its seashores and on its continental shelves. The tides on Earth are optimal for recycling nutrients and wastes. They provide the potential for a rich and abundant ecology.

### 8. Astrosphere Habitable Zone

This is a recently discovered astrophysical phenomenon that limits the region around a star where a potential life-sustaining planet can reside.[33] Researchers observe that a star's "wind" (release of radiation) pushes outward against the cosmic radiation all around it, radiation emanating from its galaxy's core and from nearby supernova explosions. This wind creates a cocoon of charged particles surrounding the star. This region, called the astrosphere, is where the wind blows strongly enough to deflect cosmic rays. The astrosphere acts as a buffer to screen the orbiting planet's atmospheres and surfaces from the high-energy cosmic radiation that would be deadly.

The buffering, however, must be delicately balanced to yield a zone safe for life. A powerful stellar wind will generate a large plasma cocoon, but such a cocoon could blast nearby planets with so many stellar particles as to either kill or seriously limit the prospects for life there. On the other hand, a weak stellar wind produces a small plasma cocoon inadequate for shielding its planets from blasts of deadly cosmic radiation.

The effective protection offered by a star's astrosphere depends on the star's mass and age, as well as on the density of the interstellar medium in which the star resides. Because stars follow orbital pathways around the galactic center, the density of the interstellar medium in any star's vicinity will vary over the course of its orbit. The question for habitability is whether, at any given time in a star's burning cycle, the star's astrosphere covers the orbit of a planet with the just-right level of protection—neither too strong of a stellar wind nor too weak, all within a region overlapping the liquid water, UV, photosynthetic, and tidal habitable zones.

To allow for the existence of any life other than the most primitive unicellular forms, all these habitable zones must overlap. They can do so only in a relatively narrow band around a star with the same mass as the Sun. Even then, however, dangers remain. As two astronomers from the University of Arizona demonstrated, for a solar-mass star, a close encounter with a dense molecular cloud will at least temporarily shrink that star's astrosphere to a size smaller than the overlapping set of habitable zones.[34] This study showed that solar-mass stars encounter 1–10 such shrinking events every billion years, leading researchers to consider a possible correlation with major extinction events in Earth's fossil record. These events have occurred once every 27 million years, on average, over the past 600 million years.[35] Astrosphere-shrinking events may account for at least a few of these episodes.

## The Essential Magnetic Fence

For the just-right organisms to be present at the just-right times to lay the foundation for a long, diverse, and complex life history, the habitable planet must be able to maintain a powerful, stable magnetic field. Without a protective electromagnetic fence, a planet's atmosphere eventually would be sputtered away by the host star's particle radiation. Without a just-right magnetic field, even a carefully balanced environment of solar and cosmic radiation will wreak havoc on surface life.

To develop and maintain a strong, steady magnetic field presents a challenge. Everything depends on the planet's internal composition. Two teams of astronomers have demonstrated that for a rocky planet to maintain a sufficiently strong and enduring magnetic field, its internal composition must closely resemble Earth's.[36] In particular, it must have a liquid iron outer core surrounding a solid iron inner core and highly specified viscosity and magnetic diffusivity values at the inner-outer core and outer core–mantle boundaries. A team of Japanese astronomers showed that the magnetic field duration (for a planet with Earth's exact core composition) slowly increases with planetary mass but sharply declines when the mass reaches 1.4 times that of Earth.[37] They concluded that for life to be sustained on a planet for as long as 4 billion years, the planet's mass must fall within the range of 1.0–1.4 times the mass of Earth.[38] Another research team showed that the planet's rotation rate history must also be similar to Earth's.[39]

## Habitable Zone Longevity

The physical properties of every star change dramatically as the star ages. The same holds true for a star's planets throughout the planetary system's history. These changes mean that the circumstellar habitable zones around any star change through time both in their distance from the star and in their breadth.

Newly forming stars brighten rapidly as they accumulate mass (as illustrated in fig. 6.2). Young stars then grow dimmer for a while as they shed some of the mass they initially accreted. After this dimming period, stars begin to brighten gradually as nuclear burning in their cores raises the core density and causes their nuclear furnaces to burn more efficiently. This stellar burning cycle places limits on the time period during which a planet with the suitable accompanying planets, asteroids, and comets orbiting an appropriately massive star possesses all the essential conditions and features life requires. The more complex the life, the deeper and more enduring the foundation must be (see appendix B).

This entire discussion of when and where life can possibly exist and persist, continuing not only to survive but also to flourish over nearly 4 billion years, substantially narrows the field of life-support candidates. However, no one can yet account for how life came to exist—here on Earth much less anywhere else—in the first place.

## The Meaning of Life's Early Origin

Earth is much more than a planet with primitive life residing upon it. It is a planet with a very long history of life, a history that led to the appearance of human beings. We are not constrained to a low population in a few restricted areas. Humans currently occupy all of Earth's landmasses. We have multiplied to a population exceeding 7 billion individuals and have achieved a high-level technology that continues to advance on a global scale.

All these features of current human existence and civilization would be impossible unless life originated on Earth as early as physically possible. These features likewise would be impossible if that first life had not been abundant and diverse. As astronomers David Spiegel and Edwin Turner pointed out, confidence that abiogenesis must be an easy step—because life *did* suddenly emerge on Earth as early as physically possible—may be misplaced. Their Bayesian probability analysis took into account "that, billions of years later, curious creatures noted this fact [of origin] and considered its implications."[40] They concluded, "The evidence is inconclusive and indeed is consistent with an arbitrarily low intrinsic probability of abiogenesis."[41]

In other words, the probability for life's origin by natural processes alone may not be high at all. In fact, it may prove as low as zero. More on this topic appears in the next chapter.

# 8

## Construction Begins below Ground

The first step in any construction job—even one as tricky as laying the foundation for the Wilshire Grand Center—tends to be the most thoroughly researched and the least complex of the total project. Such is the case with our planetary home. Scientists have identified and mapped all the chemical building blocks that comprise the simplest cells, which form the foundation for life. The chemical pathways through which these building blocks interact with one another have become so well understood that biochemical research labs are able to redesign cells to serve various therapeutic functions.[1] The physical and chemical conditions at the time of life's origin no longer remain a mystery.

Enough has been discovered that a model for life's origin can now be proposed and assessed. This model identifies when and where life first arose and indicates what kind of organisms emerged first. It even narrows in on the means by which life did—or did not—arise.

As a graduate student at the University of Toronto, I once had the opportunity to hear astronomer and science popularizer Carl Sagan present a lecture series on life's origin. Sagan described a vast ocean densely packed with the chemical building blocks for DNA, RNA, proteins, and membranes that percolated for about a billion years. So many prebiotics and so much time, he asserted, would virtually guarantee the spontaneous production of a simple bacterium, at least.

Today we can affirm that Sagan was right about the existence of a vast ocean. Earth at the time of life's origin could be described as a water world, with liquid water enveloping almost its entire surface. However, research now challenges his claim about the contents of this ocean. Just how densely packed was it with the chemical building blocks of life molecules?

## The Search for Building Blocks

How helpful it would be to have actual fossils of Earth's earliest life-forms! A team of researchers in Germany and Switzerland proposed a new tool that may lead to unearthing the next best thing.[2] They found that certain iron-oxidizing bacteria produce twisted stalk-like structures that can survive high heat and high pressure, such as that produced by extensive diagenesis (transformation of sediments at temperatures and pressures less extreme than those required to form metamorphic rock). They observed such structures in material taken from 1.9-billion-year-old rock formations deep inside a silver mine in Germany's Black Forest. Testing showed the twisted stalks to be remarkably heat and pressure resistant.[3] If similar structures were to be discovered in the 3.8-billion-year-old metamorphic rocks of Greenland, they would provide strong evidence that bacterial life existed very early in Earth's history.

Until this finding becomes available, studies rely primarily on geochemical markers for life. The long-term effects of plate tectonic activity, volcanism, and erosion have nearly destroyed the chances of finding intact fossils of earliest life—at least on Earth's surface. The good news is that while these fossils were being obliterated on Earth, they might well have been transported, in pristine form, to the Moon.

At the time of life's origin, comets, asteroids, and meteorites heavily bombarded Earth. These colliders ejected large amounts of Earth's surface material into outer space, and a substantial quantity of that material would have ended up on the Moon. Astronomers have calculated that each square kilometer of a region around 50° west and 85° south on the smiling face of the Moon received some 300–500 kilograms of Earth material, all of it arriving via low-velocity impacts.[4] For 43 percent of these impacts, the vertical arrival speed would have been less than 1 kilometer per second.

Researchers can expect to find the fossilized remains of Earth's first life embedded in the material wafted up to the Moon from collision events on Earth. Given the slow-speed impacts and the lack of geological activity on the Moon in the era since life originated on Earth, in all likelihood the pristine fossils of first life still remain on the Moon.

Missions to the Moon focused on recovery of these fossils could help us resolve a major debate. Nontheists and theists tell very different stories about Earth's first life. Nontheists propose that the first organism was a single species of minute bacteria, less than 0.1 microns in diameter, low in abundance, and at least as simple as the simplest single-celled life-form existing today. Theists, by contrast, propose that the origin of life was the sudden appearance of a complex ecology of abundant single-celled organisms, many as large or larger than a micron in diameter. A targeted lunar mission could potentially go a long way toward settling this question.

Nevertheless, Earth's earliest life has left behind some clues. The planet's crust contains telltale isotope signatures. When living organisms use inorganic material to build biomolecules, they preferentially select lighter isotopes from that material. For example, life and the remains of life contain higher ratios of carbon-12 to carbon-13, nitrogen-14 to nitrogen-15, and sulfur-32 to sulfur-34 than does material that was never part of an organism.[5]

Organisms use certain building block molecules to manufacture proteins, DNA, RNA, lipids, and polysaccharides. The most critical of these building block molecules are amino acids, nucleosides, fatty acids, and five- and six-carbon sugars.

When organisms die, they first decay into these building block molecules and then further break down into a suite of carbonaceous substances. Isotope analysis of the building block molecules and carbonaceous substances found in ancient crustal deposits allow researchers to distinguish whether or not this material arises from the decay of once-living organisms.

To date, isotope analysis of Earth's oldest rocks reveals that none of the building blocks and carbonaceous substances found there came from inorganic sources.[6] All bear the signatures of decay from once-living organisms. These results indicate that Earth never carried a rich, or even a dilute, supply of prebiotics. On this basis alone, the once widely accepted "primordial soup" scenario is off the table—or the stove.

A physical explanation for the absence of prebiotics on the early Earth comes from the oxygen-ultraviolet paradox. Research shows that the presence of oxygen, even in a minute amount in the ocean or atmosphere, effectively stymies prebiotic chemistry.[7] At the same time, the lack of oxygen in Earth's environment means no ozone can form to protect the planet from the Sun's ultraviolet radiation—such radiation unimpeded proves equally catastrophic to prebiotic chemistry.

Abiogenesis depends crucially on the availability of a highly concentrated supply of prebiotics. At the time of life's origin prebiotics were neither abundant on Earth nor concentrated. In fact, they seem to have been nonexistent. This finding has led to considerable debate over the timing of Earth's first life.

## Strategic Timing

More than a decade ago, evidence indicated that the origin of life occurred within an immeasurably brief time span. The late heavy bombardment (LHB; see ch. 6) raised the temperature of the entire planetary surface so high as to evaporate all its water and melt all its rocks. Then, according to multiple isotope studies,[8] just as soon as the surface temperature cooled enough for the possibility of life's existence, life appeared. This evidence prompted paleontologist Niles Eldredge to comment, "One of the most arresting facts that I have ever learned is that life goes back as far in Earth history as we can possibly trace it. . . . In the very oldest rocks that stand a chance of showing signs of life, we find those signs."[9]

To address this obvious challenge to a strictly natural origin of life, many researchers scoured the scientific landscape for indications of a much wider time window. One approach called into question the early dates for the isotope signatures found in Earth's oldest rocks.[10] The other suggested that the LHB must have been less intense or else extended over a much longer time period.[11]

### The Dating Challenge

In the 1990s, a research team published an origin-of-life date of 3.86 ± 0.01 billion years ago.[12] They used zircon minerals to determine the age of the graphitic quartz-rich rocks (that's graphite in apatite grains embedded in banded quartz-pyroxene-magnetite rocks) containing life's carbon isotope signature (a low ratio of carbon-13 to carbon-12). However, other researchers suggested that the zircon minerals used might have come from some unspecified older material infused into the rocks.[13] So the team performed a more precise dating of their best sample. The result came back with a date of 3.825 ± 0.006 billion years ago.[14] They also showed that the minerals in the suspect zircons are consistent with their having crystallized from their host rocks.[15]

Another basis for challenging the early date arose from questions about the banded quartz-pyroxene-magnetite rocks (mentioned above). Perhaps they had been misidentified as metamorphosed sediments. Further studies showed that while the formations in which these rocks were found do not exactly resemble other organic-rich banded iron formations, they do look very much like metamorphosed marine sediments.[16]

Additional support for the early date of Earth's first life came from a study by earth scientists at the University of California, Los Angeles (UCLA). This team used three-dimensional molecular-structural imaging to confirm that "inclusions of graphitic carbon, wholly contained within apatite grains, occur in the same quartz-pyroxene-magnetite bearing Akilia metasediment," as those studied and dated by the team that published the 3.825-billion-year date.[17] The UCLA team then used secondary ion mass spectrometry to show that the graphite inclusions indeed contain the carbon isotope signature of life.[18]

The UCLA team's samples indicated that life was present on Earth at least 3.830 billion years ago.[19] Their conclusion: "It seems likely that the record of life on Earth is as old as the oldest sedimentary rocks now known."[20]

Another research team found the carbon isotope signature of planktonic organisms in metamorphosed shale dating to 3.70+ billion years ago.[21] In the same shale they measured a high ratio of uranium relative to thorium. This finding indicated a sequence whereby organic debris produced a local reducing environment that precipitated uranium deposited in the shale sediment by oxidized ocean water. The presence of this oxidized water implies that oxygenic photosynthetic life was abundant prior to 3.70 billion years ago. Given that the simplest oxygenic photosynthetic bacteria contain over 2,000 gene products, this finding suggests that highly complex unicellular life already existed some time before that date.

A team of Japanese and Danish geochemists recently addressed the challenge of whether the graphitic carbon was indigenous to the early dated rocks or was precipitated from less ancient metamorphic or igneous fluids.[22] First, they affirmed the carbon isotope signature for life by using transmission microscope observations. These observations showed that graphite occurs in these rocks as nanoscale polygonal and tube-like grains—typical of biotic graphite, but in sharp contrast to abiotic graphite, which appears as flakes. Next, the team's Raman spectroscopy and geochemical analyses established that their samples had formed in "clastic marine sediments that contained $^{13}C$-depleted carbon at the time of their deposition."[23] Finally, they noted that the distorted crystal structures and disordered stacking of graphene sheets observed in their samples matched what would occur during metamorphism. On these bases, the team concluded that the graphitic carbon really is indigenous to the early dated rocks and that life must have flourished in the oceans as far back in time as the formation of Earth's oldest known sediments.

Stanford University teams led by geophysicist Norman Sleep have demonstrated that black shale constitutes a biosignature.[24] Earth's black shales reveal that sulfide and probably iron-oxide-based anoxygenic photosynthesis were well established by 3.8 billion years ago. This marine photosynthesis would have caused organic carbon to accumulate in shales. Dates for black shales "indicate that the Earth teemed with life by the time of the earliest preserved rocks, ca. [about] 3.85 Ga [billion years ago]."[25]

The presence of widespread silicates and abundant granite 3.7 to 3.8 billion years ago could also qualify as signatures for life. Scientists know that photosynthesis harvests solar energy and channels that energy into geochemical cycles. Today photosynthesis contributes about three times more energy to these cycles than does heat flow from Earth's interior.[26] If abundant photosynthetic life on and just below the planet surface appeared early in Earth's history, it would explain the advent of aggressive, sustained silicate production.[27] Such silicate production may also explain the unique great abundance of granites on Earth, as contrasted with other planetary bodies, and why stable continents appeared only *after* the origin of life.[28]

## The LHB Challenge

Given that life does date back to 3.82–3.83 billion years ago, the timing of the LHB, which peaked at about 3.9 billion years ago, leaves the narrowest imaginable time window for life's origin. If the bombardment created as much heat and devastation as researchers thought it did, Earth's surface would not have cooled and stabilized enough for life to survive, let alone originate, until 3.83–3.85 billion years ago.

To widen that life-origin time window, some researchers hypothesized an earlier date for the LHB, a longer and less intense LHB, or some combination of these options. The introduction of this hypothesis led to a new round of studies—a more thorough investigation of the LHB. The results have been striking.

Detailed analyses of lunar samples collected by Apollo astronauts (looking at argon-argon, uranium-lead, rubidium-strontium ratios) indicate that the LHB did, indeed, remain intense until 3.85 billion years ago.[29] Similar analyses of lunar meteorites support this conclusion even more definitively.[30] When planetary scientists studied the Argyre Basin on Mars, they saw evidence for the LHB's intensity. The basin resulted from a giant impact on Mars between 3.8 and 3.9 billion years ago.[31] Evidence showed that this impact raised Mars' surface temperature by several hundred degrees, causing a runaway loss of water vapor. It permanently transformed Mars into a cold, dry planet. Given Earth's much greater mass and density, Earth would have absorbed at least ten times the damage suffered by Mars.

A team of Australian geologists went on to uncover terrestrial evidence for the LHB. They found an anomalously low abundance of tungsten-182 in metamorphosed sedimentary rocks dating 3.7–3.8 billion years ago in western Greenland and northern Labrador (Canada).[32] The low abundance of this tungsten isotope, never observed in strictly terrestrial rocks, resembles the composition of sedimentary deposits heavily contaminated by meteorites. (Meteorites have a particularly low quantity of tungsten-182.) Discovery of nickel and chromium in these rocks, in quantities characteristic of iron and chondritic (rocky, carbon-rich) meteorites, added further confirmation.

The "tepid" LHB model[33] proposes that the impactors all came from the main belt of asteroids, that the number of impacts to Earth totaled no more than 17,000,[34] and that the LHB deposited no more than about 200 tons of extraterrestrial material per square meter over Earth's entire surface.[35] The latest research on lunar samples points to a more intense scenario. It reveals that some 80 percent of the lunar face was "resurfaced" by impacts during the LHB.[36] The magnitude of the lunar collision effects, when scaled to account for Earth's size and mass, tell us Earth took roughly 23,000 major hits within a relatively brief period.[37]

The notion that the LHB impactors came from the main belt has been countered by analysis of meteorites from the asteroid Vesta, a resident of the main belt. These meteorites provide evidence that Vesta suffered high velocity bombardment analogous to the lunar bombardment associated with the LHB.[38] We can be sure this bombardment did not come from within the main belt, where impact velocities among main-belt asteroids average less than 5 kilometers per second, a small fraction of the LHB impact velocities. Thus, Vesta's high-velocity impactors must have come from beyond the main belt.[39]

The Nice model for early solar system development (see ch. 6) shows that the LHB colliders came from a massive disruption of the Kuiper Belt. This scenario received potent confirmation from a geochemical study of Earth's earliest rocks, wherein samples of three types of 3.8-billion-year-old metasedimentary rocks were found to contain 7.5 times more iridium than does the ocean crust today.[40] This level of enrichment aligns with the lunar cratering rate as well as the LHB's corresponding contribution to Earth's crust, given that most of the influx came from comets rather than asteroids. The total mass of the impactors that struck Earth during the LHB adds up to at least 1,000 tons per meters squared.[41] The LHB comets delivered the equivalent of a one-kilometer-deep global ocean.[42]

The question about the duration of the LHB has been addressed by recovery of zircons from the Jack Hills region of Western Australia. These zircons exhibited key indicators of intense bombardment—higher abundances of uranium and hafnium, a lower thorium to uranium ratio, and lower abundances of cesium and phosphorous—that continued from 3.91 to 3.84 billion years ago.[43]

Multiple indicators would seem to confirm that the LHB persisted with great intensity until about 10 million years or less prior to the origin of life, allowing only that astronomically brief time window for Earth to recover from the bombardment's physicochemical effects. However, one more challenge lingered, and to meet it required additional research.

## The Recovery Hypothesis

On the assumption of a bombardment composed of only asteroids from the main belt and that lasted nearly 200 million years, planetary scientist Oleg Abramov and geologist Stephen Mojzsis proposed an alternate model for the timing of life's origin. Their computer simulation demonstrated the possibility of a few local refuges, two or more kilometers below Earth's surface, where temperatures during the LHB could have fallen below 110°C (230°F).[44] Such refuges, they argued, would have permitted the survival of deep benthic life (life-forms living in subseafloor sediments), in this case hyperthermophiles, bacterial species capable of tolerating temperatures a little above water's boiling point, that later recovered (after the LHB) and evolved into more complex life that eventually proliferated upon Earth's surface.

Abramov and Mojzsis's simulation implied that the LHB might not have been a total sterilization event. While it rendered the entire surface of Earth impossible for life and eliminated any subsurface mesophiles—organisms that thrive at moderate temperatures, typically between 5°C and 45°C (40°F and 115°F)—it might have harbored hyperthermophiles in a few deep pockets. This proposal raised hopes within the origin-of-life research community that the maximum time window for the origin of life could be widened from less than a few million years to perhaps as much as several hundred million years.

To support the hypothesis that life's origin could be stretched out over several hundred million years, Abramov and Mojzsis cited a few terrestrial zircons shown to be between 3.9 and 4.4 billion years old. The existence of these zircons indicates that liquid water must have been present, at least in the time frame and geographical region where the samples were found.[45]

These lone terrestrial survivors, a few zircons dating previous to 4.0 billion years ago, can hardly carry the weight of the hypothesis resting on them. If liquid water had, in fact, persisted on and in Earth's crust from 4.4 billion years ago until the first life appeared 0.57 billion years later (according to its isotope signature), scientists should be able to find more evidence of it than just a handful of high-temperature resistant zircons in Western Australia (Jack Hills), western Greenland (Akilia Island), and in one small area of Canada's Northwest Territories (west of Great Slave Lake).[46]

A more likely explanation for the limited rock and zircon remains previous to 3.9 billion years ago is that liquid water existed intermittently and in a few limited spots on and in Earth's surface between 4.4 to 3.9 billion years ago. The intermittent liquid water conditions within a few refuges leaves open the possibility that life appeared even earlier than isotope signatures yet convey. If so, it might have appeared, disappeared, and reappeared multiple times during the LHB era. Such a scenario would assume either highly efficient abiogenesis or multiple creations.

A strike against the possibility of efficient abiogenesis comes from recent reanalysis of ancient cratering events on Mercury, the Moon, and Mars. This study shows that bombardment of Earth must have been very intense even *before* the LHB.[47] Early colliders included an estimated one to four bodies 1,000 kilometers in diameter, three to seven roughly 500 kilometers in diameter, and a great many more between ten and a few hundred kilometers in diameter. Bombardment of such a magnitude implies that liquid water must have been limited to brief moments in tiny pockets either deep inside Earth's crust or quickly driven there by the impacts. If any life ever did exist in these temporary refuges, scientists would face the challenge of explaining not just one but rather multiple rapid origin events.

What's more, hyperthermophilic (able to survive in extremely hot environments) organisms are the only life-forms that could possibly have existed in these extreme conditions—and they are a poor candidate for abiogenesis. In 2004, a research team demonstrated that extremophiles, owing to both how unstable life's building block molecules are under extreme conditions and to the additional biochemical complexity required for the extremophiles to survive, are essentially irrelevant to naturalistic origin-of-life hypotheses.[48] Although life can survive under extreme physical and chemical conditions, its likelihood to originate under such conditions defies reality.

High temperatures prove especially catastrophic for naturalistic origin-of-life models. The higher the temperature, the shorter the half-life of all the crucial building blocks. For example, at an ideally neutral pH (neither acidic nor alkaline), a sample of ribose, a five-carbon sugar crucial to every nucleotide component comprising RNA, will break down, losing half its molecules in 44 years at 0°C (32°F). At 100°C (212°F), the ribose half-life drops to just 73 minutes.[49] Such an extremely brief half-life guarantees that the concentration of ribose consistently remained too low to sustain a naturalistic pathway for spontaneous RNA assembly—even at 0°C (32°F).

Another challenge to the early, rapid origin and survival of hyperthermophilic life through the LHB epoch comes from the narrow range of temperatures hyperthermophiles can withstand. As Abramov and Mojzsis noted in their paper, the surface material in the vicinity of an impact that generated a 2,000-kilometer- (1,250-mile-) wide crater would take 10 million years to cool to a level within the appropriate range for life, and an impact generating a 20-kilometer- (12.5-mile-) wide crater would take 100,000 years.[50] In each case the window of time during which temperatures match the appropriate level for hyperthermophilic life to exist appears far too brief for even the most optimistic abiogenesis scenario.

In one context, the less intense but longer-lasting LHB proposed by Abramov and Mojzsis makes things more difficult for a naturalistic explanation of life's origin. In the standard LHB scenario, a concentrated bombardment turns Earth's crust into a molten state followed by a general cooling that brings much of Earth's surface into a temperature range suitable for liquid water. However, in the Abramov-Mojzsis scenario a more extended and varied bombardment would have meant that everywhere on

Earth temperatures would have been changing erratically, too much so for either the origin or survival of life.

Even mesophilic forms of benthic life would have difficulty recovering from an impact event. A 1.76-kilometer (1.1-mile) core drill into the 35-million-year-old impact crater beneath Chesapeake Bay (eastern United States) demonstrated this point. The core data showed that the microbial community at depths below 1.5 kilometers (0.9 miles) has *not yet* recovered from the impact that produced this crater.[51]

An additional consideration comes from the huge price hyperthermophiles pay for their capacity to live at temperatures above 100°C (212°F). Much of their biochemical machinery focuses on repairing the chemical damage generated by high temperatures. These limitations are even more severe for hyperthermophiles living deep below Earth's surface. At a depth of two or more kilometers, nutrient availability declines dramatically, slowing metabolic and reproductive rates and increasing exposure to radiation from radioactive decay. Furthermore, at the time of the LHB, radiation from radioactive decay in Earth's crust was about five times greater than it is today. All these constraints impair both the rate and degree to which such species can undergo adaptive change. The hypothesis that such deep underground hyperthermophiles evolved into mesophiles defies credibility.

In 2009, when Abramov and Mojzsis published their hypothesis, microbes in the subseafloor sediments were thought to be extremely abundant. University of Georgia microbiologists had calculated that microbes in subseafloor sediments comprised nearly one third of the total global biomass.[52] In 2012, a team of five geomicrobiologists discovered that microbial abundance in subseafloor sediment can vary by factors of 100,000 times among different sites. Taking into account this variation, they determined that subseafloor microbes most likely make up just 0.6 percent of Earth's total biomass.[53] This low figure presents yet another significant challenge to the Abramov-Mojzsis proposal.

Finally, the suggestion that life might have existed previous to the LHB has been all but ruled out by evidence of extensive weathering in Earth's crust prior to the LHB. The Jack Hills zircons dated between 3.9 to 4.4 billion years of age reveal extremely high lithium abundances and anomalous lithium isotope ratios.[54] These abundances and ratios suggest that

Earth's crust during that era experienced extensive weathering indicative of acid rain.

Even though acid-tolerant microbes (acidophiles) can and do live under acidic conditions, they cannot *originate* under those conditions. Acidic conditions inhibit key prebiotic reactions and also promote the breakdown of proteins and DNA. In other words, the presence of acid rain would have frustrated any origin-of-life possibility during this extremely early era.

## An Unsolved Mystery

Perhaps the greatest challenge to abiogenesis comes from the homochirality problem. Amino acids cannot be linked together to make proteins unless all the amino acids have the same left-handed configuration. (Nineteen of the 20 bioactive amino acids exist in two different geometric configurations: one where a hydrogen atom is bonded on the left side of the molecule and the other where it is bonded on the right side.) Neither can the nucleobases be linked together to make DNA and RNA unless they are connected by sugars all with the same right-handed configuration. Outside of organisms, amino acids and sugars exist in racemic mixtures, that is, random mixtures of left-handed and right-handed configurations. No natural source can be found, either on Earth or anywhere else in the universe, for homochiral amino acids or sugars.[55] Neither has any natural source been found for the five-carbon sugars[56] that all DNA and RNA molecules need. Nor has research identified any possible natural source for the basic amino acids arginine, histidine, and lysine.[57]

The quest for deeper understanding of nature and its processes propels scientific advance. So efforts to discover how life originated rightfully focus on how nature might have generated the leap from nonlife to life. However, as in the case of the origin of the universe, when research runs head-on into nature's limits only *scientism*, not science, would rule out consideration of any cause other than nature. At such places, to invoke the possibility of a power and intelligence beyond nature may be the most rational response. That's not to say research should be discontinued, but rather that supernatural causality warrants respectful consideration by scientists, rather than immediate and unquestioning dismissal.

By whatever means life first arose on Earth, evidence shows that it came early and flourished in abundance in complex ecosystems of unicellular life-forms. When it arrived, it began to play a critical role in preparing Earth for more life, for all Earth's future inhabitants. The next chapter explains some of the ways it served later life's needs.

# 9

# Up to Ground Level

The Wilshire Grand Center's foundation did not fill the deep hole dug beneath the planned structure. It filled a hole *beneath* that five-story-deep hole. Much work remained before any permanent part of the building would appear at or above ground level, all of it anchored in one way or another by that first concrete slab. The story of our home planet's construction again invites comparison. The origin of life in the deep past and beneath Earth's surface in a vast global ocean simply anchored the transformative work to follow, an enormous complex of tasks.

To accomplish these tasks, life itself had to change, first from cells containing only a little more than a thousand gene products to cells containing several thousand, from anaerobic to aerobic—and on from there.

### A Major Step Up

The first major changes—the boost in gene products and respiration—most likely occurred almost immediately, if not simultaneously with life's origin. The simplest organism capable of independent survival today is a bacterium, *Pelagibacter ubique*, with a genome consisting of 1,308,759 base pairs (1,354 gene products),[1] considered the theoretical minimum.[2] This bacterium obtains the energy it needs for survival and growth anaerobically; that is, without oxygen.

A wide energy efficiency gap exists, however, between anaerobic and aerobic life. Anaerobic metabolism yields fifteen times less energy than does aerobic metabolism. Of course, oxygen is a prerequisite for aerobic respiration, and oxygen comes from photosynthesis. So for aerobic life to become abundant and widespread, organisms capable of photosynthesis had to become abundant and widespread.

Widespread aerobic life provides something loosely resembling the Wilshire Grand Center's plumbing system. It sets up the chemical and nutrient cycles vital for the needs of eventual residents, advanced animal life. In fact, these cycles must be sustained for a few billion years before animal life can even move into Earth's habitat (see ch. 11). Because the time window for the possible existence of animal life is fixed and relatively brief (see chs. 11–13), these crucial cycles must be launched quickly and aggressively following the origin of Earth's first life.

By quickly, I mean abundant aerobic life must be present within a few tens of millions of years following the first appearance of life. The rapidity (scientifically speaking) with which these first major changes occurred on Earth should not be taken for granted. They defy all realistic estimates and actual measurements of natural process change rates. In fact they have led to some remarkable probability calculations.[3]

We can compare the simplest bacterium (described above) with the simplest oxygenic photosynthetic bacterium, *Prochlorococcus marinus*, to glimpse the difference. This bacterial species contains 1,751,080 base pairs (1,884 gene products).[4] However, *P. marinus* lacks the phycobilisome antenna essential for efficient light capture across a broad spectrum. Given the conditions on Earth previous to 3 billion years ago, when the Sun shone more faintly (see ch. 12), the atmosphere blocked out more light (see ch. 12), and all life was marine life, bacteria without this antenna would have been inadequate for the task. In fact, an abundance of phycobilisome-possessing photosynthetic bacteria would have been essential.

The simplest photosynthetic bacterium possessing a phycobilisome is *Thermosynechococcus elongatus BP-1*, which contains 2,593,857 base pairs (2,475 gene products).[5] The most complex photosynthetic bacterium contains 9.2 million base pairs.[6]

The difference in structural complexity between simple anaerobic bacteria and photosynthetic bacteria employing a phycobilisome antenna may be compared to the difference between a bicycle and an automobile. The reader is free to speculate by what means this transformation—and others described in the paragraphs and pages ahead—came about. It's worth noting that of all Earth's microorganisms, photosynthetic bacteria are by far the most genetically diverse. This diversity enables them to occupy a broad range of habitats across all latitudes. They are abundant not only in benign habitats but also in the severe conditions of hot springs as well as saline, acidic, basic, and high-ultraviolet-exposure environments.

These abundant and diverse photosynthetic bacteria cohabited early Earth alongside abundant and diverse nonphotosynthetic bacteria. Chemical analysis of Earth's most ancient banded iron formations (BIFs), dating back to 3.7–3.8 billion years ago,[7] reveals that sulfate-reducing bacteria (SRB), methanogens (methane-producing bacteria), and methanotrophs (methane-consuming bacteria) proliferated at an early date.[8] The research team that conducted this analysis concluded that diverse communities of organisms, including cyanobacteria, SRB, methanogens, methanotrophs, and eukaryotes, emerged "very early in Earth's history, probably by the time the oldest BIFs (ca. 3.8 Ga [about 3.8 billion years ago]) formed."[9]

This great diversity and abundance established early in life's history drove the carbon, nitrogen, oxygen, and sulfur cycles to levels eventually sufficient for the entry of advanced life. The sulfate-reducing bacteria played an especially critical role. Their metabolic reactions transformed much of the soluble metal resources in the oceans and crust into insoluble concentrated metal ore deposits. Thus, a potentially poisonous environment for advanced life became an optimal resource repository, one that would later allow humanity to quickly transition from Stone Age machinery and tools to metallurgy-based technologies.

All of these changes in metabolic levels and other transformations had to take place before the Sun became too luminous and Earth's rotation period too long for more-advanced life's survival needs. Again, the timing proved precisely right for the sake of later life-forms.

## Achieving Ground Level

Although today we consider earthquakes a dreaded danger to life, research reveals a synergistic relationship between Earth's life and Earth's movable crust. Life needs plate tectonics to persist; and plate tectonic activity needs life to persist. It especially needs photosynthetic life. (The metabolic rates exhibited by photosynthetic life are orders of magnitude greater than those in nonphotosynthetic primary organisms.) This interdependence between photosynthetic life and plate tectonics was first recognized in 2006.

A team headed by geologist Minik Rosing noted that relic heat from Earth's accretion origin and heat from the decay of radioactive isotopes were the primary drivers of differentiation of Earth's interior into a core, mantle, and crust. However, at our present time, photosynthetic organisms contribute three times more energy to Earth's geochemical cycles than does interior heat.[10] Rosing's team surmised that the emergence of photosynthetic life about 3.8 billion years ago "modified Earth's geochemical cycles and ultimately stimulated the production of granite during the earliest Archaean, which led to the first stabilization of continents."[11] Thus, the presence of abundant photosynthetic organisms at or very soon after the origin of life likely explains Earth's transition from a water world to a world with both oceans and continents.

In 2015, two geophysicists, Eugene Grosch and Robert Hazen, noted that subsurface fluid-rock microbe interactions could result in more efficient hydration of the early Earth's oceanic crust.[12] This hydration would promote bulk melting leading to the production of felsic crust (igneous rocks rich in feldspar and quartz) which, being lighter than basaltic crust, in turn would generate microcontinents. That is, Earth's first microbes, by facilitating extensive hydrothermal alteration of ocean floors, yielded extensive mineral diversification that soon resulted in the formation of several minicontinents.

Even with abundant, enduring photosynthetic life, a half billion years passed before small stable continents emerged. Certain tectonic conditions

111

that existed on isolated regions of Earth's surface along with rapid erosion and deposition of sediments led to "localization of rock uplift" and "higher topography."[13] This higher topography augmented the erosion rates, which led to an increased transport of certain compounds that react with water (under pressure) to form lubricants that facilitated the subduction of tectonic plates.[14] Increasing tectonic activity enlarged the continents as well as the amount of eroded material. Life on the continents and continental shelves, in turn, greatly enhanced chemical erosion rates.

Without abundant photosynthetic life, plate tectonic activity on Earth would have shut down relatively quickly, making the crust a stationary lid over anything and everything beneath it. Without plate tectonics, the removal of greenhouse gases from Earth's atmosphere would have shut down (see ch. 13). Without removal of greenhouse gases, the Sun's increasing luminosity (see fig. 6.2 and ch. 12) would have raised Earth's surface temperature beyond what life can tolerate. Earth would have become permanently sterile.

## Breaking Inertia

Enduring plate tectonic activity cannot be taken for granted. As geophysicist Craig O'Neill has pointed out, the window of opportunity for enduring plate tectonics is quite narrow.[15] Location and timing are just two of the crucial factors. Mass density is another. The closer a rocky planet is to its host star during planetary formation, the denser it will be. (The star's more intense radiation drives off much of the lighter weight materials.) Earth is the exception, however. Due to its extraordinarily complex formation history (see chs. 4–5) Earth's density actually exceeds that of Mercury. Typically, planets more massive than Earth and residing in a region where all the habitable zones could possibly overlap would have diameters much larger than Earth's. Mantle convection simulations show that the larger a planet's diameter, the lower the planet's ratio of tectonic-driving forces to crustal resistance to stress.[16] Thus, planets larger than Earth are "likely to be in an episodic or stagnant lid regime."[17] That is, larger rocky planets are likely to experience only a few brief episodes of plate tectonic activity or none at all.

Many more factors play critical roles in determining whether or not a planet can sustain plate tectonics for billions of years:

1. Percentage of the planet's surface covered by continents (not too little or too much)[18]
2. Thermal history of the planet's interior[19]
3. Planet's average surface temperature[20]
4. Planet's surface temperature changes[21]
5. Percentage of the planet's water that remains permanently frozen[22]
6. Degree, kind, and duration of continental erosion[23]
7. Slab pull generated by upper mantle slab weights and lengths[24]
8. Slab suction generated by descent of lower mantle slabs[25]
9. Quantity of long-lived radioactive isotopes in the planet's interior[26]
10. Quantity and duration of life on the planet's surface[27]

Without sufficient quantities of long-lived radioactive isotopes, a planet will lack the interior heat flow that is crucial for launching and sustaining plate tectonics. Because of the solar system's and Earth's extraordinary origin and development (see chs. 5–6), Earth's crust and interior layers became superenriched with these heavy radiometric elements, especially thorium and uranium. Superenriched seems an understatement, really. Relative to the element magnesium, thorium is 610 times more abundant in Earth's crust than it is in the rest of the Milky Way Galaxy. Uranium is 340 times more abundant.

No accurate measurements exist for the abundance of thorium and uranium in Earth's interior. However, scientists do know these elements are vastly more abundant there than in the crust. The great abundances of thorium and uranium in Earth's interior and their enduring half-lives (thorium-232 = 14.1 billion years, uranium-235 = 704 million years, and uranium-238 = 4.46 billion years) establish that they contribute most of the heat flow—the driving engine—propelling much of the planet's plate tectonic activity over the past 4 billion years. (Potassium-40, with a half-life of 1.3 billion years, was a significant contributor to internal heat flow during Earth's youth.) The extreme abundance of thorium and uranium causes many scientists to conclude that Earth may well be alone in its capacity to sustain aggressive plate tectonic activity for billions of years.[28]

If a planet's interior is too hot, however, the viscosity of the mantle often will be too low to produce stress fractures sufficient to break the crust up into plates. On the other hand, if the planet's interior is too cold, the velocities of the flow eddies in the mantle will be too slow to generate any movement of the plates relative to one another. In either case, the planet would develop a stagnant lid (a permanently fixed, unmovable crust). As geophysicists Mark Jellinek and Matthew Jackson explained in a recent paper, the composition of long-lived radioisotopes in the planet interior must be exquisitely fine-tuned for Earth to have a long and stable plate tectonics history.[29] Even when the planet's interior manifests the right temperature for tectonic activity, by far the most common outcome is episodic tectonics—brief epochs of plate movement interspersed by long periods of a lid stagnation.[30]

While origin-of-life researchers have established a relatively firm date for the onset of photosynthetic life, geophysicists have yet to establish more than a rough date for the origin of plate tectonics. Geophysicists do know, however, that the higher radioisotope abundance in Earth's interior some 3–4 billion years ago must have made the mantle hotter and lowered its viscosity.[31] Lower mantle viscosity would have led to faster and larger flow eddies in the mantle—generating more crustal plate movement. Meanwhile, between 3.5 and 3.8 billion years ago giant asteroids and comets were bombarding Earth, generating variations in the thickness and density throughout the crust.[32] These variations, in turn, generated local crustal stresses that helped initiate a process called subduction, where one crustal plate begins to slide under another.[33]

Geochemical, petrological, and geological data reveal a third stimulant to early tectonic activity. According to this data, Earth's mantle has been increasingly hydrated throughout the past 3.8 billion years, lowering its viscosity through time.[34] In other words, the mantle was much drier, and thus more viscous, 3–4 billion years ago than it is today. A drier mantle means a lesser viscosity difference between the asthenosphere (the top 150 kilometers of the mantle) and the crust. This lesser differential makes slippage and subduction easier, leading to the launch of complex plate movements.

The presence of iron- and sulfur-based anoxygenic photosynthetic life 3.80–3.85 billion years ago (as mentioned in ch. 8) helped produce an abundance of black shale, which is more buoyant than seafloor basalts. Black shales also hold high concentrations of heavy radioisotopes, especially uranium isotopes. Radioisotope decay in these shales produces a high heat flow, and this heat flow combined with the shales' greater buoyancy, weakens the crust around them.

Continental nuclei (basement rock) of the Pilbara (Australia) and Kaapvaal (Africa) cratons (small stable continental platforms) took shape as thick volcanic plateaus about 3.5 billion years ago (see fig. 9.1). These cratons would have generated local dynamic stresses that might have stimulated tectonic activity.[35]

Researchers analyzing mineral inclusions in diamonds discovered that a significant shift in diamond composition occurred 3.0 billion years ago.[36]

**Figure 9.1. Location and Size of the Pilbara Craton**

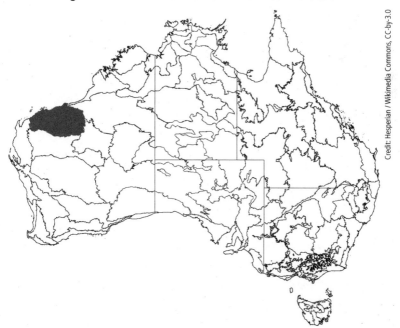

**Figure 9.2. Location and Size of the Kaapvaal Craton**

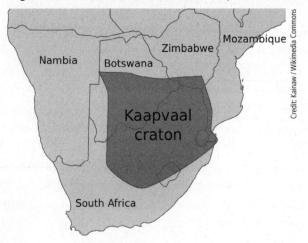

Simultaneously, a major alteration took place in Earth's geodynamics.[37] This shift and alteration indicate that plate tectonics had become a global, aggressive phenomenon by that time.

Paleomagnetic data show that Earth has possessed a strong geodynamo (the ongoing convection process in Earth's electrically conductive liquid core that maintains the magnetic field) for at least 3.5 billion years.[38] However, excess nitrogen and light noble gases in lunar samples recovered by the Apollo 14 and 17 missions indicate that Earth lacked a strong dynamo 3.9 billion years ago.[39] (A strong dynamo would have generated a geomagnetic field. If Earth had had a magnetic field 3.9 billion years ago, that field would have prevented the transfer of nitrogen and noble gases from Earth to the Moon.) These findings reveal that sometime shortly after the origin of life, geodynamics and tectonics both began.

Researchers can give no firm date for the onset of plate tectonics because the onset likely was a process. Scientists see evidence that protosubduction and subduction zone melting began 3.9 billion years ago.[40] Large crustal slabs altered by subduction began to appear 3.6 billion years ago.[41] However, not until 3.0 billion years ago did plate tectonics become a sustained, aggressive, and globally manifested phenomenon. Between 3.8 and 3.0 billion years ago Earth's crust changed. What began with just a few small isolated plates became an all-encompassing mosaic of large and small crustal plates.

The presence of life helps explain the process by which plate tectonics began and took hold. As life persisted and abounded from 3.8–3.0 billion years ago, it chemically transformed Earth's atmosphere, crust, and mantle in ways that ensured plate tectonics would continue on a global scale. Once continents were fully in place with abundant life inhabiting oceans and land, tectonic activity became continuous.[42] And scientists expect it to remain so until the brightening Sun raises Earth's surface temperature, on average, by 60°C (140°F). Such a temperature rise will force Earth into a permanent stagnant lid era.[43]

Unless plate tectonics had become established as a sustained, aggressive, globally manifested phenomenon as early as 3.0 billion years ago, Earth's surface might never have attained the necessary conditions for advanced life in the time window between the Late Heavy Bombardment and the Sun's brightening to catastrophic levels. (How Earth has remained a fit habitat for advanced life despite the Sun's increasing luminosity is the subject of ch. 12.)

The maintenance of long-lasting plate tectonics requires abundant co-existing life, especially abundant photosynthetic life.[44] Photosynthesis takes water, carbon dioxide, and other compounds from the surface environment to form carbohydrates, starches, fats, cellulose, etc. Erosion, volcanic activity, and plate tectonic subduction transport these photosynthesized products into the mantle where water is released.

Apparently, Earth had a mantle wet enough to begin convecting before plate subduction began. Subduction of photosynthesized products makes for a wetter mantle, which enhances mantle circulation, which in turn enhances plate tectonic activity.[45]

Life contributes to plate tectonics in another way. Life enhances the erosion of continents. Eroded continental material accumulating at subduction zones in the oceans in turn accelerates tectonic activity. Advanced plants are especially efficient continental eroders. When the energy flow from long-lived radioisotopes in Earth's interior declined to a level that threatened the shutdown of plate tectonics, advanced plants appeared to stimulate tectonic activity.

For life to endure for billions of years, plate tectonics must continue at a high level for billions of years. For plate tectonic activity to persist for billions of years, life must persevere for billions of years. As chapters 13 and 14 explain, both plate tectonics and life must remain at certain levels at different times throughout the past 3.8 billion years so that the history of life and of plate tectonics will produce all the resources for humanity's eventual existence and launch of global, technologically advanced civilization.

# 10

# Air-Conditioning

One of the biggest and most complex challenges for constructing any building, be it a single-family house or the Wilshire Grand Center, is the air-conditioning system. The air must be filtered, raised or lowered to the appropriate temperature, and then pumped throughout the building via a labyrinth of ducts. If the system is not designed and maintained carefully, imbalances in the carbon dioxide and oxygen levels in the building will cause considerable discomfort for the building's occupants. In a worst-case scenario, failures in the air-management system can result in the death of some or all of the building's occupants.

The air on our planet likewise must be precisely managed to prevent the undue suffering or death of its life-forms. However, different kinds of life at different times in Earth's history possessed different atmospheric requirements. Typically, the more advanced the life-form, the more atmospheric oxygen it needed to thrive. Thus, Earth's preparation for advanced life entailed appropriate oxygenation of the atmosphere.

## The Great Oxygenation Event

Despite the abundance of photosynthetic life from 3.8 to 2.45 billion years ago, the atmospheric oxygen ($O_2$) level remained low—no more than 0.001

percent of the current atmospheric level (21 percent)—according to certain sulfur isotope ratios,[1] and no less than 0.0001 percent, according to biomarker isotopes.[2] From 2.45–2.32 billion years ago, the oxygen level jumped up to just over 1 percent of its current level.[3] This episode, known as the Great Oxygenation Event (GOE), occurred just after an explosive increase in continental crust volume.[4] Analysis of sulfur isotope ratios from 2.32 billion years onward indicate that oxygen levels never again sank below the 1 percent mark.[5]

Other biomarker isotopes establish that photosynthetic life-forms were pumping prodigious amounts of oxygen into the atmosphere for at least a few hundred million years before the GOE. However, the oxidation of elements in Earth's surface layer consumed this oxygen nearly as fast as it was produced. This oxidation process might have been completed more rapidly, but lower solar luminosity (see fig. 6.2) and much higher atmospheric methane levels—at least 100 parts per million by volume[6]—slowed it down.

A large quantity of methane in the atmosphere requires a huge abundance of methanogens (methane-producing bacteria) on Earth's surface. These methanogens work in tandem with photosynthetic life to transform carbon dioxide and water into methane and oxygen. Photosynthesis splits water into oxygen and hydrogen. Methanogenesis combines hydrogen with carbon to manufacture methane ($CH_4$). The net chemical reaction of photosynthesis + methanogenesis is $CO_2 + 2H_2O \rightarrow CH_4 + 2O_2$. As this methane and oxygen are released into the atmosphere, bright sunlight generates the following reaction: $CH_4 + 2O_2 \rightarrow CO_2 + O_2 + 4H$. Because hydrogen is the lightest of all elements, it easily escapes Earth's gravity and dissipates into outer space. Thus, the net result of this reaction is $CO_2 + 2H_2O \rightarrow CO_2 + O_2$.

Two limiting factors came into play here. First, because methane is an effective greenhouse gas, removal of methane from the atmosphere lowered Earth's surface temperature to within the 0–30°C range (32–86°F); and the lower the temperature, the less efficiently photosynthesis operates. Second, the dimmer the Sun the less efficiently sunlight transforms methane and some of the oxygen into carbon dioxide and hydrogen.

Up until 2.45 billion years ago, oxygen production lowered atmospheric methane levels, which lowered atmospheric temperatures, which, in turn, decreased photosynthetic oxygen production, which then permitted a restoration of methane levels. This ongoing cycle, small back and forth swings about equilibrium, kept atmospheric oxygen and methane at roughly fixed levels from 3.83 to 2.45 billion years ago.

This delicate balance between atmospheric oxygen and methane caused a gradual removal of water from Earth's surface. The reactions described above removed between 10 and 26 percent of the water from Earth's early oceans.[7] Water removal exposed more and more continental crust to the atmosphere. This increased exposure, plus an explosive increase in continental crust volume just prior to 2.45 billion years ago, increased the ratio of above-water volcanic activity to below-water volcanic activity. Submarine volcanoes soak up much more oxygen than do above-water volcanoes.[8] So the transition from predominantly submarine volcanoes to a mix of submarine and above-water volcanoes reduced volcanic oxygen consumption, which allowed a dramatic rise in atmospheric oxygen.[9]

The near completion of the oxidation of Earth's crust also contributed to the rise in atmospheric oxygen. So did nickel depletion in the oceans. By 2.50 billion years ago, nickel concentrations in the oceans had fallen by a factor of two.[10] (A possible explanation for falling nickel concentrations may come from the partial lull in plate tectonics that lasted from 2.45 to 2.20 billion years ago.)[11] Because nickel is a critical co-factor in the functioning of several methanogen enzymes, the decline in ocean nickel abundance stifled methane production, which in turn bumped up atmospheric oxygenation. A study completed in 2015 convincingly affirmed that "a nickel (Ni) famine at the end of the Archean caused a catastrophic collapse of atmospheric methane ($CH_4$), that then allowed for the rise of atmospheric oxygen."[12]

Between 2.45 and 2.32 billion years ago atmospheric oxygen increased from 0.00001 of the current atmospheric level to at least 0.01 and perhaps as much as 0.03 of the current level.

## Impact of the Great Oxygenation Event

The GOE permanently changed Earth's biology, chemistry, and physics. For one thing, the GOE relegated methanogens to oxygen-starved deep ocean basins because methanogens can barely survive even trace levels of oxygen. They typically die off within days when subjected to oxygen levels approaching 0.01 percent of the current atmospheric level.

At the time of the GOE, the Sun was about 15–25 percent less luminous than it is today (see fig. 6.2). The demise of most of Earth's methanogens deprived the planet of the methane it needed to maintain surface warmth. While the minor variations in the oxygen and methane levels from 3.83 to 2.45 billion years ago generated at least one ice age (about 2.9 billion years ago),[13] the GOE generated three major glaciation events followed by a slushball event.[14]

A slushball event is a glaciation that extends from the poles to within 5–15° of the equator, with icebergs populating the entire equatorial zone. By this time, though, the Sun had brightened just enough from its minimum luminosity to prevent the slushball Earth from becoming an iceball that lasts for tens or even hundreds of millions of years. (An iceball event is glaciation that covers the entirety of Earth's surface.) With the Sun brightened, greenhouse gases in volcanic emissions plus methane released from methane hydrate deposits (in due time), always delivered enough greenhouse gas to the atmosphere to melt the ice from this slushball event and from subsequent glaciation episodes.

The temperature swings between the GOE glaciation events and the warm interglacial epochs were extremely severe. This severity resulted in the laying down of some of Earth's richest ore deposits.[15]

Before the GOE, the low partial pressure of oxygen in the atmosphere (pressure of atmospheric oxygen if it alone made up all the atmosphere) constrained Earth's elements, especially metals, to low oxidation states, thus limiting the number of minerals that could form from these elements. After the GOE, an explosive diversification of minerals occurred.[16] This diversification included, in addition to several nitrogen compounds, a variety of iron, sulfur, and molybdenum minerals.[17] The presence of these minerals and nitrogen compounds made possible, for the first time, an enormous variety of eukaryotes (life-forms with cells containing nuclei and organelles such as mitochondria and the Golgi apparatus). Before the GOE only a few eukaryote species existed, never approaching the abundance levels of the much simpler prokaryotes. Thus, the GOE became a dramatic turning point.

Combined effects of the GOE, glaciation that quickly followed the GOE, and the cyanobacterial blooms that immediately followed each glaciation event, produced the deposition of some 80 percent of Earth's manganese economic resources.[18] Manganese, an important resource for technologically advanced civilization, belongs on the list of "vital poisons." Too little of this element in the appropriate mineral forms is associated with several serious diseases (arthritis, osteoporosis, diabetes, and neurological disorders, for example[19]), but too much leads to even more serious ailments.[20] Without the availability of certain manganese minerals neither advanced photosynthetic plants nor high-metabolism animals would be possible. In particular, manganese enzymes are essential for detoxifying the superoxide free radicals that plague all animals living in a high-oxygen environment.

Events surrounding the GOE also laid down the first of the large biodeposits. Immediately following the slushball event, Earth's climate became globally warm and humid, which spawned the greatest biological productivity the planet has ever experienced. Carbon isotope evidence shows that 2.20–2.056 billion years ago—in a time known as the Lomagundi event—tectonic activity buried an enormous quantity of this life and its remains. Then, the Shunga event at about 2.0 billion years ago transformed these deposits into petroleum, kerogen, and bitumen, all of which became petrified.[21]

## Precise Timing

The timing of the GOE carries great significance for the possibility and timing of human civilization. The window of time during which advanced civilization is possible remains open (at most) just a few tens of thousands of years[22] (see ch. 15). Therefore, if the GOE had occurred any later, eventual resources—necessary for the launch and sustenance of global civilization—resulting from the boost in atmospheric oxygen would have been severely limited. On the other hand, if the GOE had occurred any earlier, the Sun would have lacked the luminosity needed to prevent Earth from becoming a long-term iceball, which would have risked the closure of the civilization time window.

The enormous quantity of petroleum produced during the GOE did not remain as petroleum. Like all petroleum reserves, over the course of a few hundred million years it eventually degraded into bitumens, kerogens, and natural gas. Over the next several hundred million years most of the bitumens and kerogens became petrified. Also, the periodic release of methane (natural gas) during and following the GOE most likely played a role in delivering Earth from frequent glaciation and slushball events during the following 2 billion years.

## Mineral Resources

The GOE laid down extensive metal ores that proved crucial a few billion years later. It also led to an explosion in mineral diversity that multiplied through time. The appearance of just-right life at just-right times not only contributed to the rise of plate tectonics and atmospheric transformation but also provided an abundance of invaluable mineral deposits.

An American-Canadian team of geochemists made an in-depth study of how Earth became so enormously rich in its diversity of minerals.[23] Earth certainly didn't start out with such a wealth. The dust particles in the molecular cloud from which the solar system formed contained only about a dozen different minerals, but through gravitational clumping within the molecular cloud and several unique features in the proto-Sun's protoplanetary disk, the meteorites out of which Earth formed contained 60 different mineral species. Subsequent aqueous and thermal alteration of the meteorites, as well as asteroidal accretion and differentiation transformed the 60 minerals into 250.

Once Earth had fully formed with a stable crust and ocean in place, biological processes produced explosive advances in surface mineralogy. In fact, research shows that with each "big bang" of life, a mineralogy "big bang" followed, such as the one that took place at the GOE. The ice ages associated with the GOE and the proliferation of eukaryotes made possible by the great increase in atmospheric-oceanic oxygen resulted in an increase from 250 mineral species to about 1,500.[24]

By far the most dramatic biomineral explosion took place much later, following the Cambrian explosion event about 543 million years ago. The reason for this explosion lies in the crucial and unique role life plays in generating far-from-equilibrium conditions. Thanks to the step-by-step addition of variety and abundance to Earth's life, the original 250 mineral species have exploded to 4,300 known distinct mineral species—many of which contributed to the launch of civilization and significantly impact the quality of human life in the twenty-first century. (More on this point in ch. 13.)

## Taking a Breather

Planetary scientists have long believed that Earth's atmosphere and oceans experienced progressively increasing oxygenation from the time of life's origin onward. However, recent research reveals a different story. Several lines of evidence now indicate a temporary "crash" occurred after the GOE:

1. Analysis of chromium isotopes in 1.88-billion-year-old banded iron formations show that atmospheric oxygen declined substantially, by a factor of 2–4 times from its maximum in the GOE.[25]

2. Sulfur minerals indicate that the pH of groundwater rose following the Lomagundi event, thus decreasing phosphate delivery from streams and rivers and causing a decline in oxygen production by marine photosynthetic organisms.[26]

3. Pyrite multiple-sulfur isotopes and organic carbon isotopes in black shales indicate a rapid rise of sulfur in the world's oceans 2.3 billion years ago followed by a decline at 2.05 billion years ago. This rise and fall would correlate with a coincident rise and fall in surface oxygen abundance.[27]

4. Oxidative state changes of uranium in organic-rich shales show that atmospheric oxygen levels dropped after the GOE and remained low up until the next oxygenation events that immediately preceded the Avalon and Cambrian explosions (at 575 and 543 million years ago, respectively).[28]

5. Nitrogen and carbon isotope ratio measurements in the FAR-DEEP core drill in arctic Russia reveal a decline in oxidation following the GOE and the waning of the Lomagundi interval.[29]

As the Lomagundi event diminished, the cyanobacteria bloom that helped generate the GOE became a net oxygen consumer.[30] Oxidation of the decaying remains of cyanobacteria contributed to the driving down of oxygen levels. This oxidation process along with lower nutrient delivery rates and the return of aggressive tectonic subduction (which caused more oxygen to be soaked up in the mantle) brought about a rapid and long-lasting decline in atmospheric and oceanic oxygen levels.

## A Beneficial Balance

Scientists still seek to understand by exactly how much the atmosphere became oxygenated during the GOE. They do know with some certainty that the oxygen level exceeded 0.01 percent of the current atmospheric oxygen level. Given the biological and mineral production that occurred during the GOE and the Lomagundi event, some researchers estimate that the oxygen level might have briefly surpassed 0.1 percent.[31]

Similarly, scientists still seek to discover by exactly how much the oxygen level fell after the Lomagundi event. They are confident that it dropped to, or a little below, 0.01 of the current level but never declined to the low levels that existed before the GOE. They also know that this oxygenation drop actually benefited the long-term survival of life. If oxygen levels had remained as high as they were at the peak of the GOE, they would have suppressed greenhouse gases (assuming no huge input from supervolcano eruptions) to a point at which those gases would have been insufficient to compensate for the faintness of the Sun at that time. A long-enduring iceball epoch would have been inevitable.

The first 1.8 billion years of life history prepared the way for much later advanced life. It allowed multiplication of minerals and transformation of ores needed to make the enzymes that would allow animals and advanced photosynthetic plants to thrive. This period provided the great fossil fuel resources.

Also, the 1.8 billion years of abundant photosynthetic life filled several of Earth's oxygen sinks (sets of physical, chemical, and biological resources that tend to soak up carbon dioxide from the atmosphere). This filling brought about future oxygenation events that eventually made possible the existence of animal life. The 1.8 billion years of abundant photosynthetic and methanogenic life also established plate tectonics on a global scale. Continent building could then proceed at rates sufficient to compensate for the brightening Sun and to sustain the geochemical cycles critical for progressively more advanced life.

By the end of the Lomagundi and Shunga events (circa 2.0 billion years ago) much of the foundation and preparation needed for advanced life was in place. The subsequent decline of the ocean-atmosphere oxygen levels initiated what geoscientists call the "boring billion," a reference to a billion years of Earth history during which nothing much happens. As the next chapter reveals, however, "boring" seems the wrong description for that next billion years.

# 11

## Invisible Progress

Delays seem inevitable with any construction project. When my office building underwent renovation, the work seemed to speed along for a few weeks. Some walls came down and the framing for new ones went up. Progress was visible on a daily, even hourly, basis. Then it stalled. Or at least it seemed to. As it turns out, framing had ceased, but not other important work, such as electrical wiring and measurements for the placement of an entirely new kind of energy-efficient lighting. The work was, indeed, advancing, just in a less obvious way.

Something similar happened during Earth's construction and renovation. After all the dramatic events of the early eras—the Moon-forming collision, the Late Heavy Bombardment, the origin of life, and the launch of plate tectonics—Earth entered a period many scientists refer to as the "boring billion." This geological era spanned from about 2.0 billion years ago until the Cryogenian slushball events, between 800 and 580 million years ago.

An apparent biogeochemical stasis throughout this era gave rise to the label. For about 1.2 billion years, Earth's geochemical cycles, ecology, and oxygen, temperature, and tectonic levels remained mostly the same. Based on the lack of any observed change in carbon isotope ratios throughout this era, researchers conclude that Earth's crustal dynamics and climate stayed remarkably stable.[1]

Stability need not imply lack of change, however. In this case, it means little or no change occurred in the *way* things were changing. The subtle alterations that took place during the boring billion indeed carried dramatic implications for future life. One research team referred to the boring billion as "the most intriguing period in Earth's history."[2] Despite its name, the boring billion holds great fascination for investigators.

## Return of the Methanogens

Throughout the period, oxygen remained scarce or nonexistent below the ocean's surface layer.[3] This oxygen deprivation permitted a restoration of methanogen populations to levels almost as high as those that existed prior to the Great Oxygenation Event (GOE).

Although the Sun shone a little brighter than it had before the GOE (see fig. 6.2), the atmosphere still needed a certain level of greenhouse gases to prevent a runaway freeze. Methane, rather than carbon dioxide, must have played the dominant role in maintaining surface temperatures warm enough for life. Isotope evidence and calcified remains of cyanobacteria indicate that carbon dioxide levels during the boring billion were less than nine times the current atmospheric level[4] while methane levels must have exceeded the current level by 40–50 times or more.[5]

Methane at such high levels could be maintained only if methanogens, once again, became dominant in the biosphere. However, because of the increased solar luminosity, they need not have been quite as abundant as before the GOE. Oxygen levels in the atmosphere and upper ocean layer after the Lomagundi event remained too high to sustain pre-GOE methanogen levels.

Throughout the boring billion the oceans remained anoxic except for the surface layers. In the ocean depths, methanogens thrived. In the upper layers, however, methanogens only occasionally survived as isolated surface ocean areas became anoxic. Similarly, in certain regions on the islands and continental landmasses, brief anoxic episodes allowed methanogens to flourish.

## Oxic-Anoxic Bacteria

To maintain just-right atmospheric conditions to compensate for the Sun's relatively low luminosity required a delicate balancing act between life-forms that could switch between oxic (oxygen present) and anoxic (oxygen not present) habitats. However, the biochemical machinery needed to survive under anoxic conditions differs radically from the biochemical machinery needed for oxic conditions. Life's persistence throughout the boring billion, then, required an abundance and variety of unicellular organisms possessing both sets of machinery.

Such organisms still exist today. Various species of euglena (flagellate protist, which is unicellular) thrive in isolated acid mine drainage environments where, as during the boring billion, conditions oscillate between oxic and anoxic.[6] These euglena are among the giants of the microbiology world. Whereas a typical bacterium may be a micron in length, euglena specimens measure from 25 to 170 microns (the latter size can be easily seen by the naked eye), not including the flagella, which can be longer than the rest of the organism.

Many species of euglena possess conserved compartmentalization of biosynthetic machinery akin to hybrid automobiles. These euglena can shut down their oxic metabolic machinery and switch on their anoxic metabolic machinery and vice versa. Many of them also possess machinery that allows them to tolerate metallic poisons, such as arsenic, or extreme environmental acidity, alkalinity, cold, or heat.[7]

Euglena-type species helped maintain a high abundance of life during the boring billion. In their photosynthetic mode, they pumped oxygen into the atmosphere and oceans. This oxygen lowered the abundance of the methanogens. With fewer methanogens, less methane was delivered to the atmosphere, which caused surface temperatures to drop. Lower surface temperatures caused photosynthetic activity to plummet. Lowered photosynthetic activity enabled methanogen populations to rebound, which brought surface temperatures back up to the level at which photosynthetic activity could resume.

These up-and-down oscillations—in surface temperature and photosynthetic and methanogenic activity—kept Earth's environment relatively stable overall throughout the boring billion despite rapid changes in local conditions. Because euglena-like species possessed the biosynthetic machinery to handle both oxic and anoxic environments, they were able to thrive regardless of changing temperature and chemical conditions.

Euglena species and others like them played a key role in keeping the boring billion boring enough for life to endure. In the context of a continually brightening Sun, the time window during which conditions would become tolerable for more advanced life would open relatively soon—within a billion years—and remain open for a limited time. So much to be done; so little time to get it done! This preparatory period required the presence of the just-right life-forms at the just-right times and in the just-right abundance. These just-right life-forms included extraordinarily large and complex unicellular organisms capable of seamlessly switching between different metabolic modes.

## Stromatolites

If Earth were ever to become capable of supporting a globally dispersed and technologically advanced civilization, a wealth of stored resources would be needed. Such a home required the buildup of rich iron ore reserves, which in turn required the early establishment of structures that could support and protect a diverse ecosystem. Stromatolites perfectly match the requirements.

During the boring billion the Sun showered Earth with much more intense ultraviolet (UV) radiation than it does today, and with lower oxygen levels in Earth's atmosphere, the ozone shield offered far less UV protection. For life to proliferate on Earth's surface, it needed something similar to tinted windows.

As the boring billion began, certain colonizing species of cyanobacteria proliferated. Excretions from these colonies would bind together fine-grain sediments to form an umbrella-like structure over the bacteria. These structures filtered just the right quantity and wavelengths of solar radiation to maximize the photosynthetic productivity of the cyanobacteria residing below. Eventually, however, the umbrella-like structures would filter out too much solar radiation. On these occasions, the cyanobacteria migrated above the structures to form overlying umbrellas.

**Figure 11.1.**
Present-Day Stromatolites at Lake Thetis, Western Australia

Over time, thousands of these filtering layers built up. Scientists call these multilayered structures and the organisms residing within them stromatolites (see fig. 11.1).

These stromatolite structures provided shelter not only for cyanobacteria but also for dozens, sometimes hundreds, of other microbial communities. Thanks to their presence, Earth was able to sustain and build up an enormous biomass and biodiversity during the boring billion.

Stromatolite structures and their resident microbes played an especially significant role in laying down ore deposits. The resident bacteria processed iron compounds and stored the iron minerals within their cells. They then released the minerals after cell death, and thus the structures acted as nucleation (clustering) sites for precipitation of iron minerals. Meanwhile, the oxygen generated by cyanobacteria facilitated the precipitation of iron minerals.[8] The stromatolite structures sheltered other ore-processing bacterial species, as well.

## Sulfate-Reducing Bacteria

Before the boring billion, Earth would have been an impossible place for animals. The concentration of soluble metals and metallic minerals was so extremely high as to make all conceivable food sources lethally poisonous. The abundance and functioning of a special kind of bacterium—sulfate-reducing bacteria (SRB)—helped bring about a dramatic change through this billion-year time span.

SRB obtain their energy by oxidizing organic compounds (or hydrogen) while reducing sulfates to sulfides. They "breathe" sulfate rather than oxygen. By feeding on sulfates, which are highly soluble, and transforming them into insoluble sulfides, SRB can transform their environment, over time, from toxic to safe habitats for more advanced life-forms.

SRB not only transform sulfates into sulfides, but they also function as pollution processors. They degrade harmful organic residues and reduce high concentrations of nitrate, nitrite, and various metal compounds. Consider them air quality control managers.

In the process of biodegrading algal products in surface ocean layers, SRB removed oxygen and produced sulfides.[9] This consumption and production inhibited oxygen transport to the ocean depths where it would have further inhibited the methanogen populations' methane production. Without sufficient methane to maintain warm temperatures on Earth's surface, a slushball event would have quickly ensued.

These enduring and abundant SRB also served to load Earth's crust with high-grade metal ores. When colonies of SRB die, they leave behind concentrated metal sulfide deposits. Different species of SRB deposit different metal sulfides. For example, some SRB species consume zinc sulfates and produce and deposit sphalerite ($ZnS$). Without long-term (2 billion-plus years of) abundant and diverse SRB, no such thing as metallurgy would be possible.

For many elements in the periodic table, transformation into appropriate abundances of minerals safe for advanced life proves no trivial matter. As mentioned in chapter 7, many elements are paradoxically vital to life and deadly to life—lethal or deleterious if overabundant or underabundant. Life requires more, however, than the just-right abundances of these elements in Earth's crust (see table 11.1). For each of these elements the ratio of soluble to insoluble mineral forms of these elements must also fall within certain narrow ranges.

All animals must continually ingest measured amounts of soluble chromium, copper, and zinc minerals, for example. If they ingest too little of these minerals, they either die or suffer serious health problems leading

## Table 11.1: Vital Poisons

The following elements are toxic if ingested in soluble form at either too high or too low a concentration level:[10]

| boron | phosphorus | vanadium | cobalt | arsenic | tin |
|---|---|---|---|---|---|
| fluorine | sulfur | chromium | nickel | selenium | iodine |
| sodium | chlorine | manganese | copper | bromine | |
| magnesium | potassium | iron | zinc | molybdenum | |

to substantially shorter life spans. On the other hand, ingesting too much of these minerals also brings calamitous consequences (organ failures, for example).

Thanks to the role played by SRB, animals have access to optimal amounts of soluble mineral forms of each essential element. For nearly 2 billion years, SRB aggressively transformed soluble mineral forms of all these elements into insoluble forms. The process had to be aggressive enough to bring levels into the safe range for animals *before* the time window for the other conditions essential to animal life closed.

Once animals arrived, SRB activity had to decrease but not terminate. During the animal era, SRB activity has kept the quantities of vital soluble mineral forms at a constant level. Any significant decrease or increase to these levels would pose health problems for animal life.

## The Gift of Dirt

What would be easier to take for granted than dirt? However basic it may seem, the ubiquity of dirt represents no small coincidence. The complex story traces back to plate tectonics.

Most people have some awareness that Earth's current configuration of seven continents and 18 large (as in 100,000 square kilometers or more) islands resulted from the breakup of the supercontinent Pangaea. Few may know, however, that geophysicists and geologists now see evidence of a supercontinent cycle. Pangaea represents just the most recent of five supercontinents.

Tectonic activity persisted throughout the boring billion. This ongoing activity increased both the quantity of continental crust and the proportion of Earth's surface covered by continents (see fig. 11.2). It also caused

### Figure 11.2. Portion of Earth's Surface Covered by Continents

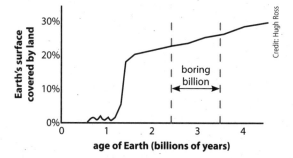

Earth began as a water world. Tectonic activity first produced volcanic islands, many of which eroded away. Ongoing tectonics generated granitic and andesitic rocks, which are less dense than basaltic rocks and which floated above them to make continents. Tectonics built up continents while erosion wore them down. Currently, tectonic buildup slightly exceeds erosion.

continents to break apart, come back together, and break apart again multiple times (see fig. 11.3).

Increasing coverage of Earth's surface by continents meant increasing erosion and increasing accumulation of sandstones and carbonates, which drew down atmospheric carbon dioxide (see ch. 13).[11] This drawdown helped compensate for the brightening Sun. As the Sun gradually brightened throughout the boring billion, the greenhouse effect of carbon dioxide gradually declined so that Earth's surface temperature remained boringly constant.

Continent growth compensated for the warming effect of the Sun's increasing luminosity in another way, as well. In 1982, physicist Kirk Hansen showed that the number, sizes, shapes, and geographical placement of the continents and their accompanying continental shelves hugely impacted the tidal torques exerted on Earth by the Sun and Moon.[12] The combined torques have worked to slow down Earth's rotation rate from 2–4 hours per day (shortly after the Moon-forming event) to its current rate of 24 hours per day. As chapter 7 explains, a slowing of Earth's rotation means its clouds can reflect more sunlight and, consequently, keep Earth's surface cooler. Thus, as continental buildup contributed to slowing Earth's rotation, it helped compensate for the warming effects of the brightening Sun.

Geoscientists have now identified five supercontinents that formed and broke up during the past 2.7 billion years. The names of these

### Figure 11.3. Breakup of the Pangaea Supercontinent

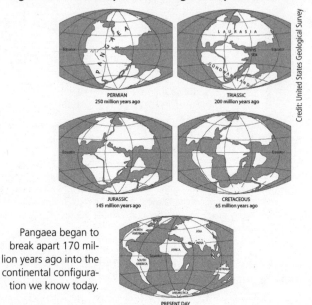

Pangaea began to break apart 170 million years ago into the continental configuration we know today.

supercontinents and the dates when Earth's landmasses joined together to form them are as follows:

| | |
|---|---|
| Kenorland | 2.7 billion years ago |
| Columbia (Nuna) | 1.9–1.8 billion years ago |
| Rodinia | 1.0 billion years ago |
| Pannotia (Vendia) | 0.60–0.55 billion years ago |
| Pangaea (Gondwana) | 0.25 billion years ago |

Each supercontinent formation event gave a boost to Earth's plate tectonic activity. A single large continent generates increased convective stresses at its boundaries. It also makes the subcontinental mantle hotter.[13] The stronger stresses and hotter subcontinental mantle produce new plate boundaries and considerable upheaval. A supercontinent era presents huge challenges for advanced life. Earthquake activity during such times is much stronger, and precipitation much less evenly distributed. A high human population would not be possible at any time within 200 million years of a supercontinent event.

Geoscientists know more about the past 750 million years of supercontinent history than about its earlier periods. Approximately 750 million years ago, Rodinia broke apart into three continents: proto-Gondwana, proto-Laurasia, and the Congo Craton. Both proto-Gondwana and proto-Laurasia rotated and made contact with the Congo Craton and together formed the supercontinent Pannotia by about 600 million years ago.

At that time, much of Pannotia sat on or near the North Pole, and its position led to a slushball event. However, by about 540 million years ago Pannotia had splintered and spread apart into four continents: Gondwana, Laurentia, Siberia, and Baltica. By about 510 million years ago, these four continents amalgamated to form Pangaea, and Pangaea remained intact as a supercontinent until about 200 million years ago.

Evidence shows that in Earth's geological history, the current continental separations and configurations represent the exception. The norm is for the landmasses to be joined together into a supercontinent. When joined together, the landmasses exert much weaker tidal torques than do widely dispersed continents. The current configuration, with well-separated north-south-oriented continents, delivers especially strong tidal torques—one reason for the slowing of Earth's rotation to 24 hours. Because they change the sea level and, thus, the amount of continental landmass exposure, glaciation events also influence the strength of the tidal torques.

As it turns out, a 24-hour rotation rate for Earth is ideal for sustaining global, technologically advanced civilization. With a slower rotation rate day-night temperature differences would be destructively extreme. With a faster rotation rate jet streams would be too laminar (flowing along streamlines with little or no latitudinal variation). Throughout the past 3.5 billion years, the number, sizes, shapes, and geographical placement of the continents and their accompanying continental shelves has delivered, step by step, the just-right tidal torques to slow Earth's rotation rate to 24 hours precisely within the narrow time window[14] in which advanced civilization is possible.

## Nutrient Recycling

The extensive mountain chains that adorn each of Earth's continents constitute one of our planet's unique features. Although erosion wears down mountains over time, the supercontinent cycle replaces them. Consider, for example, the ongoing collision between the Indian subcontinent and Asia, which raised and still is raising the Himalayas. This erosion and uplift cycle provides enduring, life-essential nutrient availability.

Extensive erosion of mountain chains contributed to the formation of continental shelves off most of the coasts of each continent. This same erosion delivered vast quantities of various nutrients to continental shelves and ocean depths, enabling these ecosystems to sustain an enormous biomass and biodiversity. This wealth of life-forms in turn provided the buildup of biofuels and biodeposits on which civilization depends. However, only the resources deposited after 600 million years ago remain in forms that are economically recoverable.

Over time, nutrients accumulated on the seafloors. The supercontinent cycle raised up new landmasses that brought these nutrients to the surface. For example, the Himalayas are composed of ocean floor material that

**Figure 11.4. Formation of the Himalayan Mountain Chain**

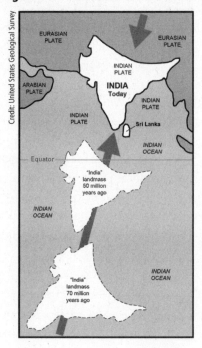

About 80 million years ago, the Indian subcontinent was located about 6,400 kilometers (4,000 miles) south of the Eurasian continent. About 10 million years ago this northward-moving subcontinent crashed into Asia. It still moves northward, driving the Himalayas to ever-higher elevations.

once separated the north-advancing Indian subcontinent from the Eurasian continental plate (see fig. 11.4).

During certain episodes of the supercontinent cycle, nutrient delivery to continental shelves and shallow seas was particularly intense. Such episodes apparently contributed to both the Avalon and Cambrian explosions of life.[15] (More on these topics appears in ch. 14.)

Geochemists report that ore deposition is similarly episodic. Banded iron formations, for example, correlate strongly with slushball events.[16] Ore genesis also correlates with periods of rapid growth in landmass coverage[17] and periods of extensive granite intrusion.[18]

The breakup or fragmentation episodes of the supercontinent cycle make its greatest contribution to the formation of ore deposits. Copper deposits, for example, commonly appear along continental rift zones.[19] Other metal ores are found along steeply dipping deformation zones and in locations where hydrothermal vents were once active,[20] both produced by supercontinent breakup. It appears that Earth's aggressive supercontinent cycle over the past 2.7 billion years allowed for life's advance beyond Stone Age technology.

## Enriching the Dirt

Scientists explain that dirt is neither common nor ordinary. Furthermore, dirt may well be humanity's most valuable resource: it allows us to grow food. But dirt wasn't here when life began or even soon afterward.

The continents began as chunks of silicate (granites, shales, and sands). However, for vascular or flowering plants to produce the food resources animals need, the granites, shales, and sands needed further transformation into prodigious quantities of soil, or dirt. Only soil possesses the water and mineral concentration and retention that vascular plants require.

A complex symbiotic ecosystem known as biological soil crust (BSC), or cryptogamic crust, turned Earth's barren landmasses into nutrient-rich surfaces that made possible the existence and flourishing of advanced plants.[21] BSC is a blend of cyanobacteria, diatoms, fungi, algae, mosses, liverworts, lichens, sand, and clay.

Cyanobacteria yield the primary photosynthesis production while algae, mosses, lichens, and bryophytes deliver secondary production. The cyanobacteria species in BSC manufactured bundled filaments and sheets of filaments that formed netlike structures to encapsulate the surrounding sand, clay, and shale particles, transforming that material into crusty bumps, balls, and sheets. Filamentous structures produced by microfungi also helped bind together sand, clay, and shale particles.

First, cyanobacteria and fungi colonized the bare ground. Once filamentary nets stabilized the soil particles, the algae, mosses, lichens, and liverworts could thrive. The fungi functioned as decomposers. The lichens and cyanobacteria functioned symbiotically by taking nitrogen from the atmosphere and using it to manufacture nitrates and ammonium minerals[22]—nitrogen fertilizers critical for the survival of advanced plants. Various combinations of algae, mosses, and lichens regulated the pH of the soil, making acidic soil less acidic and alkaline soil less alkaline.[23] By working together and dividing their labor, cyanobacteria, fungi, algae, mosses, lichens, and liverworts were able to thrive and greatly expand the habitats in which they could continue to live and thrive.

The BSC layers (see fig. 11.5) ranged 1–150 millimeters in thickness. The top crust cover acted as a filter to protect cyanobacteria and algae residing just below from the especially intense ultraviolet radiation the Sun generated between 2.0 and 0.6 billion years ago. The upper BSC layers provided resistance to wind and water erosion,[24] increased soil aeration, and provided surfaces where mineral formation could occur.[25] The surface roughness of BSC also captured significant quantities of nutrient-rich wind-driven dust.

The surface roughness of BSC and the pigmentations of its upper crustal layers that helped shield life below from harsh UV radiation made BSC surfaces much darker than the surrounding landmass. Because of its darkness, BSC absorbed much more heat from the Sun. Compared to adjacent surfaces, BSC can be up to 12°C (22°F) warmer. As BSC gradually spread out over Earth's landmasses, the planet's albedo, or reflectivity, lessened. Thus, the need for superabundant greenhouses gases in Earth's atmosphere to compensate for the Sun's early dimness declined.

Thanks to ever-expanding BSC colonies and the slowly brightening Sun, the makeup of Earth's greenhouse gases toward the end of and just after the boring billion transitioned from methane dominated to carbon dioxide dominated. This transition played a major role in the second great

Credit: Hugh Ross

**Figure 11.5.** Biological Soil (Cryptogamic) Crust. A complex symbiotic community of "primitive" organisms is transforming a barren rock surface in the Selkirk Mountains (British Columbia) into soil suitable for sustaining advanced plants. The dark raised bumps are biological soil crust.

oxygenation event, which made possible the introduction of animals (see ch. 13).

From 2.0 to 0.6 billion years ago, BSC expanded to create extensive soil coverage on all Earth's landmasses. BSC chemically conditioned those soils, enriching them with the nitrogen, phosphorus, and potassium minerals[26] to fertilize and sustain advanced plants. BSC gave those soils their essential, high water-retention capability and transformed the pH of much of Earth's crust from hostile levels to benign. As BSC spread over the continents, it helped oxygenate the atmosphere and gradually reduced the greenhouse gas levels needed to compensate for the slowly brightening Sun. When occasionally covered with sand, BSC could triple its production of nitrogen mineral fertilizers.[27]

The complex symbiotic relationships among cyanobacteria, fungi, algae, lichens, mosses, and liverworts that existed in colonies at precisely the right time in Earth's history and spread over Earth's landmasses at a precise rate for a period of 1.4 billion years made possible the proliferation of advanced plants. These plants, of course, were exactly what land animals needed for their existence and survival.

## Ready for the Next Stage

No one can honestly say that nothing much happened during the boring billion. While Earth's surface temperature and various processes remained relatively stable and consistent, dramatic changes took place. Step by step the terrestrial scene took on the precise features and conditions that set the stage for two of the most dramatic events in Earth's history—the Avalon and Cambrian explosions. The specific events that most effectively ushered in Earth's first animals are described in chapter 13. First, however, another aspect of the story warrants attention—how the repeated just-right introductions and removals of life throughout the past 3.8 billion years served to compensate optimally for the Sun's changing luminosity.

# 12

# Heating and Ventilation

The larger a structure and the more temperature sensitive its occupants, the more complex its heating, ventilation, and air-conditioning (HVAC) system. The temperature range and other conditions outside it present more complications. In the mild Southern California climate, the architects of the vast Wilshire Grand Center HVAC system faced only a minor challenge compared to the design of the Burj Khalifa in Dubai or the Amundsen-Scott South Pole Station. The Burj Khalifa, soaring more than 2,700 feet above the scorching Arabian desert, depends on more than 1.8 million square feet of specially manufactured heat-and-light reflective glass to assist its robust air-conditioning system. The Amundsen-Scott South Pole Station relies on a unique adjustable elevation feature, plus precisely angled walls with rounded corners and three jet-fuel-powered generators, to keep its inhabitants from freezing.

The challenge of keeping our earthly home in a temperature range appropriate for life over the span of nearly 4 billion years makes these human HVAC engineering efforts seem less difficult than flipping a switch. The effort to unravel the mystery of how this feat was accomplished involves a vast network of researchers in a wide variety of scientific disciplines and continues to this day. The faint Sun paradox presents the central dilemma. This striking enigma has intrigued astronomers for over four decades. Ironically, it has been largely ignored by the one discipline most significantly impacted by it: evolutionary biology (see chs. 13–15).

### Faint Young Sun

Carl Sagan and his astronomer colleague George Mullen first articulated the paradox in a 1972 paper in *Science*.[1] As they explained, the Sun fuses hydrogen into helium in its nuclear furnace, and this fusion gradually increases the Sun's core density. A higher core density increases the fusion efficiency of the nuclear furnace with the net result that as the Sun ages it progressively brightens. Sagan and Mullen calculated that the Sun is about 30 percent brighter today than when life originated on Earth 3.8 billion years ago.

The faintness of the youthful Sun poses a problem, a *major* problem, because the existence of life on Earth requires a relatively fixed surface temperature. Studies show that a solar luminosity change of as little as 2 percent would make Earth uninhabitable![2] And yet, despite the Sun's dramatically increasing brightness, life has somehow persisted on Earth's surface for all this time.

To solve this puzzle, scientists have proposed one hypothesis after another, each one like the first foray into an enormous maze. As each solution is tested, it moves the researchers forward, but always to another turn, where additional problems must be solved and a new direction taken, perhaps closer to, perhaps farther from, the prize: a more complete and comprehensible picture of what actually occurred.

### Initial Ideas

Sagan and Mullen suggested that early Earth's atmosphere contained a sufficient endowment of greenhouse gases to adequately compensate for the dimmer Sun. They proposed the presence of ammonia at several parts per million in Earth's ancient atmosphere as a viable resolution to the faint

Sun paradox. However, atmospheric chemists soon determined that ammonia is an unstable component of Earth's atmosphere, not only today but also throughout the past 4 billion years.[3] Neither could they discover any conceivable source for such a vast quantity of ammonia.

The abandonment of ammonia's candidacy led to consideration of other heat-trapping gases. In the 1980s, a team headed by geochemist James Kasting proposed the less potent greenhouse gas, carbon dioxide, as the resolution to the paradox. Kasting's team calculated that for life to survive on Earth 3.8 billion years ago, the primordial atmosphere must have contained from 100 to 1,000 times as much carbon dioxide as it does today.[4]

To answer the question of where so much carbon dioxide came from, the team suggested volcanic gas emissions. It seemed reasonable enough at the time. So, until the end of the twentieth century, scientists considered that this extra carbon dioxide provided an adequate resolution.

## The Methane Proposal

In 2003 and 2004, several research teams overturned the notion that carbon dioxide, by itself, could compensate for the lower solar luminosity.[5] To offset a 25–30 percent difference in the Sun's brightness at the time of life's origin would have required not only a vastly greater concentration of carbon dioxide than exists today but also a *steady* concentration of it at the level of 0.3 bars.[6] (A bar is a unit of air pressure. It is about equal to Earth's atmospheric pressure at sea level. A 0.3 bar level of carbon dioxide equals about 1,000 times Earth's present-day level of carbon dioxide.) At such a high concentration, however, carbon dioxide would have condensed as a solid (dry ice) at Earth's poles, thereby dropping its atmospheric concentration below the needed 0.3 bars.[7] Additional research on paleosol (fossil soil) composition found a deficiency of iron carbonate ($FeCO_3$), indicating that atmospheric carbon dioxide concentrations were at least five times below the level needed to compensate for the fainter Sun.[8]

Having shown the weakness of the carbon dioxide explanation, space scientist Alexander Pavlov and Kasting and their colleagues next proposed methane as a possible solution.[9] Because methane has a short half-life in Earth's atmosphere (due to photo-oxidation and, to a much lesser degree, escape from Earth's gravity), getting the atmospheric methane abundance up to the necessary levels (180 times higher than today's level) presented a challenge. Some source was needed to provide a steady influx of methane at a level 10–20 times higher than we see today.

Pavlov and Kasting's team hypothesized that life's emergence spawned an enormous proliferation of methanogens (methane-producing bacteria). For this model to work, however, would mean that life originated under extremely cold conditions—far too cold, as it turns out, for life even to survive. Three additional factors undermined this proposal. First, a study of the mineralogy of Archean sediments (2.5–3.8 billion years old) in general proved inconsistent with a vast abundance of methanogens.[10] Second, banded iron formations within Archean sediments showed "the ubiquitous presence" of mixed valence iron oxides (magnetite), a finding that's impossible to reconcile with the presence of an enormous abundance of methanogens.[11] Third, a calculation of the known metabolic constraints of methanogens rules out the possibility they could have produced the necessary level of methane concentration.

## Maybe Nitrogen

With the elimination of ammonia, carbon dioxide, methane, or some combination of the three as the complete resolution to the faint Sun paradox, atmospheric chemists and physicists searched for ways to enhance or complement the heat-sustaining effectiveness of the available greenhouse gases. A team led by British geophysicist Colin Goldblatt hypothesized that all or nearly all the nitrogen currently trapped in Earth's crust and mantle was somehow released into Earth's atmosphere during the epoch of the faint Sun.[12]

Although nitrogen is not a greenhouse gas, its presence in the atmosphere has the effect of increasing the capacity of both methane and carbon dioxide (by broadening their absorption spectral lines) to absorb more of the Sun's heat. However, a number of problems cast a shadow over this proposal. From a hypothetical standpoint alone, no one could suggest a reasonable scenario for the release of all this nitrogen from Earth's crust and mantle into the atmosphere, nor could they devise a hypothesis to explain what might have kept it from returning back into the crust and mantle. Atmospheric physicists and chemists note that the balance of nitrogen in Earth's atmosphere, crust, and mantle prove extraordinarily stable. What's more, nitrogen is a crucial life nutrient. Without adequate nitrogen reserves in Earth's ocean and crust, life would not have survived.

Fossilized raindrop evidence places a hard limit on the nitrogen-enhancement hypothesis. In South Africa, volcanic ash blanketing a riverbed preserved the splash pattern of raindrops that fell 2.7 billion years ago. The size and depth of the drops that created the splash pattern give clues to air pressure. In this case, the splash pattern showed that Earth's atmospheric pressure 2.7 billion years ago was somewhat greater but certainly no more than double what it is today.[13]

This finding shows that the quantity of nitrogen in Earth's ancient atmosphere would have been insufficient to boost methane and carbon dioxide heat absorption to such a high level as to compensate for the faint young Sun. Even if enhanced by the presence of the greatest possible amount of nitrogen, the maximum possible quantities of carbon dioxide and methane in Earth's ancient atmosphere still would have been insufficient to compensate for the faint young Sun.

## Volcanic Effects

Researchers began to consider volcanic activity as a source of the compensation. Earth's interior layers contained more gases during those early days than they do today, and volcanoes served as release valves for those gases. Some of what volcanoes emit, such as carbon dioxide and water vapor, trap heat effectively. Other emissions, however, effectively diminish the amount of sunlight that penetrates Earth's atmosphere. Various sulfur oxides fall into this second category. Particulates and ash from eruptions also block sunlight and contribute to the cooling of Earth's surface.

One hypothesis suggested that just before life's origin, volcanoes aggressively pumped greenhouse gases into the atmosphere *without* emitting light-blocking, cloud-producing aerosols, particulates, and ash. Then gradually, with perfect timing, volcanoes transitioned to emitting progressively less greenhouse gas or more heat-blocking aerosols, particulates, and ash or both. As two Japanese astronomers pointed out, sometimes a hypothesis seems too good, too complete in and of itself, to be true. In this case, the amount of fine-tuning to make this scenario work would be monumental, to say the least.[14] The chances of its unfolding naturally on *any* planet in our galaxy seems more than remote. Nevertheless, volcanic degassing must have played some part, and certainly must be accounted for, in life's long history.

## Reflectivity

A team led by Danish geologist Minik Rosing proposed that a much lower albedo on early Earth played a major role in compensating for the fainter Sun.[15] Albedo is a measure of reflectivity. If less of the Sun's light and heat bounced back into outer space in the early eras of life, Earth might have retained enough of the Sun's heat and light to compensate for fainter luminosity. Rosing's team postulated that the much lower continental landmass coverage of Earth's surface (see chs. 8–11), combined with a lower level of biologically induced cloud condensation during the fainter Sun era, could have lowered Earth's albedo sufficiently to compensate for the inadequacy of the greenhouse warming provided by atmospheric methane and carbon dioxide.

This new model raised considerable discussion among researchers. Some pointed out that water reflects very effectively, better than virtually any continental land area except areas covered by snow and ice. Even where snow and ice dominate, the model gains no advantage. Frozen ocean water reflects light just as well as frozen landmasses do.

Although clouds reflect light more effectively than either surface water or surface land, the notion that less cloud cover existed during the era of the faint Sun remains questionable. Most atmospheric chemists would say that the greater quantity of greenhouse gases in the atmosphere during the faint Sun's fainter days would have generated more clouds, not fewer. And the idea that biologically induced cloud condensation nuclei were less abundant during that time frame remains an open question. Their abundance might actually have been greater.

Performing radiative calculations within the framework of their global atmospheric models, Goldblatt and astrobiologist Kevin Zahnle demonstrated that lower cloud and surface albedos on the ancient Earth fell short by at least a factor of two from resolving the faint young Sun paradox.[16] The lower albedos could reasonably add only 5–20 watts/meter$^2$ of surface heating. This heat is far short of the 50 watts/meter$^2$ required to compensate for the faint young Sun, given the low atmospheric carbon dioxide levels acknowledged by the Rosing et al model.[17]

Two research teams found geochemical data to challenge the low atmospheric carbon dioxide levels acknowledged by others and argued that perhaps carbon dioxide levels were high enough to resolve the paradox.[18] Rosing and his team responded that while a little more atmospheric carbon dioxide might have been available, the persistent preservation of magnetite in all Archean era banded iron formations still means atmospheric carbon dioxide and methane levels were too low to compensate fully for the faint young Sun.[19]

Biological soil crusts (described in the preceding chapter) manifest a much lower albedo than do other parts of Earth's land area. The problem, here, is that these cryptogamic (microbial) colonies take considerable time to multiply. Not until a later era did they cover enough of Earth's landmass to substantially lower the planet's albedo. While BSC certainly did help compensate for a dimmer Sun during the Proterozoic era (2.45–0.8 billion years ago), they could not have been a major factor during the Archean era (3.83–2.45 billion years ago).

## Faster Rotation Rate

Some additional warmth during the Archean era likely came from Earth's more rapid rotation rate at that time (see chs. 6 and 11). A faster rotation rate plus less continental landmass coverage would generate much more laminar (constant in strength, nonturbulent, and with little or no latitudinal variation) atmospheric jet streams and ocean currents than exist today. Such laminar flow patterns would have inhibited heat flow away from the tropics and toward the poles.

On Archean Earth, then, the tropics were warmer and the polar regions colder, regardless of atmospheric greenhouse gas levels. Thus, in spite of a dimmer young Sun, Earth's tropics might have been warm enough for water to remain liquid and for life to survive. So here at least lies the possibility of a partial resolution to the faint Sun paradox.

Three-dimensional simulations of the Archean climate and recent general atmospheric circulation models, however, show that the tropical warming effect due to higher rotation rate is real but not great.[20] Nevertheless, these sophisticated simulations and models reveal that cloud droplets during the Archean were, indeed, larger than what climatologists had previously thought. Larger cloud droplets, higher rotation rate, smaller landmass coverage, minimal disruption to laminar flow patterns—all these features converge to provide a possibility that at least some survivable temperature zones for life prevailed.[21] Thus, they might have prevented global glaciation.

One team discovered an efficient cloud feedback mechanism that operates over cold ocean water.[22] This mechanism permits the possible existence of ice-free water up to 25° from the equator *if* and *when* landmass coverage in the tropics was nonexistent or very minor (a few small isolated islands) and Earth's atmosphere contained no methane and just four times its current amount of carbon dioxide.

## Interstellar Dust

As it penetrates Earth's atmosphere, interstellar dust produces an effect similar to that produced by volcanic ash and particulates. The dust particles reflect sunlight while allowing much of Earth's heat to dissipate into space. That is, interstellar dust has an antigreenhouse effect on the planet surface.

Astronomers note, however, that the density of interstellar dust through which Earth passes varies as the solar system follows its orbital path around the center of the Milky Way Galaxy. A team of American and Russian geochemists has shown that the solar system encounters giant molecular clouds (and their cooling effect) at least once every billion years and possibly as frequently as once every 100 million years.[23] A possible correlation exists between such encounters and the occurrence of slushball events (see chs. 10 and 11) in Earth's history.

Just as the solar system at times passes through exceptionally dusty regions, at other times it passes through dust voids. The less dust, the less cooling of Earth's surface as a result of the dust. The fact that the solar system currently resides in a relatively dust-free region means that appealing to an interstellar dust void to account for increased warmth in the distant past does only a little, at best, to explain what compensated for the young Sun's faintness. The combined effects of reduced levels of interstellar dust and volcanic dust, while they do help, still add up to providing less than one-fifth of the extra warmth needed to compensate for the dimmer Sun.

## Rotation Axis Tilt

In 1993, while studying Earth's rotation history, Australian geophysicist George Williams proposed that the angle of Earth's obliquity (the tilt of its rotation axis) might have changed over time, decreasing from 54° or more to its current tilt, 23.5°.[24] When atmospheric scientist Gregory Jenkins produced a set of global climate model simulations in 2000, he used obliquity values from 54–70° and found that high obliquity could yield warmer oceans and cooler landmasses.[25]

In one of his models, Jenkins came up with enough extra heat to resolve the faint Sun paradox. This model invoked a 65- to 70-degree obliquity, a faster rotation rate, an ocean covering the entire planet surface except for a small mountainous supercontinent at the equator (with mountains oriented north-south), and an atmospheric carbon dioxide level nearly ten times greater than the current value.

A serious challenge for Williams's model, however, comes from the viscosity of Earth's outer core. It is too low[26] to generate the hypothesized core-mantle torques. This leaves just one mechanism to significantly lower Earth's obliquity. If the continental landmasses congregated at the poles, if they developed high average elevations, if they became overlaid with thick layers of ice, and if they remained in the polar positions for a long time period, then an obliquity-oblateness feedback (oblateness refers to Earth's shape being wider at the equator) might have reduced the obliquity by a few tens of degrees.[27] Earth's plate tectonics characteristics and the planet's history, however, make this scenario extremely unlikely.

A challenge for any obliquity reduction model comes from the Moon's strong tidal torque. It serves as a powerful stabilizer of Earth's obliquity. While this stabilizing effect might have been a bit less powerful during the Archean era, too many other factors (sizes, positions, and shapes of landmasses, the makeup of greenhouse gases, rotation rate, and albedo, for example) would have had to fall within exact ranges for obliquity changes to compensate for the fainter Sun. A recent analysis demonstrates that, regardless of any possible orbital perturbations in the solar system or in the Earth-Moon system, Earth's obliquity has remained relatively unchanged over the entire history of life on Earth.[28]

## Cosmic Ray Flux

During its youth the Sun generated a stronger stellar wind. This stronger wind provided Earth with a more effective shield against cosmic rays. This shower of cosmic rays (which was lower than it is today) might mean Earth's low-altitude clouds were once less extensive. Cosmic rays generate atmospheric ionization, which stimulates the formation of condensation nuclei, which augments the formation of low-altitude clouds.[29] These low clouds typically possess a higher albedo than the surface below, so they have a cooling effect on Earth's surface. Thus, the Sun's stronger wind might have contributed to warming the planet surface by keeping more cosmic rays away and preventing more low-altitude clouds from forming.

The warming effect from a stronger solar wind remains a possibility only because scientists are uncertain about what other factors influence cloud formation and by how much. Neither is it clear how much stronger the youthful Sun's stellar wind might have been or exactly how much wind would effectively reduce the generation of condensation nuclei in Earth's atmosphere.

## Initial Solar Brightness

From the 1990s onward, a suspicion grew among astronomers, physicists, and geologists that some critical data about the early Sun must be missing. Based on their accumulated knowledge and understanding, no set of physical and chemical conditions on early Earth could possibly compensate fully for a 25–30 percent less luminous Sun at the time of life's origin. At the same time, planetary scientists encountered frustration in their attempts to explain how the Martian surface became warm enough, for a brief time nearly 4 billion years ago, to permit the existence of liquid water on its surface.[30]

These suspicions and frustrations led some astronomers to question the Sagan-Mullen model for the history of the Sun. In 1995, a team headed by Daniel Whitmire demonstrated that if the Sun were 3–7 percent more massive during its youth, the extra mass would make the Sun luminous enough to answer the Mars question. It showed that liquid water could have been present on the Martian surface 3.8 billion years ago.[31]

In 2003, California Institute of Technology astronomers Juliana Sackmann and Arnold Boothroyd pointed out, using helioseismology measurements, that the Sun during its *youth* (as opposed to its infancy) experienced a loss of at least 4–7 percent of its mass.[32] Sackmann and Boothroyd's finding indicated that the Sun's brightness at the time of life's origin on Earth was 15 percent, not 30 percent, less luminous than it is today (see fig. 12.1).

### Figure 12.1. Sun's Luminosity History according to Sackmann and Boothroyd

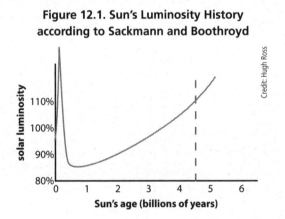

In Sackmann and Boothroyd's solar model, the Sun continues to lose significant mass, not just for its first 300 million years, but rather throughout its first 800 million years of existence. Thus, instead of being 25–30 percent less luminous at the time of life's origin (see fig. 6.2), it was only about 15 percent dimmer. The origin of Earth's first life and first animal life occurred when the Sun was about 740 million and 4 billion years old, respectively.

Recognition of this mass loss during the Sun's first 800 million (rather than 300 million) years goes a long way toward resolving the faint Sun paradox. To compensate for luminosity 15 percent lower represents a less daunting challenge. It means a lesser quantity of greenhouse gases in Earth's atmosphere would have been able to keep the surface of Earth warm enough for life. As Sackmann and Boothroyd pointed out, the essential greenhouse gas quantities no longer exceeded all reasonable possibility. In addition, a Sun just 15 percent less luminous than today would help explain the evidence for substantial quantities of surface (liquid) water on Mars some 4 billion years ago.

## Revised Numbers

In support of their not-so-faint young Sun model, Sackmann and Boothroyd referred to several observational studies showing that very young stars of mass roughly equivalent to the Sun's do, in fact, measurably lose mass at rates consistent with their model. They then called for more extensive and definitive observational programs to determine the mass-loss history of solar-type stars.

Such programs have already produced some meaningful results. Radio wavelength observations of a 300-million-year-old star with a mass similar to that of the Sun provide an upper limit on its loss rate ($5 \times 10^{-11}$ solar mass/year).[33] If this mass-loss rate is applied to the first 800 million years of the Sun's history, it adds up to a total mass-loss of up to 4 percent.[34] Another program is now under way to employ large arrays of radio interferometers to measure the mass-loss rates of multiple young solar-type stars directly.[35]

By observing X-ray flares emitted from 32 young solar-type stars (so young that hydrogen burning had not yet ignited in their nuclear furnaces), a team of astronomers calculated mass-loss rates ranging from $10^{-12}$ to $10^{-9}$ solar masses per year.[36] However, this mass-loss rate may not be relevant because it corresponds to the Sun's mass loss when it was less than 50 million years old, not 740 million years old, as it was at the time of life's origin.

When astronomers Joyce Guzik and Katie Mussack reworked the Sackmann-Boothroyd models using updated measurements of the Sun's elemental abundance profile (its elements heavier than helium, that is), they found encouraging results.[37] With an initial mass 15 percent greater in one case, or 30 percent greater in a second case, and an exponentially declining rate of mass loss over its first billion years, the model yielded a good match—not a perfect match, but an intriguing one—with helioseismology measurements. The first model yielded a close fit for the Sun's inner layers while the second, a close fit for the Sun's outer layers.

Figure 12.2 shows the effect the two models have on the Sun's luminosity history. Instead of the Sun being 25–30 percent less luminous at the time of life's origin (Sun's age at that time = 0.74 billion years), it would be 20 percent less luminous for the 1.15 initial solar mass model and 10 percent less luminous for the 1.30 initial solar mass model. However, for both models a minimum solar luminosity, 22 and 20 percent less luminous, respectively, occurs when the Sun is 1.30 billion years old.

**Figure 12.2. Sun's Luminosity History according to Guzik and Mussack**

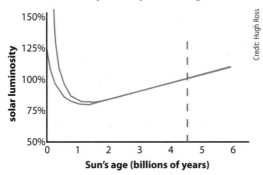

The dotted line indicates the Sun's current luminosity. The top curve represents the 1.3 initial solar mass model. The bottom curve represents the 1.15 initial solar mass model. The zero point for the Sun's age is taken to be that time when the Sun completes its accretion of mass from the solar disk.

Guzik and Mussack concluded the report on their research findings by commenting that an even better fit with observations might be achieved by modeling smaller mass loss, different rates of mass loss, different initial mass accretion, and varying opacity in the Sun's outer layers and atmosphere. Future studies will bring greater refinement.

It's worth noting that Guzik and Mussack's models offer the advantage of a much more luminous Sun at the time of life's origin than does the Sagan-Mullen model. If Earth's first life-forms were dominated by methanogens, those methanogens conceivably could have pumped enough methane into Earth's atmosphere to compensate for lower solar luminosity that, in the Guzik-Mussack models, occurs 540 million years later.

Meanwhile, recent observations of young solar analogs (stars that approximate the Sun's mass) as well as solar neutrino and solar seismology measurements indicate that the Sun might not have reached a stable mass until it was 770 million years old.[38] The latest observations of X-ray and ultraviolet (UV) radiation variability reveal that young solar analogs can, indeed, lose up to 30 percent of their mass. Based on these findings, a team of astronomers proposes that during its youth the Sun lost at least 20 percent of its mass, and, with this loss stretched over as long a time period as their model implies, the Sun was approximately 15 percent dimmer at the time of life's origin than it is today.

Harvard astrophysicists Ofer Cohen and Jeremy Drake reviewed the full range of observational efforts to determine the mass-loss rate of young solar analogs.[39] They noted that the stellar winds had not been directly observed and measured in these studies. They went on to conclude that the use of multiple indirect methods for determining mass-loss rates and the observational uncertainties and assumptions inherent in each method accounted for the lack of consistency in results.

Cohen and Drake then developed a grid of detailed theoretical models for mass-loss rates in young solar-like stars. What they observed was an added complication: "Mass loss rates in general are largely controlled by the magnetic field strength [the stellar dipole field]."[40] So far, this field can be measured only for the Sun. Nevertheless, they demonstrated a relationship between the dipole field and rotation rate for hydrogen-burning stars and they produced a stellar-rotation-period versus stellar-mass-loss-rate correlation curve (see fig. 12.3). Other astronomy research teams are engaged in ongoing studies of solar analog stars to help identify and reduce remaining uncertainties. They hope to show a better rotation-versus-age relationship for the Sun.[41]

Astronomers cannot yet discern the exact brightness of the Sun at the time of life's origin. However, they can determine with some level of certainty what does and does not constitute a reasonable range of possible luminosity figures. In summary, physicists and geologists conclude that the Sun could not have been 25–30 percent less luminous at the time of life's origin. Astronomers conclude that the Sun was unlikely massive enough at the time of life's origin to have been only 10–15 percent less luminous

**Figure 12.3. Rotation Rate Correlation with Mass Loss (Cohen and Drake)**

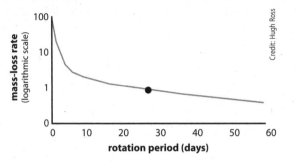

The dot shows the Sun's current position on the curve. The mass-loss rate is relative to the Sun's present value of 2.5 x 10⁻¹⁴ solar masses per year. The mass-loss rate scale is logarithmic.

than it is today. However, astronomers also say that the Sun's mass-loss rate at the time of life's origin was likely at least several times greater than at present. Therefore, we can reasonably conclude that at the time of life's origin, the Sun would have been between 18 and 23 percent less luminous than it is today.

If these numbers are reasonably accurate, they could help solve another puzzle that has stumped planetary astronomers for years: how a planet as distant from the Sun as Mars is could have experienced a warm, wet episode about 4 billion years ago (see "Could Mars Have Been Warm and Wet?" on page 158). Neither of these mysteries has a single solution; each requires a combination of solutions.

## Multiple Contributors

Abundant evidence for the presence of liquid water and life on Earth about 3.8 billion years ago confirms that a resolution to the faint Sun paradox exists. What also seems obvious is that some combination of factors must have worked together to keep Earth's surface warm enough for liquid water and life.

Just how many operational factors were required, and in what intricate combination, research has yet to reveal, but scientists know the resolution to the paradox involves at least some of those addressed in

## Could Mars Have Been Warm and Wet?

When Mars was less than 300 million years old, outgassing from its magma oceans and magma interior as well as delivery of volatiles from planetesimals and comets might have enveloped the planet with a copious quantity of greenhouse gases. With the planet surface warmed by these gases, liquid water might have been present for up to 12 million years.[42] The Sun's X-ray and UV radiation flux—nearly 100 times greater then—would have limited water's duration, as would frequent large impact events and Mars' low surface gravity.

At about 4 billion years ago, when Mars was about 560 million years old, the Sun's X-ray and UV radiation flux would have declined to just 10 times greater than at present. By then the Martian crust was fully formed, and impact events had become less frequent and less catastrophic. A combination of factors—including volcanic outgassing, delivery of volatiles via comets, and the Sun's slightly greater mass—might well have permitted a brief epoch of warm, wet surface conditions on Mars.

This warm, wet episode, however, would have ended abruptly with an event called the carbonate catastrophe. Liquid water reacts with carbon dioxide to form carbonic acid. As this acid inevitably rained on Mars, it would have produced carbonates, which leach greenhouse gases, water vapor, and carbon dioxide from the atmosphere. Such leaching would have swiftly transformed Mars into a dry, cold wasteland despite the continued brightening of the Sun. Earth avoided such a carbonate catastrophe because of its unique geological history and its abundance of specific life-forms that helped to sustain plate tectonics. Tectonics, in turn, established a carbon cycle that transformed carbonates into water vapor and carbon dioxide and spewed those gases back into Earth's atmosphere.

the paragraphs above. By way of review, the list of compensating factors includes these:

1. More carbon dioxide in Earth's atmosphere
2. More methane in Earth's atmosphere
3. More nitrogen in Earth's atmosphere
4. Greater volcanic release of greenhouse gases
5. Lesser volcanic output of aerosols, particulates, and ash

6. Lower albedo

7. Cryptogamic soils

8. Less continental landmass coverage

9. Supercontinent configuration

10. Landmasses positioned at high latitudes

11. Less reflective cloud cover

12. Faster rotation rate

13. Lower incident cosmic ray flux

14. Greater obliquity

15. Less interstellar dust

16. Greater solar mass (during the Sun's youth)

None of these factors individually seems to play the dominant role in resolving the faint young Sun paradox. Some might have played an insignificant role or no role at all. For example, at the time of life's origin, interstellar dust density and Earth's obliquity were likely too low to have been contributors to the compensating warmth.

Factors that undoubtedly played critical roles include greater amounts of carbon dioxide and methane in Earth's atmosphere, greater volcanic release of greenhouse gases, less continental landmass coverage, a faster rotation rate, a lower cosmic ray flux, and a slightly more massive young Sun. Factors that likely played at least some role include a little extra atmospheric nitrogen, less reflective cloud cover, and the sizes, positions, and configurations of Earth's landmasses.

These factors and any others yet to be identified must have converged in precisely the right ways, right times, and right levels or we would not be here to observe and consider them. What seems even more remarkable, the Sun's changing luminosity has required *ongoing* compensation and intricate adjustments throughout life's history.

## Thermostat Adjustments

In the context of an ever-brightening Sun, repeated mass extinction events followed quickly by mass speciation events provide exactly what is needed, step by step, to lower either the heat-trapping capacity of Earth's atmosphere or the planet's albedo (reflectivity) or both. Certain species of life are less efficient at consuming greenhouse gases or reflecting sunlight or both. Due to this efficiency difference, certain species must be removed and replaced with different species that are more efficient at compensating for changes in the Sun's luminosity. This process must occur at just-right levels to maintain life-optimal conditions on Earth's surface for a few billion years. In other words, life plays a critical role in its own survival—and in making room for different kinds of future life. Organisms compensate for the brightening Sun in five specific ways.

### 1. Silicate Erosion

Since the origin of life, the coverage of Earth's surface by continents and islands has grown from 0 percent to 29 percent (see fig. 11.2),[43] and silicates dominate the composition of these landmasses. Silicates are metallic elements (represented by the letter $m$) bonded to silicon trioxide ($mSiO_3$). As water in the form of streams, rain, mist, and other types of precipitation makes contact with exposed silicates in the presence of carbon dioxide, it acts as a catalyst to generate a chemical reaction. Here is an example of that reaction, where the metal is calcium, Ca, and $Ca^{++}$ represents doubly ionized calcium:

$$CaSiO_3 + 2CO_2 + H_2O \rightarrow Ca^{++} + 2HCO_3 + SiO_2$$
$$Ca^{++} + 2HCO_3 \rightarrow CaCO_3 + CO_2 + H_2O$$
Net reaction:
$$CaSiO_3 + CO_2 \rightarrow CaCO_3 + SiO_2$$

As calcium silicate reacts with carbon dioxide it produces calcium carbonate ($CaCO_3$) and sand ($SiO_2$). Water facilitates the reaction but remains unchanged. Looking at it another way, as water makes contact with exposed silicates, it promotes the removal of carbon dioxide from the atmosphere and the addition of carbonates and sand to the landmasses. Gradual removal of carbon dioxide from the atmosphere through this silicate reaction means that as the Sun gradually brightens, Earth's atmosphere becomes less efficient in its capacity to trap solar heat. In this way, water's contact with exposed silicates helps compensate for the brightening Sun.

Just as importantly, water's contact with exposed silicates promotes the production of carbonates and sand, vast quantities of which eventually served as the raw materials for many of the buildings and transportation systems that comprise both ancient and modern civilizations. For example, carbonates and sand are the most important ingredients used in the manufacture of concrete.

Carbonates and sand also played critical roles in allowing and sustaining an abundance and diversity of advanced plants and animals. For example, carbonates and sand are crucial components in both stromatolites and biological soil crusts, which made possible the survival of vascular (flowering) plants. Thanks to carbonates, crustaceans and vertebrates could proliferate. However, one reason vascular plants, crustaceans, and vertebrates appear so late in life's history is that it takes a very long time to build up the necessary quantities of cryptogamic soils, carbonates, and sand.

In building up Earth's landmasses both horizontally and vertically, plate tectonics and volcanism expose greater amounts of silicate to liquid water. Life-forms then erode silicates, and in doing so expose more silicates to liquid water. Throughout life's history, we see this pattern: life-forms less efficient at eroding silicates were repeatedly replaced by life-forms more efficient in doing so.

Life-forms can differ dramatically in their silicate-eroding capacity. For a vivid example we look to vascular plants, the latest plants to appear on Earth. Compared to earlier plant life, vascular plants enhance silicate erosion by as much as two to four times. The roots of certain conifers can penetrate and break apart mountains of solid granite (see fig. 12.4).

Looking back over the entire construction process, we see this evidence: first life helped launch plate tectonic activity; later life sequentially sustained that activity and progressively eroded more silicates to make way for still later life; that life had even greater capacity to provide what future life would need next, and so on. Not only must the timing, geographical locations, and silicate-eroding capacities of these removals and replacements of life-forms prove just right, but this process must also keep perfect

**Figure 12.4.** Pines and Fir Trees Eroding Cathedral Peak in Yosemite National Park

pace with the changing physics of the Milky Way Galaxy, Sun, Earth, and Moon for 3.8 billion years.

### 2. Organic Carbon Burial

When photosynthetic life dies, decay processes break down its tissues (sugars, starches, fats, and cellulose) and release carbon dioxide back into the atmosphere—*except* when these tissues are buried before the decay processes can operate. If this burial is deep and enduring, such as when catastrophic floods and lava flows occur, it keeps the carbon dioxide from returning to the atmosphere and instead sequesters it in the crust. When crustal plates get subducted, the carbon dioxide can become sequestered for long periods of time in the mantle. Such events bring about a reduction in the quantity of atmospheric carbon dioxide.

Today the burial of life tissues is responsible for about 20 percent of the removal of carbon dioxide from Earth's atmosphere. The erosion of exposed silicates accounts for the other 80 percent. Over the past billion years, however, this ratio has varied. At times, and as needed by life at those times, an alteration of this ratio resulted in greater or lesser compensation for the Sun's increasing luminosity.

### 3. Atmospheric Composition

Different species of life either add to or subtract from the carbon dioxide, water, methane, oxygen, ozone, and aerosols in Earth's atmosphere. Because carbon dioxide, water, and methane are greenhouse gases, their additions and subtractions alter atmospheric heat-trapping capacity. Aerosols tend to increase precipitation, which in turn boosts silicate erosion, which in turn decreases the quantity of carbon dioxide in the atmosphere. Most aerosols also tend to increase Earth's albedo. Depending on the kinds and quantities of aerosols produced by various life-forms, the clouds reflect light (and its warming effect) away more or less effectively.

While the atmospheric proportions of carbon dioxide, water, methane, oxygen, and ozone help determine what species of life are possible and at what population levels, these species also influence the composition of the atmosphere. In other words, a certain ecosystem can alter the atmospheric chemistry so as to make possible the introduction of new life-forms, including those that are more efficient at removing greenhouse gases from the atmosphere.

### 4. Cloud Cover Variations

The different quantities of carbon dioxide, water, methane, oxygen, ozone, and aerosols that life adds to or subtracts from the atmosphere also determine the extent of Earth's cloud cover and the characteristics of that cover. Certain types of clouds reflect light better than others. By reflecting away more sunlight, clouds can keep Earth's surface at a temperature cool enough for life as the Sun brightens.

But cloud cover can create problems as well. If it proves too effective in blocking sunlight, cloud cover can stymie the growth of the life-forms most needed, such as photosynthetic bacteria and plants, to remove greenhouse gases from the atmosphere. Thus, to be sustained, life requires just-right kinds of clouds in just-right locations at just-right quantities and for just-right durations.

### 5. Change in Earth's Albedo

The various species of life exhibit distinct colors and surface patterns. Some colors and patterns help absorb light while others reflect it away. Life's colors and patterns alter the reflectivity of the oceans by only a little. However, no life at all can change the albedo of the continental landmasses by as much as a factor of three.

As noted in chapter 11, the early proliferation of cryptogamic soils on Earth's emerging continental landmasses helped keep the albedo low enough that in spite of the fainter Sun at that time, temperatures on Earth's surface remained within a survivable range. As the Sun has continued to brighten since that early time, life-forms with greater light-reflecting capability have gradually replaced those with less light-reflecting capability. Meanwhile, land has continued to cover more of Earth's surface area and more life-forms have covered that land. Here again life in just the right forms, quantities, and habitats acts as an effective thermostat, compensating for an ever-brightening Sun.

## Timing of Extinction and Speciation

Although the astronomical jury still deliberates over exactly how much the Sun has brightened in the past 3.8 billion years, solar brightening models all tend to agree on one point: over the past 2 billion years, the Sun has brightened by about 12 percent. Given that life can help compensate for the Sun's increasing luminosity and that life shows some degree of adaptability to its environment, mass extinction events followed by mass speciation events would likely have been relatively infrequent. That is, if preservation of relatively simple life-forms constituted the whole story.

What scientists see instead points to something much different, much greater. We see multiple mass extinction and mass speciation events repeatedly making room and preparing conditions for more advanced life in greater variety, greater complexity, and greater abundance, even stockpiling resources that could only benefit not-yet-existent humans and something called civilization. Once the HVAC system was appropriately established, the building process could move into high gear.

# 13

# The Structure Rises

The shape, size, and virtually all other features of the Wilshire Grand Center, the Burj Khalifa, the Amundsen-Scott South Pole Station, and any other residential structure reflects its owner's intended use, as well as the needs and wants of its prospective occupants. The Wilshire Grand Center combines retail space, office space, condominiums, hotel units, parking space, swimming pool, restaurant, and observation deck. The Burj Khalifa boasts 27 acres of parkland and a 30-acre lake, in addition to residential and hotel units, offices, shops, and restaurants. The Amundsen-Scott Station houses 150 people from November to February and about a third of that number from mid-February through October, along with a greenhouse and all the equipment necessary to conduct research in astronomy, astrophysics, biomedicine, geophysics, glaciology, meteorology, and upper-atmospheric physics.

Likewise, Earth's cosmic habitat, history, and natural resources reflect the needs of its inhabitants (and we would argue its Owner's intent). As noted in chapter 2, Earth currently hosts $8.7 \pm 1.3$ million eukaryotic species (that's 6.5 million land species and 2.2 million marine species) as well as 0.1 million to 10 million prokaryotic species, along with all the supplies and structures to sustain their existence. These numbers approach Earth's theoretical maximum capacity for occupancy. In other words, Earth cannot carry, at one time, a *significantly greater* number of species, especially if that total includes the many high-population, large-bodied species currently populating the planet.

Achieving this nearly maximal profusion and diversity of life has required a step-by-step process, as the preceding chapters show. Beginning with a primordial Earth that was "formless and void" (Gen. 1:2), life gained a foothold. This earliest life served to transform Earth in ways that allowed for a greater diversity and complexity of life. As conditions became inhospitable for some of these kinds of life, other forms arrived to replace them. Each new generation of organisms further transformed Earth so that it could sustain an even greater diversity and complexity of life—up to a point, the point where humanity took up residence.

## Earth's Atypical Resources

Earth could sustain its maximal profusion and diversity of life throughout the past 3.8 billion years because of its unique inventory of elements and water. The water and carbon on which all life depends are abundant in the universe. Too much of these good things, however, would have ruined the possibility of advanced life. As chapter 5 shows, if Earth had retained its primordial inventories of water and carbon, its ocean would have been so deep that continents would never have arisen, and its atmosphere so thick that lungs would have been incapable of functioning.

Compared to what astronomers expect to find on planets possessing the same mass as Earth and orbiting at the same distance from a Sun-like star, Earth has about 1,200 times less carbon and 250 times less water.[1] These extremely atypical abundances turn out to be exactly what Earth needs to support advanced life.

Many elements besides carbon also exist in highly atypical abundances on Earth. These unusual quantities result from the solar system's unique birth and the extraordinary events in its early history, as well as Earth's exceptional transformations during its youth (see chs. 4–6). The 32 elements that are essential for the existence of advanced life and for sustaining advanced civilization are present on Earth in especially atypical abundances. Table 13.1 lists the abundances of these elements relative to what would be expected for other gas-poor bodies (bodies lacking the gravity to retain hydrogen and helium in their atmospheres) in the Milky Way Galaxy (MWG).

### Table 13.1: Relative Abundances of Heavy Elements Critical to Advanced Life in Earth's Crust

The fractional abundance of magnesium (by mass) in Earth's crust is nearly identical to the fractional abundance of magnesium in the entire MWG. (The light elements, hydrogen and helium, that escape Earth's gravity are not included.) Thus, magnesium provides a helpful measuring stick for comparison purposes. For each element listed below, the number indicates how much more or less abundant it is in Earth's crust, relative to magnesium's abundance, as compared to its average abundance throughout the MWG, relative to magnesium's abundance. Asterisks denote "vital poisons," essential elements that if overly abundant in human bodies would be toxic or lethal, but would also be toxic or lethal if too underabundant. The water measure compares the amount of water in and on Earth relative to the minimum amount planet formation models would predict for a planet the mass of Earth orbiting a star identical to the Sun at the same distance from the Sun.[2]

| Element/Compound | Abundance Relative to Magnesium |
|---|---|
| carbon* | 1,200 times less |
| nitrogen* | 2,400 times less |
| fluorine* | 50 times more |
| sodium* | 20 times more |
| aluminum | 40 times more |
| phosphorus* | 4 times more[3] |
| sulfur* | 60 times less[4] |
| chlorine* | 3 times more |
| potassium* | 90 times more |
| calcium | 20 times more |
| titanium | 65 times more |
| vanadium* | 9 times more |
| chromium* | 5 times less |
| manganese* | 3 times more |
| nickel* | 20 times less |
| cobalt* | 6 times less |
| copper* | 21 times more |

| Element/Compound | Abundance Relative to Magnesium |
|---|---|
| zinc* | 6 times more |
| arsenic* | 5 times more |
| selenium* | 30 times less |
| yttrium | 50 times more |
| zirconium | 130 times more |
| niobium | 170 times more |
| molybdenum* | 5 times more |
| silver | 3 times more |
| tin* | 3 times more |
| antinomy | 10 times more |
| iodine* | 4 times more |
| gold | 5 times less |
| lead | 170 times more |
| uranium | 340 times more |
| thorium | 610 times more |
| water | 250 times less |

The elements listed in table 13.1 rarely occur in pure form. Rather, they exist as minerals. As chapter 11 describes, billions of years of sulfate-reducing bacteria processed soluble metal minerals that would have poisoned later advanced life, transforming them mostly into concentrated deposits of insoluble metal minerals. These deposits made possible the metallurgy that helped propel humanity's leap from the Stone Age into civilization.

Thanks to the long history of progressively more advanced life-forms, the mineral inventory in Earth's crust grew from 250 minerals up to its present stock of 4,300 distinct minerals (for a description and explanation see ch. 10). Many of these minerals have made possible the technology and standard of living humanity enjoys today.

Billions of years of life appearing in progressively more advanced forms also provided humanity with an enormous treasure chest of biodeposits. This treasure includes several feet of rich topsoil and humus (amorphous organic matter) on sedimentary plains all over Earth's landmasses—essential for extensive, intensive cultivation. Earth's long history of life and tectonic activity also laid down vast stores of fossil fuels and building materials. (Table 13.2 presents a partial list.) That history speaks of a rich endowment that built up over billions of years of speciation events, deaths and extinctions, new speciation events, more deaths and extinctions, and more life.

Table 13.2: Inventory of Biodeposits: Fuel and Building Material[5]

| Source | Quantity (in quadrillions of tons) |
| --- | --- |
| coal, oil, and natural gas | 0.009–0.013 |
| clathrates | 0.020–7.17 |
| kerogen | 0.9–90 |
| organics in limestone | 75–120 |
| Total | 76–217 |

## Mass Extinction Timing

In a paper titled "On the Uniqueness of Earth as a Harbor of Steady Life,"[6] astronomer Gennady Kochemasov first noted (in 2007) that Earth resides in a planetary system with unique asteroid and comet belts (see ch. 6). He then demonstrated that Earth has the best possible orbital path in the solar system to receive the kinds and frequency of asteroid and comet collisions that would "pace" Earth's mass extinction events. The pace of these events matches what life needs to compensate for the Sun's changing luminosity and to build up rich biodeposit reserves of particular benefit to humanity. If these extinction events had been totally random in their timing and intensity, these diverse and abundant reservoirs would not be here. More significantly, the atmospheric heat-trapping capacity might have easily gotten out of sync with the Sun's changing luminosity, enough to sterilize Earth permanently.

The nonrandom nature of mass extinction events was first noted in 1984.[7] Subsequent research by University of Kansas astronomers revealed an apparent 27-million-year periodicity to these events, meaning that major extinction episodes have occurred roughly every 27 million years, over the last 500 million years (see fig. 13.1).[8] When a comprehensive revision of the geological timescale came forth (in 2012),[9] the Kansas astronomers performed a reanalysis of their findings to see if the proposed periodicity

## Figure 13.1. Extinction of Marine Animal Genera since Cambrian Explosion

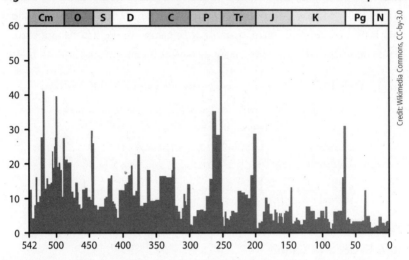

The x-axis extends back 542 million years. The y-axis shows the percentage of marine animal genera that went extinct at any given time.

would still match the geological record.[10] Not only did it match, but the statistical significance of the periodicity also improved.

The research team concluded that mass extinction events exhibit a "highly regular period" and a "relatively narrow bandwidth."[11] The exact cause of the mass extinction periodicity has yet to be determined with any certainty. The z-axis cycle in the solar system's orbit about the galactic center (see ch. 4) is a candidate. It has a period of about 33 million years. Because the density of matter is much higher in the galactic midplane than in regions above and below the plane, the z-axis cycle influences the tidal pull of the galaxy on the solar system. Thus, every 30–35 million years this tidal pull disturbs Oort cloud comets, which could send many of them hurtling into the inner solar system.[12] This hypothesis seems fairly consistent with the dates for Earth's impact craters larger than 35 kilometers in diameter, which show a 35-million-year periodicity.[13]

Geologist Michael Rampino has suggested that the passage of the solar system through the galactic plane could expose it to dense clumps of exotic dark matter (clumps of weakly interacting massive particles).[14] The capture and subsequent annihilation of exotic dark matter particles in Earth's core could heat its interior. This source of periodic heating, Rampino pointed out, aligns with what geologists observe as an approximately 30-million-year periodicity in Earth's tectonic and volcanic activity.[15] Thus, the z-axis cycle might have generated a periodicity in both terrestrial geological activity and comet or asteroid impact events that together would account for the periodicity in mass extinction events.

Space does not permit a detailed analysis of how all the known mass extinction and mass speciation events specifically prepared the way for later life and particularly for human beings and advanced civilization. What follows, however, is a brief description of known benefits associated with a few of the most notorious events that occurred during the 300 million years following the boring billion (see ch. 11). Descriptions of the major events following this 300-million-year period—events during the 500 million years that preceded humanity—appear in the next chapter.

## Neoproterozoic Oxygenation Event

By the end of the boring billion, everything that small-bodied, low-metabolism animals need to survive was in place *except* for their required atmospheric oxygen levels. After the close of the boring billion, an oxygenation event far more dramatic than the earlier Great Oxygenation Event (see ch. 10) occurred. This second oxygen boost, called the Neoproterozoic Oxygenation Event (NOE), came about immediately after the Cryogenian era (750–580 million years ago).

The Cryogenian era featured three major glaciation events: (1) the Sturtian, which persisted from 750–700 million years ago[16] and peaked at 717 million years ago;[17] (2) the Marinoan, which started 660 million years ago and ended 635 million years ago;[18] and (3) the Gaskiers, which occurred 582–580 million years ago.[19] The Sturtian and Marinoan glaciations were slushball, or near slushball, events whereas the Gaskiers glaciation most likely covered less than half Earth's surface. Just before 750 million years ago, the Rodinia supercontinent started to break up.[20] Magmatic events accompanying this breakup produced huge basalt landmasses.[21] Since exposed basalts weather about eight times more rapidly than typical continental silicates, the newly formed basalt landmasses significantly increased global weathering. As noted previously, such an increase removes enormous quantities of carbon dioxide and water (basalt + water → silicate) from the atmosphere, causing global mean temperatures to plummet.

The Marinoan ranks as the greatest known ice age in Earth's history.[22] Glacial ice sheets reached the tropical oceans. Nevertheless, recently re-covered fossils establish that photosynthetic organisms, including several benthic macroalgae species, survived throughout the Marinoan.[23] The geo-graphical locations of these fossils establish that photosynthetic organisms survived not only in equatorial ocean waters but also in a few continental shelf refuges at mid-latitudes.

Repeated cycles of ongoing landmass buildup followed by release of volcanic carbon dioxide into the atmosphere most likely explains the three major glaciation events and warm interglacial episodes that followed each.[24] These glaciation events and their accompanying interglacials resulted in the transition from a methane-dominated to a carbon-dioxide-dominated climate system, thus paving the way for more advanced life.[25] An increase in the abundance of sulfate-reducing bacteria accompanied by slowly rising atmospheric oxygen levels caused a sharp decrease in methane production by methanogens.[26] With a now brighter Sun, photosynthetic organisms no longer needed a methane-dominated climate system to thrive. The combina-tion of new landmasses and altered climate now permitted the introduction of new species of land plants.

These land plants stimulated clay mineral formation and the delivery of phosphorus into the oceans.[27] This delivery of large quantities of phos-phorous and other nutrients into the oceans ignited a multiplication of photosynthetic marine organisms. With most of Earth's oxygen sinks now full, this major increase in the population of photosynthetic organisms gave rise to the NOE. Just after the end of the Gaskiers glaciation (580 million years ago) another profound change in global oxygenation occurred.

## First Avalon Explosion

Until 575 million years ago, prokaryotes (unicellular organisms that lack a membrane-bound nucleus) dominated Earth's life.[28] Some eukaryotes did exist throughout the Proterozoic era (2.5 billion to 542 million years ago), but they were confined to shallow water environments, their morphological diversity was limited, and their body sizes remained microscopic.

None of this history is surprising. Not until after the Gaskiers glaciation event did bottom ocean waters transition from anoxic to oxic and surface ocean waters from pockets of oxic conditions to ubiquitously oxygen-rich.[29]

What *is* surprising is how rapidly large, architecturally complex organisms appeared after this oxygen enrichment event. As soon as oxygen reached the minimum level for their survival, they were here, with little or no measurable delay.[30] Evidence shows sudden rather than gradual change in body size, systemic sophistication, and morphological complexity.

The first metazoan (large-bodied) fossils were unearthed in the Avalon peninsula of Newfoundland (eastern Canada). Some of these 575-million-year-old fossilized creatures measured two meters in length.[31] Body shapes included fronds, discs, and segmentation.[32]

So sudden and profound did this transition from microscopic biota (life-forms) to large-bodied creatures occur that paleontologists referred to it as the Avalon explosion. The body size, diversity, and morphological complexity of the Avalon biota took maximal advantage of the oxygen levels, food supplies, and nutrients newly available after the Gaskiers glaciation event.

These metazoan creatures did not replace all the life-forms that preceded them. While some of the pre-Avalon species did go extinct or decline in abundance, most survived. Overall, the Avalon explosion constituted a huge upsurge in Earth's biomass and biodiversity.

The Avalon explosion also brought about an immediate extension of symbiotic relationships into the metazoan world.[33] A defining feature of Avalon animals is their very large surface-area-to-volume ratios. The many sponge species that arose provide a good example. These creatures greatly enhance the living space over which photosynthetic bacteria and algae can thrive. In return, the bacteria and algae living on and within the bodies of these Avalon animals supply them with abundant photosynthetic products. The symbiotic relationships that developed demonstrate how the introduction of new species of life, rather than replacing former species or greatly diminishing their numbers, can actually increase their populations and make possible a diversification of their kinds.

For physical and chemical reasons, the Avalon explosion could not have occurred any earlier in Earth's history. And yet the Avalon animals manifest the greatest diversity and complexity physically and chemically possible at that time. This observation warrants thoughtful consideration.

## Second Avalon Explosion

Although the initial Avalon animals were large, they lacked certain features such as eyes, ears, a mouth, an anus, and a digestive tract. These early filter-feeding organisms lived predominantly on the seafloors.[34] Their fossils show no evidence of mobility; most were permanently attached to the sea bottom by a holdfast structure. The existence of more-complex animals would require the presence of more oxygen in the atmosphere, oceans, and lakes.

As soon as oxygen levels in shallow marine environments stabilized, 560 million years ago, more changes occurred.[35] New habitats opened up for more-advanced animals—creatures with bilateral-like symmetry and at least a limited capacity for movement or for burrowing within the microbial mats upon which they grazed.[36] By 550 million years ago, thinly calcified tubular and goblet-shaped organisms began to appear.[37] These animals, along with calcimicrobes, constructed the first skeletal reefs. By 545 million years ago, the first predatory animals appeared. However, as with the first Avalon explosion, none of these life-forms yet possessed eyes, ears, or digestive tracts.

Then, between 544 and 543 million years ago, Ediacaran biota (Avalon explosion animals) suffered a mass extinction event. So catastrophic was this event that the number of Ediacaran species that survived into the subsequent era "can be counted on the fingers of one hand."[38] Carbon isotope measurements confirm that, indeed, the extinction event devastated the biosphere.

What caused the mass extinction of Ediacaran biota remains a matter of debate. A short-lived global anoxia event offers the most probable explanation.[39] Tectonic activity, for example, could have disturbed a number of methane hydrate deposits, releasing huge quantities of methane into the atmosphere, which would have generated a global warming episode and brought about a temporary but steep drop in oxygen levels in many of the world's oceans. Other proposed explanations include a possible collapse in the microbial mat populations at the base of the Ediacaran food chain and some combination of an anoxia event with a food chain collapse.

## Cambrian Explosion

Less than a million years following the mass extinction of Ediacaran biota, the first animals manifesting bilateral symmetry and hard body parts appeared. These first skeletal animals arrived not in just one or two phyla (basic body plans). Fossils unearthed in southern China and in the Canadian Rockies reveal that 50–80 percent of the animal phyla known to exist at any time in Earth's history appeared within no more than a few million years of one another, as the Cambrian geological period began, 542–543 million years ago.

This sudden appearance of new life-forms, called the Cambrian explosion, included every kind of skeleton known to have existed, past or present:

- internal and external
- rigid and flexible
- rod-based, plate-based, and combinations of rods and plates
- calcium carbonate, calcium phosphate, chitin, or silica
- fixed, molting, or remodeling

A team of geologists at Franklin and Marshall College showed that of the 182 animal skeletal designs theoretically permitted by the laws of physics, 146 appear in the Burgess Shale (Canadian Rockies) fossils.[40] Given the ecological and habitat constraints existent at that time, this number of skeletal plans—which constitutes 80 percent of all physically conceivable designs—stirs a sense of amazement and wonder.

Until the Cambrian period, sea chemistry did not permit the formation of skeletons. The Cambrian explosion occurred just as the oceans and seas attained for the first time—via a protected and widespread continental erosion episode called the Great Unconformity—high abundances of phosphorus, magnesium calcite, silica, and aragonite (calcium carbonate).[41] This change in seawater chemistry occurred on a global scale,[42] and so did the proliferation of Cambrian biota.[43]

When first confronted with fossil evidence for the Cambrian explosion, paleontologists presumed that the Cambrian event involved invertebrates only. Vertebrates (animals possessing a backbone) were thought to have arrived much later. But this perspective changed when a team of Chinese and British geologists discovered fossils of jawless vertebrates in the early Cambrian fossil beds at Chengjiang in southern China.[44] The discovery of similar fish in the Burgess Shale revealed that these creatures must have been widespread.[45] These finds pushed the date for the first fish back by nearly 70 million years.

The Chengjiang fossil beds yielded other important members of the Chordata, the most complex phylum to which humans belong. One well-preserved fossil exhibited "a heart, ventral and dorsal aorta, an anterior branchial arterial, gill filaments, a caudal projection, a neural cord with a relatively large brain, a head with possible lateral eyes, and a ventrally situated buccal cavity with short tentacles."[46] An international research team found fossils of shrimp-like creatures that possessed a brain and optic neural lobes,[47] as well as a heart and a fully developed cardiovascular system.[48] In the words of one research team, "The co-occurrence of stem-group deuterostomes [e.g., sea cucumbers] and agnathan [jawless] fish are consistent with an 'explosion' of metazoan body plans in the latest Neoproterozoic and early Cambrian."[49]

The first optical devices in animals appeared during the Cambrian explosion. These first eyes included reflectors, lenses, and cornea.[50] Nearly every eye design that exists today has been found in Cambrian organisms—compound eyes with numerous hexagonal facets, freely movable eyes on top of both short and long stalks, and inset eyes.[51] These multiple eye designs all appear in the fossil record at the same time.

The Cambrian period features the simultaneous occurrence of animals that flourish in the open ocean with the bottom-dwelling animals.[52] Evolutionary models had predicted that the bottom dwellers would appear long before the open-ocean swimmers, which needed appropriate biomechanics for buoyancy, locomotion, and exploitation of open-water nutrients. And yet both the bottom- and open-ocean animals appeared early and simultaneously.

Optimized ecological relationships also surprised researchers. Instead of a slow, gradual development of predator-prey relationships, these relationships appeared at the outset of the period. Paleontologist Simon Conway Morris commented that the Cambrian fauna attained this optimization without any measurable delay.[53]

To say that scientists were and still are astounded by what the Cambrian fossils reveal would be an understatement. Numerous books and research papers convey their profound amazement:

- "At no other time in Earth's history has there been such a profusion, such an exuberance, and such an overwhelming diversity in so short time, within one million years."[54] (Andrew Parker, zoologist)
- "The Cambrian strata of rocks, vintage about 600 million years, are the oldest ones in which we find most of the major invertebrate groups. And we find many of them already in an advanced state of evolution, the very first time they appear. It is as though they were just planted there, without any evolutionary history."[55] (Richard Dawkins, evolutionary biologist)
- "No single environmental or biological explanation for the Cambrian explosion satisfactorily explains the apparent sudden appearance of much of the diversity of bilaterian animal life."[56] (Jeffrey Levinton, marine ecologist and evolutionary biologist)
- "The Cambrian 'explosion' of body plans is perhaps the single most striking feature of the metazoan fossil record. The rapidity with which phyla and classes appeared during the early Paleozoic, coupled with much lower rates of appearance for higher taxa since, poses an outstanding problem for macroevolution."[57] (Gregory Wray, evolutionary biologist)
- "Elucidating the materialistic basis of the Cambrian explosion has become more elusive, not less, the more we know about the event itself."[58] (Kevin Peterson et al., evolutionary biologists)

Paleontologists and evolutionary biologists in search of a naturalistic cause for the Cambrian explosion appeal to the proliferation of extreme genetic diversity through mutation events from a common ancestor as a possible explanation.

Based on estimates of the genetic diversity and mutation rates of the Cambrian fauna (animals), estimates derived in part from known genetic diversity and mutation rates of currently existing species that share similar body structures, sizes, functions, and feeding habits, evolutionary biologists have calculated when, at the latest, the presumed common ancestor might have existed. That date lies between 777 and 851 million years ago.[59] Even if they apply extremely high and admittedly unreasonable, unworkable mutation rates, evolutionary biologists come up with a divergence date (from one or more common ancestors) still no further back than 586 million years ago.[60]

The fossil data stand in contradiction to these molecular clock dates. Fossil evidence indicates that the great radiation (first appearance and diversification) of Cambrian fauna occurred sometime after 542 million years ago. Physical and chemical conditions on Earth between 586 and 851 million years ago also present an intractable problem. For example, lack of oxygen and mineral nutrients during that epoch rule out the survivability of any conceivable common ancestor.

In a review paper on the Cambrian explosion, marine ecologist Jeffrey Levinton wrote, "It is likely that the assumptions of the models of molecular evolution may influence the outcomes too strongly to allow any significant confidence in estimates of molecular dates for the divergence of the Bilateria."[61] Oxford evolutionary biologist Thomas Cavalier-Smith wrote in a review of life history, "Evolution is not evenly paced and there are no real molecular clocks."[62]

## Later Explosions

The Avalon and Cambrian explosions were just the beginning. Several more mass extinction and mass speciation events occurred thereafter. And, like the Avalon and Cambrian explosions, these subsequent events profoundly challenge naturalistic explanations for life's history. They also demonstrate, again, how just-right introductions and removals of life at just-right times in just-right places continued to compensate for the ever-brightening Sun and the changing dynamics of the Earth-Moon system. These same events, all the while, built up a vast store of physical and biological resources for later life, specifically humanity. The next chapter describes how this provision came about by explaining some of the more significant later mass extinction and mass speciation events.

# 14

## Finishing Touches

Once the framing is up, the wiring and pipes in place, and the HVAC ducting positioned, the final phase of construction can get under way. At this stage, the residential structure begins to take on its beauty. It becomes more than a mere skeleton or shell. This stage in some ways resembles what occurred once the Avalon and Cambrian explosions marked the beginning of animal life. The mass speciation events that followed saw increasingly advanced plants and animals—more diverse in color, size, function, and vitality.

With each new burst of more complex and diverse species, researchers see that the life that existed ahead of it transformed the physical environment in ways that proved critical and beneficial for the more advanced organisms that followed. This progression of life not only compensated for ongoing changes in the solar system but also transformed the terrestrial environment, step by step, adding to the accumulation of biodeposits and introducing a wider array of species to fill out various phyla.

Geologists refer to the stages in the step-by-step progression as geological eras and periods and they mark the boundaries between them. Table 14.1 lists these eras and periods and their timing in Earth's history. Geologists classify Earth's history since the Cambrian explosion into three geological eras according to the physical conditions and the life-forms that existed at the time. They also identify a number of periods within each of these eras. A few of these periods are further subdivided. For example, the Carboniferous often is referred to as the Mississippian (359–324 million years ago) and the Pennsylvanian (323–299 million years ago) periods. The numbers in the table refer to millions of years ago.

Table 14.1: Geological Eras and Periods since the Cambrian Explosion

| cenozoic (66–0) | | | | | |
|---|---|---|---|---|---|
| Paleogene 66–23 | | | Neogene 23–2.59 | Quaternary 2.59–0 | |

| mezozoic (252–66) | | | | | |
|---|---|---|---|---|---|
| Triassic 251–201 | | Jurassic 201–146 | | Cretaceous 146–66 | |

| paleozoic (542–251) | | | | | |
|---|---|---|---|---|---|
| Cambrian 542–488 | Ordovician 488–444 | Silurian 444–416 | Devonian 416–359 | Carboniferous 359–299 | Permian 299–251 |

Credit: Hugh Ross

### Ordovician-Silurian Transition

One hundred million years after the Cambrian explosion, and 444 million years before our current era, the Ordovician-Silurian transition in Earth's environment and life occurred. Earth's mean atmospheric carbon dioxide content dropped from about 7,000 parts per million to about 4,500 parts per million (for comparison, the preindustrial human era level = 280 parts per million).[1] This drop correlates with volcanic eruptions that increased the amount of silicates exposed to the atmosphere. The erosion of these new silicates (see ch. 12) drew a significant quantity of carbon dioxide out of the atmosphere. Meanwhile, atmospheric oxygen content rose from 13 percent by volume to 14 percent, mean surface temperature rose from 16°C (61°F) to 17°C (63°F)—about 3°C (37°F) above the present level—and sea level dropped from 220 meters (720 feet) above the present level to 180 meters (590 feet).

This transition marked the widespread appearance of three kinds of life: (1) jawed and bony fish in the oceans and seas; (2) arthropods, or invertebrate animals with exoskeletons, segmented bodies, and jointed appendages; and (3) vascular land plants, or plants with tissues that transport nutrients and food. These first vascular plants were small, shallow-rooted, moss-like species that hugged lakes, streams, and coastlines. Marine animals appeared that were larger in size than their predecessors. Some species of sea scorpions attained several meters in length.

The mass extinction event that occurred at the beginning of the Ordovician-Silurian ranks as the second most devastating mass extinction event yet known. One hundred marine families were wiped out—a destruction that constituted 49 percent of all animal genera and about 85 percent of all marine species.[2]

The Ordovician extinction event resulted from the migration of the Gondwana supercontinent (see ch. 11 for names and dates of ancient supercontinent landmasses) into the South Pole region. This movement brought about extensive glaciation, global cooling, and a dramatic drop in sea level as more water froze.[3] The decline in sea level eliminated the vast shallow intracontinental Ordovician seas that had sustained most of Earth's marine life until then. A second contributor to the Ordovician extinction was a huge rise in volcanic activity that created steeply sloped mountains on the landmasses. Erosion of these newly formed mountains played a role in drawing atmospheric carbon dioxide levels down to 4,500 parts per million.

The mass speciation event that marked the beginning of the Silurian period coincided with the beginning of a transition from cold to warm conditions. Warm, benign conditions returned nearly halfway through the Silurian after erosion had worn down the taller landforms and the Gondwana supercontinent had migrated back toward the equator. Continental landmasses remained relatively flat and, thus, the removal of carbon dioxide from the atmosphere via erosion stayed relatively low. Warm shallow seas covered much of the equatorial landmasses, creating habitats for a profusion of diverse plant and animal life.[4]

The drop in atmospheric carbon dioxide that occurred during the Ordovician-Silurian helped compensate for the ever-increasing solar luminosity. As vascular plants proliferated during the Silurian, they enhanced the erosion of silicate landmasses, thereby accelerating the removal of carbon dioxide from the atmosphere. The fact that the Silurian vascular plants were moss-like flora that grew near bodies of water proved a plus. More extensive or more advanced vascular plants would have drawn too much carbon dioxide from the atmosphere and, thus, would have overcompensated for the brightening Sun. The existence of limited, small vascular plants also served the needs of the first land animals. Paleontologists have uncovered mid-Silurian fossils of small terrestrial invertebrates such as millipedes.[5]

## Lau Event and Devonian Explosion

The Lau event, 424 million years ago, witnessed the extinction of two-thirds of Earth's fish taxa.[6] The appearance of marine stromatolites, oncoids (layered structures formed by cyanobacterial growth), and subtidal wrinkle structures marked the reduction or disappearance of higher life-forms at this time.[7] Sedimentary changes and discontinuities, the cause of which is still under investigation,[8] might have brought about an initial drop in atmospheric carbon dioxide levels.

Following the Lau event, the Euramerica continent formed from the convergence of Laurentia and Baltica. Next, Euramerica and Gondwana began to approach one another in the southern hemisphere—the start of Pangaea's assembly. Meanwhile, to the north, the Siberian continent began to form.

During the Devonian period, 420–359 million years ago, a wide variety of new plant species successfully colonized all the continents in an event referred to as the Devonian explosion. These new plants included ferns, horsetails, and lycophytes (large seedless plants with primitive leaves). For the first time plants with true roots and leaves appeared. These plants increased the rate of silicate erosion, thereby drawing more carbon dioxide from the atmosphere and further compensating for the Sun's brightening.

Toward the end of the Devonian period, the first trees with true wood and the first seed-bearing plants appeared.[9] These trees and seed-bearing plants further augmented silicate erosion, producing more carbonate and sand deposits. Then, some major geological event or combination of events during the late Devonian caused widespread burial of forests. The combination of enhanced silicate erosion and forest burial removed still more carbon dioxide from the atmosphere.

In fact, atmospheric carbon dioxide fell from 4,400 parts per million down to 2,200 parts per million toward the end of the Devonian period. The resultant cooling—to a global mean surface temperature of 20°C (68°F)—allowed Earth to maintain an enormous biomass and biodiversity despite the brightening Sun and the warming effects of continental movement toward the equator.

Meanwhile, the proliferation of new terrestrial plant species helped raise the atmospheric oxygen content to nearly 16 percent by volume by the end of the Devonian (~360 million years ago). This extra oxygen made wildfires possible for the first time.[10] Wildfires injected charcoal into soils, a critical nutrient for the more advanced plants yet to come. The extra oxygen also made possible an explosion of new fauna. Fish species multiplied and diversified. The first four-footed animals walked upon the land. Insects appeared.

These first insects and seed-bearing plants also marked the introduction of obligate symbiosis. Certain insects and seed-bearing plants appeared, neither of which could thrive without the other. Both somehow came on the terrestrial scene at the same time and location.

## Devonian Ends, Carboniferous Begins

About 374 million years ago, a major extinction event wiped out nearly 50 percent of genera. Relatively soon thereafter, about 359 million years ago, another extinction event took out 44 percent of the higher-level marine vertebrates. With this event, the Devonian period came to a close. The net impact of these two late Devonian extinctions was the loss of 55–60 percent of all Devonian genera and roughly 70–82 percent of all Devonian species.[11] Scientists have yet to determine what, exactly, caused these extinctions. We do know that an anoxic black shale layer accompanied the latter event.[12]

The lack of oxygen in the ocean inhibited decay. So partially decayed organic matter accumulated on and in the porous rocks of the vast reefs that existed during the late Devonian. This organic matter ultimately became a wealth of petroleum.

The introduction of advanced vascular plants' engineering systems (xylem and phloem conduit systems) during the latter part of the Devonian might well have contributed to the marine life extinctions. These systems allowed plant heights to jump from 30 centimeters to 30 meters (1 foot to 100 feet). The roots of these huge plants fractured upper bedrock layers, exposing more silicates to weathering. This enhanced weathering, in turn, dumped enormous amounts of nutrients into rivers, lakes, and oceans (too much of a good thing), causing eutrophication (explosive growth of plants and algae and the subsequent death and decay of those organisms that remove huge quantities of oxygen from the water) and anoxia.[13]

Increased silicate weathering, combined with burial of organic carbon, caused yet another dramatic drop in atmospheric carbon dioxide levels, from 2,200 parts per million down to 800 parts per million by volume. This drop again helped overcome the effects of increasing solar luminosity, enough to transition Earth out of the warm Devonian into the relatively cool climate that persisted throughout the Carboniferous and Permian periods.

Following the Late Devonian extinction events came the Carboniferous mass speciation event. During this next period, from 359 to 305 million years ago, the dominant animals were amphibians, and vast forests grew up on virtually all Earth's landmasses. Trees pumped up atmospheric oxygen to about 30 percent by volume[14] and contributed to the drawdown of atmospheric carbon dioxide.

Carboniferous trees averaged a bark-to-wood ratio of 8 to 1, compared with modern trees at a ratio of 1 to 4. Given that Carboniferous animals, fungi, and bacteria could not digest bark, vast quantities of it were deposited in Earth's crust, later to become the enormous coal beds found in Carboniferous layers all over the world—a critical factor in the launch of the Industrial Revolution.

With added oxygen in the atmosphere, wildfires grew more frequent and extensive. Increased wildfires enhanced Earth's soils with an added abundance of charcoal, plus nutrients, conditioning, and water retention characteristics that supported the more advanced vascular trees and plants to arrive during later geological periods.

During the latter part of the Carboniferous period, crinoids, brachiopods, and bryozoans—all marine invertebrates—became especially abundant and diverse. Their great abundance and diversity helped produce large stores of limestone and petroleum. As with coal, these deposits eventually helped initiate and sustain industrialization.

### Rainforest Collapse and the Permian Era

About 305 million years ago Earth's climate changed rapidly from warm and humid to cold and dry. This change resulted from the assembly of supercontinent Pangaea, which meant large areas of land existed far from the oceans. Pangaea's shape and orientation at that time also positioned much of Earth's landmass at high latitudes, which resulted in extensive glaciation and a consequent drop in sea level.

These changes led to destruction of nearly all the Carboniferous rainforests, causing the atmospheric oxygen level to drop to 23 percent by volume. Carbon dioxide rose slightly to 900 parts per million. The overall drying and cooling of Earth wiped out many amphibian species and severely reduced the populations of those that remained. However, the dry, cool conditions also created vast habitats ideal for the introduction of diverse reptile species.

The arid climate of the Permian period favored gymnosperms, seed-bearing plants with protective skins or shells. Thus, the first conifers appeared. A great variety of both crawling and flying insects arose, including cockroaches, beetles, and true bugs.

### Permian-Triassic Mass Extinction

The greatest of all known mass extinction events occurred 252.3 million years ago.[15] This cataclysm wiped out 90–96 percent of marine species and at least 70 percent of land species.[16] It even wiped out the insect species.[17]

No single cause can explain this event, referred to as the Permian-Triassic catastrophe. Just before it occurred, however, massive volcanic eruptions in Siberia expelled 1–4 million cubic kilometers of lava, enough to pave Earth's entire surface area to a depth between 2 and 8 meters (7 and 26 feet). Some scientists cite evidence of a huge impact event in Antarctica as a possible trigger for the volcanic eruptions.[18]

Whatever caused them, the volcanic eruptions might have released enough carbon dioxide to raise global temperatures by as much as 5°C

(9°F). Such warming would have melted some of the clathrate (methane gas trapped in a lattice structure of frozen water) reservoirs below the ocean floor and released methane to further warm Earth's surface. Alternately, or in combination, the eruptions ignited wildfires[19] and may have ignited some of the coal beds laid down during the Carboniferous and Permian periods. This burning could have released large amounts of carbon dioxide to the atmosphere, thereby pushing the global mean temperature even higher. All this warming would have deprived the ocean depths of oxygen, and oxygen deprivation gives rise to vast blooms of hydrogen sulfide–producing bacteria.

Hydrogen sulfide is toxic to most species of life. It can also degrade or destroy Earth's ozone shield. Whatever life survived the toxic gas would likely have been destroyed by incident ultraviolet radiation. Other contributors to the Permian-Triassic mass extinction would probably include acid rain, acidification of oceans and lakes as a result of increased carbon dioxide levels, rising sea levels from melting ice, and movement of the Pangaea supercontinent.

## Triassic Recovery

The Triassic period (251–201 million years ago) is best known as the epoch during which dinosaurs and mammals first appeared. However, these creatures did not show up until 20 million years into this period. Conditions needed further adjustment.

Oxygen-18 to oxygen-16 ratios in apatite minerals within microfossils provide good proxies for ocean temperatures. Measurements of such ratios reveal that leading up to the Permian-Triassic catastrophe, surface seawater temperatures rose from 21° to 32+°C (70–90+°F) within less than 800,000 years.[20] Just a million years later surface seawater temperatures may have surged even higher. They remained above 32°C (90°F) for the next 5 million years, gradually declining thereafter.

Such high temperatures severely limited photosynthetic activity, eventually bringing the atmospheric oxygen level down to about 16 percent by volume. Heat also brought about enhanced continental weathering, which dumped minerals and nutrients into the oceans that proved detrimental to marine ecosystems. Researchers recently used strontium isotope ratios to confirm the timing and degree of this continental weathering.[21] Eventually it removed enough carbon dioxide from the atmosphere to bring Earth's mean surface temperature down to 17°C (63°F) globally, an ideal level for many forms of advanced life.

As the temperature dropped, Pangaea split into two large continents: Laurasia and Gondwana. This split produced new habitats. With the return of benign conditions for more advanced life and the availability of more habitats, another mass speciation event began. Once again, a multitude of new species burst onto the scene—as soon as the physical and chemical conditions permitted. For the first time seed plants became the dominant flora on the landmasses. Frogs, turtles, dinosaurs, mammals, and flying vertebrates suddenly appeared, all in great diversity. They appeared with balanced and mutually beneficial ecological relationships already in place. That is, herbivores, carnivores, parasites, and detritivores all possessed morphological features from the start that brought health and vitality and optimal population levels for all life.

## Triassic-Jurassic Mass Extinction

Life flourished again until 201.564 ± 0.015 million years ago.[22] The Triassic-Jurassic extinction event (TJEE) extinguished at least half of all species existing on Earth at the time. The magnitude of the TJEE equaled or exceeded that of the later Cretaceous-Paleogene event that wiped out all the dinosaurs.[23] For continental organisms, it was at least as devastating as the Permian-Triassic extinction event.[24]

The TJEE timing correlates closely with the eruption of the Central Atlantic Magmatic Province (CAMP).[25] Within a 580,000–610,000 year period, four eruption events poured out a total of 2–3 million cubic kilometers of lava, a quantity sufficient to pave Earth's entire surface 4–6 meters (13–20 feet) deep. The first and most violent of the eruption events caused the global extinction.[26]

This first CAMP eruption also spewed a prodigious quantity of sulfur dioxide and carbon dioxide into the atmosphere. The sulfur dioxide, a reactive gas with a relatively short-lived impact, brought about an immediate

1- to 10-year global cooling.[27] The carbon dioxide gave rise to a subsequent 100- to 100,000-year global warming period,[28] intensified by destabilization of seafloor methane hydrates.[29] The global warming and volcanic gases produced widespread ocean anoxia and euxinia (sulfidic conditions).[30] In addition to warming, the carbon dioxide acidified the oceans,[31] wiping out all pH-sensitive marine organisms.[32] Deposits of charcoal and polycyclic aromatic hydrocarbons (tars) dated to the Triassic-Jurassic boundary show that the eruption ignited vast wildfires across the landmasses.[33]

These wildfires and volcanic ash fallout[34] snuffed out many terrestrial life-forms, both flora and fauna. Greenhouse gas buildup destroyed others. In fact, these gases raised leaf temperatures above the lethal limit, resulting in the death of more than 95 percent of all terrestrial megaflora species,[35] plus all the animal species dependent upon them.

## Jurassic Recovery

Evidence of both cyclic variations in Earth's orbit and of reversals in Earth's magnetic field permeates the strata in which the fossils and footprints of creatures living just before and just after the TJEE appear. As a result, accurate, astronomically calibrated dates exist for these fossils and footprints. The Jurassic speciation event is the only speciation event earlier than a few tens of millions of years ago for which accurate dates can be given. And these dates reveal a remarkable recovery.

Although the TJEE nearly equaled the worst devastation yet known, the mass speciation event that followed proved surprisingly quick and robust. Within 10,000 years or less after the TJEE, large theropod dinosaurs appeared.[36] Less than 100,000 years later, the diversity of dinosaur species attained a stable maximum.[37]

Not only do the body size and complexity of the new species astound researchers, but so also does their timing. They appeared while environmental conditions were still hostile. The worst of the four CAMP eruption events had barely subsided when the first large theropod dinosaurs appeared. Dinosaur diversity rose to a maximum while climate changes remained extremely harsh.[38]

The extreme brevity of the 10,000-year (or narrower) time window between the TJEE and the appearance of theropod dinosaurs perplexes biologists who hold to a naturalistic interpretation of life's history. None of their models is capable of explaining such a rapid and dramatic evolutionary advance. Furthermore, long-term evolution experiments performed in real time show that even with the aid of extreme laboratory manipulation in the most evolutionally flexible species—bacteria and yeast—nothing more than microevolutionary changes occur.[39]

The Jurassic speciation event has led to the hypothesis that a few small-bodied reptiles somehow survived the severity and extent of the TJEE and, in response to the extremely hostile, rapidly changing environmental conditions and lack of competing species, quickly evolved into a huge population of diverse, complex, large-bodied dinosaurs.[40] However, conservation biology research contradicts this scenario.

An experiment performed on tiny crustaceans with a reputation for adaptability and evolvability demonstrated that their rate of evolution, even when assisted by selective breeding managed by human experimenters, could not keep pace with even a modest change in average temperature.[41] In a study of butterfly species with a similar reputation for adaptability and evolvability, researchers found that the butterflies suffered "reduced fitness" and "a significant loss of adaptive variation" when subjected to relatively modest changes in climate and habitat.[42] Jurassic speciation occurred when climatic conditions changed rapidly and with far greater severity and extent.

Numerous studies confirm that when an animal species suffers a population collapse and faces environmental stress, if not quickly and aggressively rescued by human intervention, it rapidly goes extinct.[43] Furthermore, the extinction risk and the speed with which a species goes extinct rises dramatically with adult body mass.[44]

## Jurassic-Cretaceous Radiations and Biodeposits

During the Jurassic and Cretaceous periods (201–66 million years ago) the ongoing breakup of Pangaea expanded coastlines, continental shelves, and shallow seas. The continental climate shifted again from dry to humid, and as it did, rainforests replaced deserts. The global mean temperature rose gradually from 16°C (61°F) to about 18°C (64°F).

The new environmental conditions made possible the introduction of a host of advanced plants and animals. Conifers became the dominant trees. Dinosaurs again became the dominant land vertebrates while fish and marine reptiles ruled the oceans and seas. During the Jurassic (201–146 million years ago), the first birds, mammals, and lizards appeared. Many new species of plankton boosted the base of the marine food chain.

During the Cretaceous period (146–66 million years ago) many new groups of birds and mammals appeared, creatures distinct from those that existed during the Jurassic era.[45] Also, the Cretaceous saw the first flowering plants.

The extinction event that marks the divide between the Jurassic period and the Cretaceous remains a mystery. Its causes have yet to be explained, but as most school children can tell you, the dinosaurs that came on the scene after that event differed noticeably from the ones before. The Cretaceous was the time of the *Tyrannosaurus rex*, *Triceratops*, and other famous "terrible lizards."

Near the end of the Cretaceous period, the first leafy trees arrived, and flowering plants became predominant. At the same time, bees and other pollinating insects showed up, along with the first ants, termites, aphids, and grasshoppers. Diatoms (algae cells enclosed within cell walls made of silica) began to proliferate in the oceans, introducing an important new biogeochemical cycle.

Only during the Jurassic and Cretaceous periods did environmental conditions—vast shallow seas, swamps, jungles, plains, and forests with little or no surface relief—permit gigantic dinosaurs to thrive. The shallow seas and swamps provided buoyancy to support the huge body masses of the largest species. The flatness of the land and of the shallow seabeds and swamps minimized these creatures' energy expenditure. The abundance and diversity of both large- and small-bodied dinosaurs during the Jurassic and Cretaceous periods indicate that life filled virtually every habitat on Earth with the full range of physically possible body sizes.

The proliferation of coniferous forests along with the introduction of flowering plants and leafy trees substantially escalated silicate erosion, enough to help compensate not only for rising solar luminosity but also for extensive carbon dioxide outgassing from volcanoes. Thanks to the balancing of all these factors, the global mean temperature rose only about 1°C (34°F) above that of the Triassic period.

The Jurassic and Cretaceous periods yielded an enormous accumulation of biodeposits. The fossilized body parts of animals that proliferated throughout the widespread warm, shallow seas led to the formation of vast thick beds of limestone and chalk. The minimal temperature difference between the equator and the poles during the Cretaceous period shut down several deep-sea currents and facilitated the formation of black anoxic shales.[46] These shales multiplied subsurface deposits of oil, gas, and phosphorite.

Within the few hundred thousand years immediately prior to the mass extinction event that marked the end of the Cretaceous period, the global ecosystem was stressed by three short-duration, mega-volcanic eruptions—the Deccan events in India.[47] These events brought on frequent, intermittent, severe cold snaps, decimating much of the life that had flourished during the long warm era. Average annual temperatures went up and down by as much as 20°C (36°F) over just tens of thousands of years or less.[48]

The cold temperatures along with the toxic gas and ash associated with the eruptions caused many species to go extinct and weakened the survivability of many or most of the remaining species.

## Cretaceous-Paleogene Extinction

The decisive blow that wiped out the already critically stressed species came from the asteroid that produced the Chicxulub impact crater in Mexico. The established date for the impact event is 66.038 ± 0.049 (including systematic and random uncertainties) million years ago, which is virtually identical to the date for the Cretaceous-Paleogene Extinction Event (CPEE).[49] The crater measures 180–200 kilometers (112–124 miles) across and about 20 kilometers (12–13 miles) deep. Based on these measurements, geophysicists deduce that the asteroid's diameter was 10 kilometers (6 miles) or more. The calculated impact energy equaled 100 terratonnes of TNT, the equivalent of 3 billion times the combined energy of the atomic bombs dropped on Hiroshima and Nagasaki.[50]

For two decades after the Chicxulub asteroid impact crater was discovered in the 1970s, researchers debated its ecological consequences, but the debate continues no longer. In a review article published in *Science* in March 2010, an interdisciplinary team of 41 distinguished scientists concluded that the impact produced these effects:[51]

- It generated a shock wave and a heat wave that instantly killed all surface life within a diameter of several thousand miles from the impact site.
- It induced multiple earthquakes of magnitude 11 and greater.
- It unleashed tsunamis cresting above 100 meters (328 feet) that crashed upon all Atlantic Ocean coastlines and rushed an average of 20 kilometers (12 miles) inland.
- It produced enough nitric oxide (NO) from shock-heated air to destroy the ozone shield.
- It acidified the surface waters of all oceans, seas, and lakes.
- It released, almost instantaneously, more than 500 billion tonnes (550 billion tons) of sulfur into the atmosphere.
- It transformed most of the released sulfur into sulfur aerosols that blocked sunlight.
- It proliferated enough dust, sulfur aerosols, and smoke (from fires ignited by ballistic ejecta as they reentered the atmosphere) to shut down photosynthesis for a few years.
- It killed off all herbivores and carnivores dependent upon photosynthetic organisms for food.
- It dropped the global mean temperature, due to sunlight blockage, by up to 10°C (18°F) for years, perhaps decades.

Discoveries since the publication of this review article show that the end-Cretaceous mass extinction was much more severe than previously thought. High-precision argon-40/argon-39 dating has established that the Deccan supervolcanoes underwent much-accelerated eruptions at the same time as the Chicxulub asteroid impact.[52] Seismic modeling shows that ground motion from the Chicxulub impactor would have triggered volcanic eruptions worldwide and would have sustained the eruption of lava, dust, and gas from supervolcanoes for millennia.[53] A five-meter (16.5

feet) thick tsunami deposit on the Dalmatian island of Hvar in the Adriatic Sea has the same elemental isotope signature as Chicxulub impact deposit material.[54] Such a large tsunami deposit so far away from the impact site sustains the conclusion that the Chicxulub impact event drove to extinction at least 75 percent of Earth's species. Paleothermometry of ocean sediments establishes a worldwide severe ocean surface temperature drop during the months following the impact event, a plunge caused by dust blocking out solar radiation.[55]

Recent fossil record research demonstrates that paleontologists had underestimated species extinctions resulting from the Chicxulub impactor. Small lizards and snakes, which had been presumed to have largely survived the event, actually suffered an extinction rate of 83 percent.[56] One hundred percent of ammonites and more than 90 percent of calcareous nannoplankton and foraminifera went extinct.[57]

A fungal spike (global fungal proliferation) that persisted for several years following the CPEE indicates that as surface-dwelling herbivores and carnivores died out, surface-dwelling detritivores (organisms that feed on dead organisms) thrived.[58] Post-impact fossils recovered near the Boltysh crater (24 kilometers in diameter) in Ukraine—an impact event dated to have occurred within a few hundred thousand years of the impact that formed the Chicxulub crater—reveal that climatic oscillations after the initial impact likely delayed vegetation recovery by many more years due to a lack of moisture.[59]

### Paleogene Recovery

Although the CPEE wiped out 75 percent or more of all species on Earth,[60] the recovery proved both quick and robust, much like that from the TJEE. The Paleogene mass speciation event took full advantage of changes in Earth's climate and geography.

During the Paleogene era (66–23 million years ago), continents continued to drift apart. Antarctica's move toward the South Pole established the Antarctic Circumpolar Current. This new current brought cooling to oceanic waters. The movement of more continental landmass toward the North Pole and the retreat of North America's shallow inland sea led to a long cooling and drying trend on the continents.

Thanks in part to the introduction of new plant species, the atmospheric carbon dioxide level during the Paleogene fell from about 1,700 to 500 parts per million. The biggest contributor to drawing down the atmospheric carbon dioxide level might well have been ants. During the Paleogene many new ant species entered the scene, and their total biomass ballooned. Field studies in the vicinity of ant colonies show that these creatures enhance the weathering of calcium and magnesium silicates by as much as 50 to 300 times.[61] The researcher overseeing the field studies concluded, "Ant enhancement of Ca-Mg silicate dissolution might have been an influence on Cenozoic cooling."[62] Thus, despite the brightening Sun, a combination of geophysical and biological events led to a slight cooling of Earth's surface.

The transition from the Cretaceous to the Paleogene was also marked by the appearance of angiosperms (plants with flat leaves and seeds embedded in fruit), which in many parts of the world all but completely replaced gymnosperms (plants with needle-like leaves and exposed seeds) as the dominant land plants. Because of the unique characteristics of angiosperm morphology, these plants could be introduced into the terrestrial environment with far greater diversity than could previous plant species.[63] At the level of individual species, angiosperms can tolerate climatic stresses and changes in nutrient availability.[64] How angiosperms could have arisen so quickly and become so predominant and diverse on the continental landmasses in such a short time remains an unsolved challenge for naturalistic models of life history.[65]

During the Paleogene many novel kinds of angiosperms came on the scene. In particular, the first grass species and the first cacti appeared. Deciduous shrubs and trees transitioned from rare to common. The grasses, deciduous plants, and cacti not only hastened the removal of greenhouse gases from the atmosphere but also provided prairies, savannas, and food supplies for new kinds of advanced birds and mammals, creatures that would later prove crucial in assisting humans to launch and sustain civilization.[66]

The explosive appearance of widely diverse angiosperm species coincided with an equally explosive emergence of diverse insects.[67] This concurrence reflects the intricate and highly specialized symbiotic relationships connecting angiosperms and insects. The explosiveness and simultaneity of these two events poses yet another challenge to naturalistic interpretations of life history.

A vast array of mammalian creatures replaced the few small-bodied mammals of the Cretaceous period. Both large- and small-bodied mammal species proliferated. Instead of just forest underbrush creatures, mammals now thrived in the treetops, savannas, prairies, mountains, lakes, streams, and oceans. The diversity of bird species also mushroomed.

All the new life that appeared and abounded during the Paleogene period added to Earth's wealth of biodeposits. The animal remains that yielded the claystone oil deposits and the Paleogene offshore oil fields held particular importance for the later arrival of human beings.

## Neogene Continental Alignment

During the Neogene period (23–2.59 million years ago), the continents migrated into their current positions and alignment. The tectonic plate associated with the Indian subcontinent had split off from Madagascar about 90 million years ago and the Indian plate first hit the Eurasian plate about 50 million years ago. About 23 million years ago, this collision closed the sea gap between India and Asia. The collision also forced the Himalayan mountain range to begin its colossal rise. Meanwhile, the Australian continent split off from Antarctica, heading in a northeast direction. Toward the end of the Neogene period, North and South America connected at the Isthmus of Panama.

This continental realignment profoundly affected Earth's climate and optimized Earth's landmasses for the support of a large human population. The linking of North and South America prevented warm Pacific Ocean currents from entering the Atlantic Ocean and thus helped keep the global climate cool. It also established a long north-south barrier to the fast-flowing, narrow air flows called jet streams, which caused these currents to move up and down in latitude. This movement allowed for a more even distribution of precipitation over the continental landmasses. The repositioning of Africa and Australia also set up north-south continental barriers.

Introduction of a still wider variety of grasses and deciduous plants facilitated the gradual cooling of Earth's surface temperature. Deciduous trees continued to replace conifers. Wild rice, wheat, oats, barley, maize, sorghum, millet, and other grains appeared in the now expansive grasslands. These grains made possible the introduction of large-bodied grazing mammals and new species of rodents.

Meanwhile ant species multiplied, and the ant biomass continued to grow. The new plant, ant, and mammal species further augmented the silicate weathering process, and this enhanced weathering brought the atmospheric carbon dioxide level down to about 280 parts per million, equal to the level that existed prior to the Industrial Revolution. Dramatic lowering of the atmospheric carbon dioxide level contributed significantly to Earth's cooling.

The positioning of Antarctica at the South Pole and the movement of landmasses toward the North Pole also contributed to the gradual cooling. And this cooling trend continued, despite the Sun's increasing luminosity and eventually introduced, for the first time in Earth's history, a short-period ice age cycle. Until recently, few people realized the significance of this cycle in providing Earth with crucial resources for sustaining a human population in the billions. The next chapter explains how the ice age cycle was established and how it ultimately enabled Earth to house such a large population of human beings with all the accoutrements of a technologically advanced civilization.

# 15

## Ready for Occupancy

Once the roof is in place, the walls are up, the plumbing, power, and HVAC systems are installed and functional, a structure may appear ready for occupancy, but no one can move in until inspectors say so. During this last phase of the construction project, experts test and fine-tune systems. Landscapers and decorators work to beautify the residence—choosing wall colors, flooring, furnishings, and fixtures.

This final stage bears some resemblance to the Quaternary period, the brief window from 2.588 million years ago to the present, when pets and people could finally move in to their home. During this brief moment of geological time, massive ice sheets cyclically advanced and retreated over much of the northern hemisphere, setting up just-right conditions for our ultimate benefit.

### Rare Chill

Ice ages have occurred only rarely in Earth's history (see fig. 15.1). Other than those associated with the two great oxygenation events, ice ages have lasted for only brief episodes.

## Figure 15.1. Ice Ages throughout Earth's History

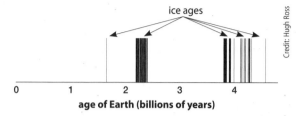

Black bars designate those times during which ice covered more than five percent of Earth's surface. Only in the present period does an ice age cycle operate.

As described in chapter 13, three major glaciation events occurred during the Neoproterozoic era: one that persisted from 750–700 million years ago, another from 660–635 million years ago, and a third from 582–580 million years ago. During the Permo-Carboniferous period (300–280 million years ago), when the southern part of the Pangaea supercontinent was centered on the South Pole, ice expanded across the continental landmass up to 45° south latitude. At the Permian-Triassic mass extinction event (252 million years ago), brief glaciation events interrupted the much longer global warming events caused by catastrophic volcanic activity.

The only other geological period of the past 2 billion years during which ice sheets persisted is the Quaternary, the current period. For the past 2.59 million years, at least 10 percent and as much as 23 percent of Earth's continental landmasses have been covered with thick layers of ice. Given that the term "ice age" refers to an era when ice covers at least 5 percent of the land area, Earth still remains in an ice age.

How astonishing that the present glacial era occurs when the Sun is at its brightest (see fig. 6.2) since the day life began! How amazing that it occurs when the atmospheric greenhouse gas abundance exceeds that of the ice-free Neogene period from 23 to 3 million years ago! How extraordinary that the current glacial era is cyclical! None of these features seem to fit naturalistic expectations.

Ice coverage of the continents rhythmically oscillates between 10 and 20+ percent. Initially that oscillation occurred every 41,000 years, and then it transitioned to a 100,000-year cycle. Only during the last 0.00057 percent of Earth's history (2.588 million years) has an ice age cycle been in operation.

And only during the last 0.00017 percent of Earth's history (800,000 years) has the ice age cycle taken on a 100,000-year periodicity—essential for the survival, as it turns out, of a large, globally dispersed, technologically advanced human population. Not one but five nearly simultaneous triggers contributed to launching the current ice age.

### 1. Landmass-to-Ocean Reconfiguration

After Pangaea broke up, landmasses replaced oceans in the high latitudes of the northern hemisphere (see fig. 15.2). Even though continents comprise just 29 percent of Earth's surface area, at high northern latitudes they dominate. The Arctic Ocean became a nearly enclosed sea. Given the lower heat-storing capacity of continents compared to oceans, this continental arrangement dramatically cooled the high northern hemisphere and played a significant role in the formation of the polar ice cap.

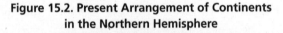

**Figure 15.2. Present Arrangement of Continents in the Northern Hemisphere**

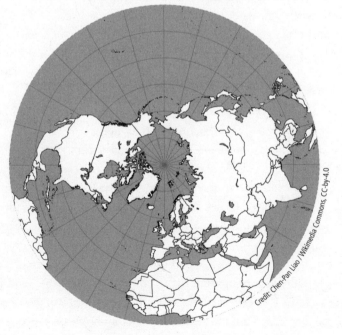

## Figure 15.3. Antarctica and the Surrounding Open Ocean

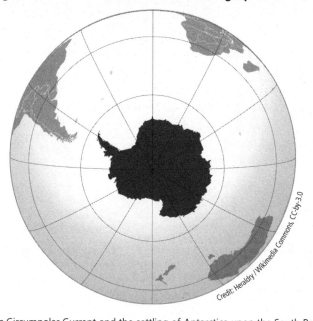

The Antarctic Circumpolar Current and the settling of Antarctica upon the South Pole led to a thick sheet of ice replacing the forests that once covered the continent.

### 2. Antarctica's Move

Meanwhile, Antarctica's landmass split off from Australia (40 million years ago), and then from the southernmost tip of South America (23 million years ago), and became centered on the South Pole completely surrounded by open ocean (see fig. 15.3). Between 3.15 and 2.75 million years ago, Antarctica accrued some 8 million cubic kilometers (2 million cubic miles) of ice.[1] This increased ice coverage and the continent's geographical location initiated more efficient heat transfer from the North Atlantic Ocean to the deep parts of the Pacific Ocean,[2] a process that brought more cooling to the northern hemisphere and, thus, contributed to its glaciation.

### 3. Isthmus of Panama Formation

Approximately 3 million years ago, converging tectonic plates led to formation of a land bridge connecting North and South America. This isthmus shut down the flow of water between the Pacific and Atlantic Oceans and, thus, forced a rerouting of ocean currents as well as atmospheric circulation. These new ocean currents and atmospheric patterns provided a more even distribution of precipitation on the continents (later a huge benefit to humans and civilization).

The new currents and winds, compared to the former, now flowed primarily in north-south directions as opposed to east-west directions, a change that enhanced global cooling. In particular, the Gulf Stream brought atmospheric moisture into the Arctic region, which contributed to the formation of a large Arctic ice cap.

### 4. Greenland's Uplift

A study by four European geophysicists revealed that over the past 60 million years Greenland has moved northward by 18° latitude (see fig. 15.4).[3] The "northward rotation of the entire mantle and crust toward the pole, dubbed True Polar Wander" moved Greenland 12° north.[4] Plate tectonic reconstructions moved Greenland another 6° north, relative to the mantle. Meanwhile, during the past 5 million years, mantle-plume pulses lifted the eastern parts of Greenland from elevations only a little

**Figure 15.4. Repositioning of Greenland**

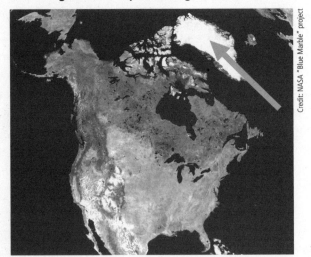

Credit: NASA "Blue Marble" project

202

above sea level to elevations exceeding 3,000 meters (10,000 feet) above sea level.

The repositioning and uplift of its landmass gave rise to a massive ice buildup that today covers more than 80 percent of Greenland. At ice age maxima, ice coverage increases to 100 percent. As this vast ice sheet grew to 1.76–2.17 million square kilometers (695–836 million square miles), it reflected away so much of the Sun's heat and light as to become a major factor in cooling the planet.

### 5. Rise of the Tibetan Plateau

About 50 million years ago, the Indian tectonic plate hit the Eurasian tectonic plate (see fig. 11.3) at the extraordinarily high velocity of 18–20 centimeters per year (7–8 inches per year).[5] Some 23 million years ago, the sea gap between India and Asia closed entirely, and the Himalayas began their meteoric rise. Since then the northeast movement of the Indian sub-continent into Eurasia has slowed a bit, to approximately 5 centimeters per year, still a fast rate that causes considerable ground shaking and uplift in the region.

About 8 million years ago, this ongoing collision between India and Asia raised the Tibetan Plateau to an average elevation slightly greater than 2,300 meters (7,500 feet) above sea level. This huge, high plateau created an air pressure gradient relative to the nearby oceans that initiated the Indian and East Asian monsoons.[6] As the uplift continued, the monsoons strengthened. Today they supply much of the water needed to sustain the intense cultivation of the Southeast Asian plains.

About 2.59 million years ago—as the Quaternary period began—the Tibetan Plateau's average elevation reached 4,000 meters (13,125 feet),[7] and permanent ice began to form, bringing a further change to the summer-winter monsoon cycle.[8] This permanent ice also resulted in the deposition of loess (fine wind-blown dust) with all of its agriculturally important nutrients all across the lowlands of China.[9]

Even today, as Earth experiences an interglacial respite, the store of ice in the Himalayas and the Tibetan Plateau exceeds 14,000 cubic kilometers (3,359 cubic miles),[10] more than the abundance of ice stored in the summer Arctic ice cap. Only the ice caps over Antarctica and Greenland hold more. The current average elevation of the Plateau stands at 4,600 meters (15,100 feet).

The low latitude of the snow- and ice-covered Tibetan Plateau (26–37° above the equator) accounts for its powerful cooling impact on the planet. Because of its location, the plateau receives much more solar radiation. Consequently, it reflects solar heat four times more efficiently than an equivalent area of icy Arctic or Antarctic landmass. Many climatologists point to the rise of the Tibetan Plateau as the predominant trigger in launching the current ice age.[11] Other than the poles and Greenland, Tibet was most likely the first region of the world to experience large-scale glaciation.[12]

Given the Sun's current brightness and the abundance of greenhouse gases in Earth's atmosphere, nothing less than the simultaneous tripping of the five tectonic triggers could have launched Earth into an ice age. However, as dramatic as these events were, they just barely launched Earth into an ice age. The current ice age is much less extensive than previous ones. The minimal nature of our current ice age, wherein Earth remains delicately balanced between no ice and extensive ice, has made possible its cyclical property.

## Milankovitch Cycles

Only during the Quaternary period, as mentioned above, has an ice age cycle occurred—the cyclical variation between lengthy highs (at 18–23 percent ice coverage) and brief lows (at 10 percent ice coverage). Research reveals a significant correlation between ice age intensity and Earth's Milankovitch cycles—the periodic changes in Earth's orbit and Earth's rotation axis. These changes have a collective, regular effect on our climate.

Earth's rotation axis "precesses" (see fig. 15.5). Though the tilt of Earth's rotation axis (obliquity) varies by only a couple of degrees, the direction its rotation axis points, relative to the stars, slowly traces out a circle about 47° (of the celestial sphere) in diameter. Currently, Earth's axis points to within 1° of the star Polaris. In about 13,000 years it will point toward Vega, and in another 13,000 years it will again point toward Polaris. A similar precession effect occurs in Earth's orbit about the Sun. As the net outcome of these cycles, Earth's northern hemisphere alternates every

21,600 years between pointing toward and away from the Sun during the northern hemisphere winter. In 2014, for example, Earth reached its farthest distance from the Sun on July 3. Because of our current place in the cycle, high northern latitude landmasses (such as England) experience milder seasonal differences than do high southern latitude landmasses (such as southern Chile).

**Figure 15.5. Precession of Earth's Rotation Axis**

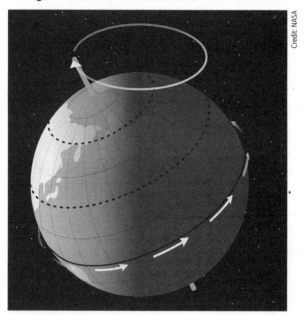

As Earth rotates, it precesses like a rapidly spinning top or gyroscope where the direction of the rotation axis traces out a cone.

The tilt of Earth's rotation axis relative to the plane of Earth's orbit about the Sun also varies. It shifts from 22.1° to 24.5° and back again every 41,000 years. The greater the tilt, the greater the temperature difference between summers and winters worldwide. Given the current sizes and configurations of the continents, lesser obliquity generates global cooling whereas greater obliquity causes global warming.

Like all planets, Earth's orbit has an elliptical shape. Eccentricity refers to the departure of the orbital ellipse from circularity. A perfect circle has an eccentricity measure equal to zero. A parabola's eccentricity measure equals one. Earth's orbital eccentricity varies between 0.000055 and 0.0679, due to the gravitational influences of Jupiter and Saturn and, to a lesser degree, of Uranus and Neptune. The two most dominant eccentricity cycles have periods of about 400,000 years and 100,000 ± 3,000 years.

The combined impact of these rotation axis and orbital cycles on global mean temperatures typically would be subtle and of no meaningful consequence to life. They have a major impact, however, when the planet sits at the delicately balanced point, as Earth now does, between no surface ice and extensive surface ice.

In fact, these factors all worked together to tip the balance: (1) the movement of Antarctica to the South Pole and several other continents to high northern latitudes; (2) the near enclosure of the Arctic Ocean; (3) the joining together of North and South America; (4) the movement and rise of Greenland; and (5) the rise of the Tibetan Plateau. Earth went from an ice-free planet (just before the Quaternary period) to a planet with permanent ice over most of Antarctica and Greenland and intermittent patches of ice over high latitude and high elevation portions of the northern continents, varying in response to the Milankovitch cycles.

During most of the Pleistocene glaciation, from 2.59 to 0.95–0.86 million years ago, the brief episodes of warmth (interglacials) occurred every 41,000 years.[13] During this early time window, as the Himalayas and the Tibetan Plateau continued their rise, each successive ice age cycle led to greater snow and ice coverage in that region. What started off as just 2–4 percent coverage at glacial maximum, grew to 29–40 percent.[14] The heat reflection from this increasing snow and ice coverage resulted in the development of snow and ice patches elsewhere in the northern hemisphere. These patches also grew larger with each successive cycle.

At 950,000 and 860,000 years ago, a major shift occurred in the cycle. In this relatively brief period the cycle transitioned from a 41,000-year period to a 100,000-year period. Climatologists have found two contributing causes for this change.

Analysis of data from South Atlantic deep-sea cores showed that a major shift in Atlantic Ocean thermohaline (heat + salt) circulation occurred about 900,000 years ago.[15] This ocean circulation change would have facilitated the simultaneous drawdown of atmospheric carbon dioxide that previous research teams had noted. Carbon dioxide removal would have helped to cool Earth sufficiently to turn off the 41,000-year cycle and turn on the 100,000-year cycle.

Other researchers point to geological evidence indicating that while the Tibetan Plateau rose from a 4,000- to a 4,600-meter average elevation over the past 2.59 million years, brief episodes of especially dramatic uplift occurred.[16] The intensification of Indian and East Asian monsoons[17] and the accumulation of aeolian dust ("yellow sand" from the Asian deserts)[18] that occurred about 0.9 million years ago can be explained as resulting from an episode of rapid uplift in the Tibetan Plateau. High-resolution magnetostratigraphy and tectonic sedimentology indeed show that such a rise took place about 0.8 million years ago.[19]

This same uplift event caused a majority of the plateau to be covered in snow and ice at the glacial maxima level.[20] The extra snow and ice coverage, combined with heightened atmospheric dust levels, cooled the planet so significantly as to enlarge the snow and ice packs at all high northern latitudes. The resultant decrease in photosynthetic activity and intensified erosion due to monsoons enhanced silicate weathering, drawing down atmospheric carbon dioxide even further and, thus, adding to the cooling.

The intensified cooling effectively stabilized the 100,000-year ice age cycle. Figure 15.6 shows Antarctic temperature changes for the last four cycles (450,000 years) as recorded in the ice core taken from the Vostok

**Figure 15.6. Antarctic Temperature Record for Previous Four Ice Ages**

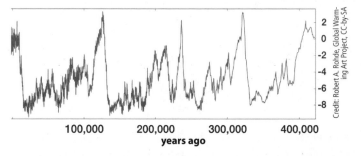

The temperature scale is in degrees Celsius relative to the current global average temperature.

site in central Antarctica. In response to the ever-increasing elevation of the Himalayas and the Tibetan Plateau, each successive ice age maximum over the past 800,000 years became progressively more severe.

About 100,000 years ago, the Tibetan Plateau experienced a tectonic uplift event of about the same magnitude as the one that occurred 0.8–0.9 million years ago.[21] Consequently, the most recent ice age maximum proved the most expansive of all (see fig. 15.7). The thickness of the larger ice sheets ranged from 1 to 3 kilometers (0.6 to 1.9 miles).[22] Ice covered the entire Antarctic continent and much of the seawater surrounding it. As much as 2.4 million square kilometers (0.93 million square miles) of the Tibetan Plateau lay under a thick ice blanket. The North American ice sheet reached as far south as 38° north latitude (the Ohio River) while the European ice sheet extended down to 48° north latitude (southern Ukraine). The Tasmanian and Patagonian ice sheets reached up to 41° south latitude. In addition to these mega ice sheets, several more covered the mountains and surrounding regions of the Andes and Venezuela, the Sierra Nevada and Sierra Madre, the Alps and the Caucasus, Kilimanjaro and the Atlas, the Japanese Alps, the Altai, the Tien Shan, and the Zagros, most of Taiwan, and the mountainous regions of New Guinea.

**Figure 15.7. Northern Hemisphere Extent of Kilometer+ Thick Ice Sheets during the Last Glacial Maximum**

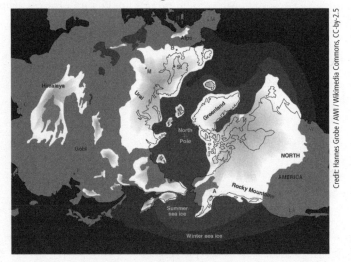

## Benefits of Cyclical Ice Ages

For the last ice age cycle, global ice volume became maximal about 21,000 years ago. However, most of this ice had melted by about 12,000 years ago.

The melting away of the great ice sheets—except those over Antarctica, Greenland, and the North Pole—helped to stabilize global mean temperatures. Until then, climate variability prevented widespread enduring agricultural and manufacturing specialization, trade, and construction of towns, roads, and ships. The climate from 120,000 to 12,000 years ago varied so radically as to render the launch of extensive cultivation and global civilization impossible (see figs. 15.8 and 15.9).[23] As one research team commented, the "last glacial climates were extremely hostile to agriculture."[24]

This extreme hostility explains why, previous to the Neolithic Revolution (circa 12,000 years ago), the only evidence for agriculture is a small-scale attempt to cultivate wild cereals along the shore of the Sea of Galilee some 23,000 years ago.[25] Researchers discovered "proto-weeds" mixed in with seeds of wild emmer, barley, and oat. The team cited numerous research studies establishing that certain weeds rapidly evolve in response to cultivation. The discovered proto-weeds showed the first signs of such evolution. The team concluded that the presence of the proto-weeds "indicates the earliest, small-scale attempt to cultivate wild cereals seen in the archeological record."[26]

Then, for reasons still unknown, the climate suddenly entered a stable phase shortly after the beginning of the last warm interglacial period. Within a brief period, large-scale agriculture emerged, as did sophisticated expressions of human ingenuity and cooperation, for example towns, specialization of industry, and organized trade. These factors, in turn, made possible the exponential expansion of civilization, technology, and human population.

The melting away of ice fields from the last glacial age continues to this day. This melt feeds the rivers that water the great agricultural plains on which nearly 7 billion people and their animals depend for food. Out from the ice fields of the Himalayas and the Tibetan Plateau, for example, flow the Ganges, Brahmaputra, Indus, Sutlej, Chenab, Narmada, Godavari, Krishna, Mekong, Yangtze, Yellow, Pearl, Irrawaddy, Salween, and Red Rivers. These rivers irrigate agricultural plains that sustain more than one-third of Earth's population. Glacier melt from other mountain ranges of Asia, as well as from the Andes, the Cordilleran mountains of North America, the Alps and Caucasus, and the high regions of eastern Africa sustain still more people. Harmonic tremors that occur within mountain glaciers also facilitate glacial melt.[27] Such humming glaciers release liquid water even when mountain temperatures are low.

Fine loess (wind-blown dust) from dried-out parts of the floodplains of glacial braided rivers carried layers of crucial nutrients onto the lowland plains below, making them richly fertile. Meanwhile, the retreating of the ice fields and glaciers exposed valuable mineral ore deposits. Thus, the ending of the last glacial era facilitated and still sustains metallurgy.

As the vast sheets of ice covering much of the northern hemisphere continents retreated, they scoured out numerous basins in which millions of lakes formed. In Canada alone retreating ice created 32,000 lakes larger than three square kilometers. Fresh water left over from the latest glacial era covers roughly 9 percent of Canada's total surface area.

This abundance of freshwater area resulted in evaporation and condensation that, in turn, supported precipitation over large swaths of land that otherwise would be drier. Lakes and rivers became habitats for marsh plants, such as wild rice and other grains, as well as for fish, crustaceans, waterfowl, muskrats, otters, beavers, moose, and many, many more creatures. Lakes and rivers also provided humans with efficient transportation corridors that facilitated specialized agriculture and industry. The flow of abundant water allowed for the generation and widespread distribution of hydroelectric power. This power conferred countless benefits, including efficient, cost-effective mass production of aluminum.

Retreating ice also carved out many calm, deep-water harbors, further enhancing the global distribution of food and other goods, as well as people. Because ice sheets had spread from shore to shore on some continents and portions thereof, their recession gouged out fjords and inlets of magnificent beauty and usefulness.

Before the ice receded, it allowed humans to migrate from their locale of origin, near the juncture of Europe, Asia, and Africa and then to spread throughout all of Africa, Asia, Australia, Europe, and North and South America. The vast quantity of ice for a time kept sea levels as low as about 125 meters (410 feet) below current levels. Thus, land bridges connected Siberia to Alaska, Britain to France, Asia Minor to the Greek Peninsula, Korea to Japan, Denmark to Sweden, and Vancouver Island and the Queen Charlottes to the British Columbia mainland. The lower sea level also facilitated relatively easy island hops between Southeast Asia and Australia. With the advent of civilization came the opportunity for people to migrate and settle on all Earth's temperate and tropical continents.

This migration and settlement was made possible by the proximity of the continents' extremities to one another. The north-south orientation of the continents' mountain ranges, with progressively higher elevations closer to the equator, also helped. Thanks to the increasing mountain elevation with shrinking latitude, melting snow and ice were more evenly distributed over the continental landmasses.

The aesthetic benefits from the latest and most severe glacial episode in the ice age cycle deserve attention, as well. Today Earth offers the most spectacularly beautiful scenery it has ever possessed. The receding ice sheets and glaciers have enhanced the relief of Earth's mountains and valleys, creating majestic waterfalls. They have produced meadows, forests, rivers, and lakes filled with an extravagant diversity of plants and animals displaying every imaginable combination of color and texture. The beauty of Earth's surface is further enhanced by the simultaneous timing of the ice age cycle with unique tectonic events, including the formation of chains of volcanoes that produced many beautiful islands, island chains, and coastal highlands.

All this stunning natural scenery and wildlife helps humans living in a high-technology, high-stress society refresh their soul and maintain their sanity. To put it another way, the richness of Earth's beauty and variety provides not only for humanity's physical needs but also for our soul's needs. Table 15.1 summarizes the more obvious benefits of the ice age cycle described above.

### Table 15.1: Ice Age Cycle Benefits for Humanity

1. Melting ice fields brought nutrient-rich alluvial silt to the plains.
2. Wind-blown dust delivered additional nutrients to the plains.

3. Melting glaciers watered the plains.

4. Ice field and glacier retreat formed an abundance of lakes.

5. Lakes and connecting rivers transformed barren deserts into productive land.

6. Geological relief yielded abundant hydropower resources.

7. Retreating ice sheets formed land bridges to facilitate human migration.

8. Glacial retreat formed deep, safe harbors.

9. Retreating ice sheets, ice fields, and glaciers exposed rich ore deposits.

10. Retreating ice sheets, ice fields, and glaciers created new habitats for plants and animals during the warm interglacial periods.

11. Retreating ice sheets, ice fields, and glaciers created spectacular scenery.

**The Long Cool Summer**

Figure 15.6 shows the variation of Earth's temperature throughout the past four ice age cycles. This graph reveals a pattern of long glacial epochs (80,000–100,000 years in duration) followed by brief warm interglacial episodes (10,000–20,000 years in length). Each interglacial is characterized by spiking temperature, a rapid rise of several degrees that peaks at about 3–4°C (5–7°F) above Earth's current level, followed immediately by an equally rapid and dramatic temperature drop, ushering in the next long glacial period. This pattern of rapid and extreme temperature rise followed by rapid and extreme temperature decline characterizes the entire Quaternary period—with one exception.

The warm interglacial period humanity currently enjoys constitutes that one exception (see fig. 15.8). As the current interglacial began, the temperature indeed rose rapidly. Between 12,500 and 9,000 years ago, the global mean temperature rose 8°C (14.5°F). However, instead of continuing to spike the usual 3–4°C (5–7°F) higher, it plateaued. For the past 9,000 years, Earth's temperature has remained extraordinarily stable—at a steady global mean temperature optimal for maintaining a large, globally distributed, technologically advancing human population.

This brief epoch of extreme climate stability is unique. At no other time during the 2.59-million-year Quaternary period has Earth experienced anything close to this degree of temperature stability.

**Figure 15.8. Temperature Variation throughout the Last Ice Age Cycle**

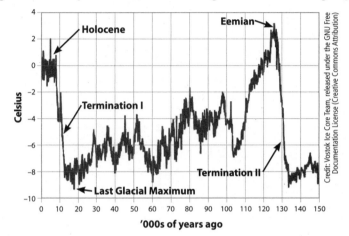

Vostok ice core (central Antarctica) supplied the temperature records here.

Evidence of this steady, global mean temperature throughout the past 9,000 years appears in all the ice cores from central Antarctica and north central Greenland (see fig. 15.9). A team of geologists used stalagmite records from caves in the Alps to show that this steady climate was, indeed, globally extensive and not just a phenomenon limited to the highest latitudes. They found that the climate in Greenland is tightly coupled to the climate in central Europe. Climatologists refer to the past 9,000 years as the long cool summer, the long warm spring, or simply as the long summer.

A cause (or causes) of this enduring, optimally benign climate has yet to be determined with any degree of confidence. However, no doubt exists about its exceptionality. In the context of everything else required to support global high-technology civilization, it constitutes a unique event in Earth's history. Given the observed cyclical nature of ice ages, the data suggest the long cool summer may soon come to an end, and it seems unlikely to repeat.

213

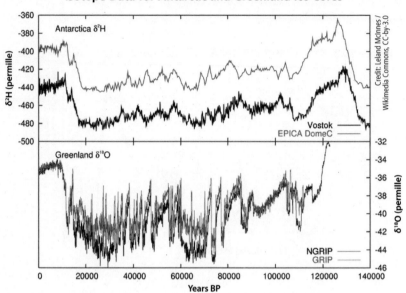

**Figure 15.9. The Long Cool Summer:
Isotope Data for Antarctic and Greenland Ice Cores**

## Optimal Solar Epoch

While cyclical ice ages are the most obvious distinguishing feature of the Quaternary, other events of this period also made human existence and civilization possible—and potentially comfortable. As figure 6.1 shows, the Sun's flaring activity, X-ray radiation, and ultraviolet radiation calmed down to their minimal values during this epoch, and the Sun entered a period of remarkable luminosity stability. Researchers have worked diligently to confirm these facts both to appreciate what's responsible for them and to predict how long these conditions might last.

With the aid of a recently upgraded neutrino detector in Italy, physicists for the first time (in 2014) observed neutrino particles produced by the proton-proton (pp) fusion reaction within the nuclear furnace at the Sun's core.[28] The observation established that the pp fusion reaction accounts for 99 percent of the Sun's energy output.

Neutrinos are fundamental particles that interact via the weak nuclear force only. Consequently, they travel through the Sun's interior and atmospheric layers at nearly the velocity of light. The photons that emerge from the Sun's nuclear furnace, however, take slightly more than 100,000 years to travel from the Sun's core to its surface. They take this long because they experience over a thousand "Compton scatterings" (inelastic scatterings of photons by charged particles, usually electrons, that increase the photons' wavelengths) before they reach the Sun's surface. Because a well-understood relationship exists between the pp neutrinos and the photons emanating from the pp fusion reaction, the Italian solar physicists were able to compare the Sun's luminosity 100,000 years ago with its current luminosity.

The two luminosities were identical, which tells us that the Sun has been in strict thermodynamic equilibrium throughout the past 100,000 years. This result is consistent with an earlier detection achieved by the Sudbury Neutrino Observatory in Ontario, Canada. The Sudbury study showed the Sun's luminosity became exceptionally stable at about 50,000 years ago and seems likely to remain stable for the next 50,000 years.[29] This era of exceptional stability in solar luminosity helped make possible humanity's launch and development of global, technologically advanced civilization.

## Optimal Supernova Moment

As noted in chapters 3 and 4, supernovae are crucial for life. They alone are responsible for producing many heavy elements essential to life, as well as many other heavy elements essential for human civilization. But supernovae can also endanger life. The more complex an organism, the more sensitive it is to radiation damage from supernova eruptions, especially those that erupt within the vicinity of the solar system.

Our galaxy's supernova rate, which has been declining since life originated on Earth, correlates with life's gradual progress from simple and microscopic to complex and macroscopic, then to high-metabolism and large-bodied, and, most recently, to human beings. As it is, the current rate of supernova eruptions in the vicinity of our solar system proves barely low enough for humans to thrive and sustain civilization.

Just 2 million years ago, the solar system passed within 130 light-years of the Scorpius-Centaurus association of giant stars.[30] Deep ocean floor samples reveal an iron-60 excess, the signature of a supernova eruption, that also dates to 2.0 million years ago. That date corresponds to that of the most recent marine extinction event.[31]

In the last 300,000 years, at least 23 supernovae have exploded within 980 light-years of Earth.[32] Four of these occurred between 22,000–44,000 years ago at distances ranging from 360 to 820 light-years (see table 15.2).[33] In the era of human civilization (the Neolithic Revolution dates back to 12,000 years ago and it marked the advent of towns, transportation systems, specialized agriculture, and manufacture), however, Earth has experienced an amazing stroke of good fortune. No supernova closer than 5,000 light-years has erupted (see table 15.3) in this period.[34] At a distance of 5,000+ light-years, supernovae pose no threat, via their cosmic radiation, either to Earth's ozone shield or to its climate stability (both are critical requirements for sustaining globally productive agriculture) or to human health.

#### Table 15.2: Recent Nearby Supernovae

| date (years ago) | distance (light-years) |
|---|---|
| 44,000 | 360 |
| 37,000 | 590 |
| 32,000 | 520 |
| 22,000 | 820 |

#### Table 15.3: Supernovae in Recorded History

Astronomers began recording bright astronomical phenomena such as novae and comets as early as 3000 BC. Therefore, with considerable confidence historians conclude that no supernovae as bright as the one that erupted in 1054 AD occurred between 3000 BC and AD 1000.

| date | distance (light-years) |
|---|---|
| AD 1006 | 5,080 |
| AD 1054 | 6,500 |
| AD 1181 | 10,400 |
| AD 1572 | 7,500 |
| AD 1604 | 9,400 |
| AD 1671 | 11,100 |
| AD 1680 | 36,000 |

Supernovae as nearby as the ones listed in table 15.3 could conceivably damage satellite electronics. However, during the past 344 years no supernovae have erupted within 10,000 light-years of Earth. In galaxies similar to the Milky Way, astronomers observe a supernova rate of at least three per century.[35] Our protection from nearby supernova events appears exceptional.

## Optimal Biological Moment

As noted in the previous chapter, the grasses so important for the welfare of ungulates (hoofed mammals) did not appear on Earth until late in the Paleogene period (66–23 million years ago), and the grains (for example, rice, wheat, oats, barley, maize, sorghum, and millet) essential for sustaining a large human population did not appear until the Neogene period (23–2.59 million years ago). Likewise, fruit trees, farm animals, transportation animals, and plants and animals suitable for the manufacture of clothing did not appear until the Neogene and Quaternary periods—the last one-half of one percent of life's history on Earth.

None of these biological resources critical for the launch and maintenance of global civilization would have been available if not for a carefully timed, step-by-step introduction of progressively more diverse and advanced species from 3.8 billion years ago onward. As chapter 2 demonstrated, not until the human epoch did Earth attain anything close to its theoretical maximum carrying capacity for number of species of life. Meanwhile, as many research biologists have pointed out, the real story of life's increasing diversity and complexity is better told by the number of families (the taxonic rank between genera and order) rather than by the number of species.

British geologist Michael Benton conducted a count of the increasing number of families throughout life's history. His study showed that the diversity of life has grown exponentially since the end of the Precambrian.[36] The total number of families rapidly increased from a few to 280 during the early Cambrian, fell to 120 by the end of the Cambrian, rose to 450 during the Ordovician, reached 600–650 by the end of the Permian, dropped to 420 at the beginning of the Triassic, ballooned up to 1,260–1,350 in the late Cretaceous, and mushroomed to 2,400 by the advent of humanity.[37]

Greater diversity translates to greater abundance, as well. Many studies have demonstrated direct correlations between biodiversity and bioabundance.[38] As the previous chapters explained, not until the present epoch did the physical conditions of our galaxy, solar system, and planet allow for such a great abundance and diversity of life. However, these optimal physical conditions will not last much longer. In several million years the Sun will be too bright, and to compensate for its increasing luminosity along the way, the quantity of carbon dioxide that will need to be removed from the atmosphere so that life can survive will begin to limit photosynthetic activity. While such a limitation will not spell the end of all life, it will mean an end to a large human population, as well as to large populations of the animals on which humans most depend. In addition, just a few million years from now, the Sun's flaring activity is expected to increase significantly.

Other factors that will begin to limit Earth's life-carrying capacity include changes in the positions and alignments of the continents and a decrease in continental landmass coverage. The present sizes, configurations, and alignments of the continents, currently optimal for maximizing Earth's carrying capacity, will change within several million years as continents continue to drift. In particular, Antarctica will move north while Greenland moves south. These movements will cause most of Earth's ice to melt, raising sea levels by more than 100 meters (330 feet) and shrinking the proportion of Earth's surface covered by land.

## Why Now?

Is it mere coincidence that our one-of-a-kind long cool summer occurs simultaneously with the following unique events: (1) the Sun becomes exceptionally stable in luminosity, with minimal flaring and ultraviolet and X-ray radiation; (2) no nearby supernova eruptions occur; (3) maximization of the diversity and abundance of life on Earth; (4) various habitable zone windows align perfectly; and (5) many other coincidences described in these pages all came together? Not likely. These amazingly arranged features should give us pause to consider the meaning of our human existence.

How is it that we humans came to be here with such a bountiful array of resources at such a uniquely optimal moment in life's long and awe-inspiring story? The last chapter addresses possible answers to this question.

# 16

## Why We're Here

When future residents move into the Wilshire Grand Center, when guests check into the Burj Khalifa, and when researchers set foot inside the Amundsen-Scott South Pole Station, they may (or may not) take for granted the extraordinary features of their accommodations. Even if they do, they certainly grasp that these amazing structures came together not of their own accord but as the result of purposeful, meticulous planning and preparation. While no analogy fits perfectly, this one does have at least some relevance to our thinking about the home into which simple life, animals, and, finally, we humans took up residence many millennia ago.

The reigning paradigm in academia today says that whether God or some unspecified spiritual entity may conceivably exist, such a being is irrelevant to Earth's history and life's history. Many (though not all) of the brightest minds of our time deem natural processes alone as the fully adequate explanation for everything astronomers and physicists, biologists and paleontologists, chemists and geologists, artists and mathematicians observe.

However, the preceding chapters describe many new, and some not-so-new, observations concerning Earth's prehistory and origin and the origin and history of life on Earth—all of which combined to represent a potent challenge to the naturalistic view. I cannot say these observations "prove" in any absolute sense that the biblical God planned and prepared Earth as a home for humans, but what explanation offers a more reasonable assessment of the data? Do we owe our existence at this time and in this place to a nearly infinite web of intricately intertwined coincidences that just happened to all come together of their own accord?

As a vocal advocate for advancing scientific research that yields deeper understanding of nature's magnificence, I simply want to encourage deep thought and a reasonable evaluation of the data. The Bible tells us that the more we investigate the record of nature, the more evidence we will find for God's existence, for his handiwork in preparing the natural realm for our benefit, and for his purposeful involvement in our lives (Job 9; 36:22–39:30; Ps. 104). I have personally found this claim to be true. Today, as scientists examine the origin and history of Earth and its life, they see more wonders and mysteries and more indicators of an intelligence and intentionality behind the reality. However, because many or most work in such highly specialized niches, they tend to assume that naturalistic or materialistic explanations for what they see reside in some other scientific discipline or subdiscipline or combination of subdisciplines.

Sometimes personal assumptions or worldview commitments get in the way. A recent article in the *New Yorker* provides an example.[1] Widely known astronomer Lawrence Krauss looked at the chain of events leading to humanity's existence and assigns godlike qualities first to the laws of physics and then to natural selection, with no reference to the source of either. He argued that "elaborating all the factors responsible for some specific event and calculating all the probabilities as if they were independent"[2] is simply a mistake because, strictly speaking, *everything* is improbable. While Krauss correctly pointed out that dependency factors must be determined before any meaningful probability can be derived, he erred in assuming that human life is nothing special and that many different sets of other physical coincidences would have led to something akin to humans. But *how* would it? To make his point Krauss needs to show at least one set of significantly different physical events and pathways that yields the equivalent of human beings. He would have to demonstrate how a set of purely physical events and pathways yields the consciousness, personality, intelligence, emotions, volition, and spiritual qualities that every person possesses. More to the point, Krauss needs to explain *why* humans have arisen—unless some driving Personal Force wanted sentient, self-aware, reasoning personal creatures to exist.

Some researchers see life's layering—the cycle of extinctions and replacements—as a haphazard, trial-and-error process that contradicts the notion of a caring, meticulous Creator. Biologist Kenneth Miller, who does acknowledge God's existence, nevertheless has stated that the record of life's history causes him to reject the notion that a Creator played any hands-on role in producing life. In his book *Only a Theory* he wrote,

> The [supposed] designer is never satisfied—or perhaps can never get it quite right. . . . Our designer doesn't just design; he does it again and again—and his designs don't last. For all of his intelligence, the most striking aspect of his work is its impermanence. His creations are swept away time and time again by extinction, requiring him to stock the pond repeatedly to keep life going. The inescapable conclusion that comes from honestly applying the idea of design to the fossil record is that the great intelligence behind ID [intelligent design] is a serial creator.[3]

What if, on the other hand, this repeated cycle of mass extinction and restocking of the pond speaks of a plan and purpose? Psalm 104:27–30, for example, says this about life's cycle:

> All creatures look to you [God]
>     to give them their food at the proper time.
> When you give it to them,
>     they gather it up;
> when you open your hand,
>     they are satisfied with good things.
> When you hide your face,
>     they are terrified;
> when you take away their breath,
>     they die and return to the dust.

When you send your Spirit,
    they are created,
    and you renew the face of the ground.

In the context of an ever-brightening Sun (see ch. 12), repeated mass extinctions and mass speciation events actually accomplished a life-sustaining purpose. The removal of certain life-forms and rapid addition of others meant that life could thrive for billions of years. By regulating Earth's conditions for the benefit of later life, creatures with progressively greater complexity and more advanced capabilities could be introduced step-by-step until the arrival of rational, relational, spiritual beings.

## Bountiful Endowment

The very long history of Earth and of its various forms has not only made possible the existence of creatures as complex as human beings but also endowed us with all the internal and external resources we would need to launch and sustain civilization. As chapter 11 described, the early, enduring, abundant, and diverse organisms helped transform Earth's crust from toxic to safe, with essential, life-nourishing minerals. Without these specialized microorganisms and their just-right populations throughout Earth's history, the vital poisons that appear in the periodic table of elements would be either overabundant or underabundant for the existence and survival of advanced life, especially humanity.

The familiar adage "You can't have too much of a good thing" doesn't hold true for Earth. Too much water would create oceans so deep that continents would never form. Too much carbon would yield an atmosphere too thick for lungs to function. On the other hand, too little of certain elements generally considered toxins would also ruin Earth's chances to serve as a life site. When Carl Sagan and others first claimed that among the universe's billions and billions of stars and planets, millions of life sites must exist, they implied that Earth is not really an unusual planet. However, research now shows that Earth is far from ordinary in multiple respects, and certainly in its abundance of elements and diversity of minerals.

These rich ore deposits enabled humans to develop beyond Stone Age civilization. Plate tectonics and bacteria helped provide the soil on which our large population depends for food. The presence of land plants and animals as early as conditions would permit provided humanity with a huge treasure chest of elements, of fossil fuels, and of fossil building materials, such as limestone, marble, and gypsum. (Tables 11.1, 13.1, and 13.2 document the enormous wealth of Earth's elemental and biodeposit treasures for humanity's specific benefit.)

## Unique Moment

With a view to events of the last few thousand years, we find ourselves in an unprecedented circumstance in Earth's history. Humans live and thrive in the *only* geological era characterized by an ice age cycle—and in the *one* enduringly warm, stable, but very brief (just 9,000 years), period within that cycle that provides the conditions appropriate for global high-technology civilization. We enjoy the beneficial aftermath of the most severe of all the glacial episodes in the ice age cycle. The well-watered, nutrient-rich plains it enhanced allows Earth to sustain more than 7 billion people. Sheltered harbors and sea routes carved by huge glaciers facilitate the efficient trading of goods. Magnificent natural scenery helps us maintain our sanity and satisfy our longing for beauty.

We also see that in many regards, Earth today is a messy, dangerous, deteriorating place. This fact must be taken into account as we consider the way the world is. Two considerations leap to mind. Both point us back to the construction analogy. When a residential or other building shows signs of damage and wear, a careful inspection reveals whether the problem lies with shoddy construction or, rather, with abuse by its occupants. In Earth's case, the structure appears fundamentally sound. Even the so-called natural evils can be shown as inherently beneficial to human existence. Hurricanes, tornadoes, earthquakes, floods, fires, and the like all played (and still play) a valuable role establishing and maintaining Earth's optimal habitability.[4] More often than not, however, humanity's lack of respect for, or understanding of, nature's forces puts people in harm's way. Even such "enemies" as viruses and bacteria serve a life-supporting role in Earth's cast of characters. But, again, human mismanagement and even malevolence have turned miniscule microbes into menacing monsters.

The second consideration focuses on permanence. Does evidence suggest to us that this earthly residence can somehow, by human effort, be made to last forever—or that it was intended to last forever? We must admit that forever is what we want. The longing for immortality can be seen not only in today's world but also in every human culture that has left any trace of its desires and values. And yet the awareness of decay, not just of our own life but also of all life and even of the physical universe as a whole, confronts us daily. As much as we prefer to live in denial, we cannot seem to rest there. The quest for a means of rescue from decay and dissolution pervades every culture and every generation, as seen in literature, music, arts, architecture, and more. Why?

## Why We're Here

Humans tend to take pride and joy in all that we have achieved, and we have accomplished a great deal since the first of our kind set foot on Earth. Although we're inclined to take full credit, we must acknowledge that whatever we've attained sprang from the preparation and provision that preceded us—on a cosmic, galactic, solar system, planetary, societal, and personal scale. Whatever we've done or become was made possible by a generous endowment of physical, intellectual, relational, and volitional capacities.

The perfect world we have *not* been able to attain—and yet still long for—gives a clue to the purpose of our existence. As we strive for peace, wars multiply. As we strive for unity, polarization intensifies. As we strive for liberty, bondage increases. As we strive for wealth, poverty spreads. As we strive for equality, intolerance grows.

Of all the proposed explanations for these realities, the one that aligns most closely and completely with the available data emerges from the pages of the Bible. We are fallen and alienated from our Creator, but this condition need not mark our permanent state. We need redemption and it is available.

This holy book (the Bible) makes sense of what *was*, what *is*, and what *will be*. It anticipates what each generation of humanity, including our own, needs to know in order to discover our origin and fulfill our destiny. It identifies a reasonable Source for nature and nature's laws, as well as for humans and their capabilities—including the compulsion to reason. Just as importantly, it identifies the ultimate aim of the created realm.

A big clue comes from noting, according to the Bible, that God planned out his works of redemption *before* he started his works of creation. Paul declares this in his letters to Timothy and Titus:

> He [God] has saved us and called us to a holy life—not because of anything we have done but because of his own purpose and grace. This grace was given us in Christ Jesus before the beginning of time. (2 Tim. 1:9)

> Paul, a servant of God and an apostle of Jesus Christ to further the faith of God's elect and their knowledge of the truth that leads to godliness—in the hope of eternal life, which God who does not lie, promised before the beginning of time. (Titus 1:1–2)

All of God's works of creation are in the context of his greater works of redemption.

All of creation makes sense in the context of a real world beyond the one we now occupy, a world of unbroken, unending, loving relationships with a host of fellow humans and with the One in whom life and love originated. I would add "possible" relationships because they involve choice. The world *is* the way it is to present us with the choice and with the opportunity to make this choice. Only those who want this everlasting life enough to acknowledge their Maker and embrace their Rescuer as the one and only Savior from their own best efforts and worst failures at being good will share in it. Gladly, we have an indication that the number of those who make this choice is huge. In Revelation 7:9 the apostle John records a God-given vision of our future:

> There before me was a great multitude that no one could count, from every nation, tribe, people, and language, standing before the throne and before the Lamb [Jesus Christ].

The Greek numbering system familiar to John extended into the hundreds of millions. So his description implies at least several billion humans standing together in this scene. Such a number means the present Earth must be able to carry an enormous human population because the Creator's plan called for a habitat that can support billions of humans.

Human history gives additional clues to the purpose of our existence on Earth—to know our good God and to make him known. In addition to the meticulous orchestration of cosmic, planetary, and life history for our existence, the direction of human history also fits this *redemptive* plan and purpose. The longing for rescue springs from the very real possibility of rescue! We see the careful timing of Abraham's migration to Canaan, the later sojourn of Abraham's descendants in Egypt and exodus from Egypt back to Canaan, the rise of the Babylonian, Persian, Greek, and Roman empires, and the timing of Jesus Christ's coming.

With the land called Canaan situated at the juncture of three continents—Africa, Asia, and Europe—what better location for the acknowledged birthplace of human civilization?[5] By about 4000 BC, large-scale agriculture, metallurgy, and trade had developed on these continents, allowing population levels to multiply. Abraham and his progeny lived in the one location where all civilized nations crossed paths. This unique location gave them opportunity to share as widely as possible the truth God had revealed to them, the truth of God's delight in blessing all who will worship him.

The first dominant world power, the Egyptian empire, emerged at the time of Abraham's great-grandson, Joseph. This young foreigner's unlikely rise to power saved countless lives, including those of his own relatives. From this family came Moses, the rescuer of an entire population of Abraham's descendants from slavery in Egypt—a vivid foreshadowing of God's ultimate redemptive plan. The power by which this rescue was accomplished compelled a very large number of Egyptians to embrace the God of their former slaves and join them in becoming "Hebrews"—followers of God.[6]

By divine guidance these people came to occupy the land of Canaan, where they could employ new technologies to establish the magnificent kingdom of David, and then of Solomon. These kingdoms drew worldwide fame for their wealth and wisdom, a fame that motivated the heads of surrounding nations to seek insight from their God.[7]

When the people of Israel lost sight of their identity and purpose, they were thrust as exiles into the power centers of the Assyrian, Babylonian, and Persian empires, where technology was advancing rapidly. Some showed such outstanding virtue, knowledge, and wisdom that the rulers of these empires promoted them to positions of great power. Daniel, for one, ruled as prime minister of both the Babylonian and Persian empires.[8] A Hebrew orphan named Esther became queen of Persia. Through her uncle Mordecai's counsel and her own daring action, Hebrews in all 127 of the empire's far-flung provinces were rescued from annihilation.[9] Furthermore, the king of the Persian empire appointed Mordecai as his prime minister over all 127 provinces.[10] The story of God's power and care spread farther.

During the rise of the Greeks and Romans, Hebrew communities sprang up in major cities across the empires. Caesar Augustus built a vast road system of such quality and durability that some roads remain in use today. This new transportation network and an emerging Mediterranean shipping industry facilitated *Pax Romana*—a period of relative peace throughout the Roman world.

Jesus of Nazareth arrived on the scene during this period. He prepared his band of followers for a new communications strategy. Instead of encouraging them to huddle together in a few large cities, he commissioned them to take advantage of every new communications and transportation option available. As eyewitnesses to his morally perfect life, his sacrificial death to atone for all the violations of God's ways committed by every human being, and his bodily resurrection from the dead, they began to spread the Good News of God's redeeming love to all the people groups around them, and through them to the rest of the world.

Most of the content in this book documents what scientists have discovered thus far about the preparation of our solar system and of Earth's physical and biological resources for humans—preparations not just for our existence but also for our globally dispersed, technologically advanced civilization. In the context of the mission God has given his followers to present his offer of redemption to every single people group that resides on Earth, the need for such a civilization becomes evident. It will take that kind of civilization to complete the mission

Jesus Christ assigned to his followers in what remains of the "long cool summer" (see fig. 15.9).

Today, we who follow Jesus Christ possess the wealth and technology to do what Jesus assigned his disciples to do. A study by the founder of the US Center for World Mission (now known as Frontier Ventures), Ralph Winter, shows an exponential increase across the centuries in the proportion of the global population who identify as Christ followers. He expressed the dramatic growth (see table 16.1), largely attributable to advancing technology, by showing the decrease in the ratio of those "who do not consider themselves Christians" to those described as "truly committed, Bible-believing Christians."[11]

**Table 16.1: Ratio of Christians to Non-Christians throughout History**

In this table Christians are defined as truly committed, Bible-believing disciples of Jesus Christ. Non-Christians are defined as people who would not call themselves Christians.

| Date | # of Non-Christians Per Christian |
|---|---|
| AD 100 | 360 |
| AD 1000 | 220 |
| AD 1500 | 69 |
| AD 1900 | 27 |
| AD 1950 | 22 |
| AD 1980 | 11 |
| AD 1990 | 7 |

Even with so much still to discover and learn about the way the world is and how it came to be this way, an abundance of evidence suggests an answer to the *why* question: we are here to seek and to find God and then to use all the resources he has so painstakingly and generously provided, within the amazingly stable and optimal climate epoch he established, to encourage people from every ethnic and cultural group in the world to receive God's redemptive offer. God's desire to bring redemption to a vast and variegated population explains why the history of the Milky Way Galaxy, the solar system, Earth, and life looks as it does.

In other words, the world is the way it is so that we can be here, and we are here so that we can be agents of blessing to every tribe on the planet for as long as his divine power holds this Earth and its life together. Then, at the just-right moment, Jesus Christ will whisk us into the new residence he spoke of as "my Father's house" (John 14:1–4), the home beyond the space-time confines of this universe, the place he is preparing for us—and preparing us for—at this very moment.

# Appendix A

# Why Not Life on a Moon?

Astronomers have speculated for more than a decade that life might possibly exist on one of the moons in our solar system—or perhaps elsewhere. They acknowledge, however, that for any moon to sustain life for a long time on its surface, it must be very large. It needs much more than just some liquid water. It needs a host of protective conditions and supportive nutrients, many or most of which depend on plate tectonics and a strong magnetic field. To manifest these features, a moon's mass must be at least 23 percent of Earth's mass. For these features to last more than a couple billion years requires a mass and density closely equivalent to Earth's.[1]

The solar system's most massive moon is Jupiter's Ganymede, at 2.48 percent of Earth's mass. Based on the typical correlation between planet mass and moon mass in our solar system (with Earth's moon as the single exception), to get a moon as massive as Earth would require a host planet at least 20 times more massive than Jupiter. Such a massive planet would inevitably generate orbital chaos for other planets in its system and, thus, for the moons in the system as well, including any moons in its own orbit.

For *any* gas giant planet to form, let alone one 20 times the mass of Jupiter, its birthing location must lie beyond the host star's snow line (the distance from the star at which water and carbon dioxide are permanently frozen). This birthing location, however, guarantees that an Earth-sized moon orbiting such a planet will accrete an atmosphere several hundred, if not thousands of times thicker than Earth's. Such a thick atmosphere rules out advanced life because lungs (or any kind of efficient respiratory organ) cannot function at such high levels of atmospheric pressures.

Another problem for lunar life is that the host planet must migrate inward from beyond the snow line to a distance from the host star where surface liquid water can be maintained at length, for a few billion years at least. So far, astronomers have discovered 54 gas giant planets beyond the solar system at least three times the mass of Jupiter that orbit their host stars between 80 and 150 percent of Earth's orbital distance from the Sun (the distance range at which surface liquid water is conceivable in the vicinity of a Sun-like star). Of these 54 planets, 50 of them exhibit high eccentricity (highly elliptical) orbits.[2] Evidently such inward migration induces orbital chaos. A host planet's highly elliptical orbit means that it and any accompanying moons will repeatedly move in and out of the range where surface liquid water can remain and where the required amount of ultraviolet radiation is possible. Even a relatively minor distance change presents a problem, however. For a lunar or planetary atmosphere to remain stable, that moon or planet must remain near enough (but not too near) to the host star to sustain both surface liquid water and the essential ultraviolet influx—and that's a very narrow distance range (see ch. 7).

A third challenge to the possibility of lunar life comes from the likelihood of tidal locking. If a moon orbits its planet closely, it becomes tidally locked, with one side of the moon perpetually facing the planet. The result would be long cold nights and long hot days. However, if a moon orbits far enough away from its planet so as to avoid tidal locking, it would experience enormous seasonal temperature differences as its orbit carries it alternately closer to and farther from the host star. While close-in tidal locking could result in an orbital period (for the moon) that would lessen the day-to-night temperature differences, such a close-in orbit would also generate destructive tides and enormous (lunar) volcanic eruptions. Depending on the strength of the host planet's magnetic field, close-in tidal locking could also wreak havoc on the moon's atmospheric layers.

Whether it orbits close in or far out, a large moon held by a large gas giant planet would experience heavy bombardment from comets and asteroids. Just as the gravity of Jupiter causes many asteroids and comets to veer into its vicinity, so, too, the gravity of any large gas giant planet would likely subject its large moon(s) to catastrophic collisions.

Moons with interior ice-water environments heated by tidal friction from the planet's gravity (such as may be the case for Jupiter's moon Europa and Saturn's moon Enceladus) lack other essential features for long-term life support. Some mechanism would be needed to compensate for the central star's increasing luminosity, and the one known mechanism is a carbonate-silicate cycle. This cycle will operate only if both continents and oceans exist on the lunar surface and only if these continents and oceans are exposed to an atmosphere wherein a water cycle operates (see chs. 8–10).

With a view to potential moon-moon interactions, tidal heating, and heat from the gravitational collapse of the host planet,[3] in addition to all the challenges listed above, a long history of life on a moon appears impossible. Advanced life needs a planetary home.

## Appendix B

# Are We Alone in the Universe?

In 1995, with the first discovery of an extrasolar planet,[1] speculations about extraterrestrial life—or at least about an abundance of potential life-sites—ran wild. At the time, most astronomers (and others) presumed that extrasolar planets would, to a large degree, mimic the planets in our own solar system, where one in eight teems with life. Surely, they surmised, life on other planets must be out there, given that life sprang up so quickly and enduringly on Earth.

As of March 2015, astronomers have detected, confirmed, and measured (at least with respect to their orbital properties) more than 1,900 extrasolar planets. Thus far, however, none of these extrasolar planets shares characteristics in common with any of the Sun's eight planets. The one that comes the closest, to date, is called Upsilon Andromedae e, with a mass nearly equal to Jupiter's (1.06+ the mass of Jupiter). It orbits its host star 1.01 Jupiter's distance from the Sun, and its orbital shape is nearly circular, like Jupiter's. However, the similarities end there. While Jupiter is more massive than all the rest of the Sun's planets combined, the system in which Upsilon Andromedae e resides contains two other planets even more massive. Upsilon Andromedae c and d weigh in at 14.57+ and 10.19+ times Jupiter's mass, respectively. Planets Upsilon Andromedae c and d also orbit their host star more closely than does e. Their orbital distances are 17 and 49 percent Jupiter's orbital distance from the Sun. The great mass of planets c and d, as well as their proximity to their host star, would generate gravitational disturbances that effectively rule out any possibility that this planetary system includes another body with the capacity to support animal life.

Given that the Milky Way Galaxy likely contains several billion planets, we can anticipate that before long one or more will be found that closely resembles Earth's mass, orbital distance, and orbital shape. Nevertheless, research findings such as those cited in chapters 3–7 cast a shadow over the optimistic expectation of finding animal life there. Unless the planetary system contains a single star that matches virtually all the Sun's properties (so far, none does[2]), unless that system contains seven other planets that replicate the properties of all Earth's planetary companions, and unless that system contains asteroid and comet belts that mimic those in the solar system, the possibility that it carries advanced life remains utterly remote. In this respect, we humans are most likely the only sentient, self-aware physical beings.

If bacterial life or some other less environmentally sensitive life-form exists beyond Earth, it may simply reflect the Creator's enjoyment in creating. No one has come close to showing that even the simplest living entity could possibly assemble itself. The existence of such life would mean, in one sense, that we're not alone as the only physical life in the cosmos. However, the Bible indicates that in another more significant sense we are not alone. The spiritual realm in which the Triune God—Father, Son, and Holy Spirit—dwells somehow intersects (for lack of a better word) the physical universe. Jesus said to his disciples, even as he was about to leave their physical presence, "Surely I will be with you always, to the very end of the age."[3] The Bible also speaks of angels, spiritual beings God created to serve his purposes. Some of them joined in Lucifer's rebellion, but most remained loyal to their Maker. He has given them access to our earthly realm and a capacity to interact with humans, to some degree. Given their presence and his, I can say we humans are not alone.

# Notes

### Chapter 1  Why Ask "Why"?

1. I have written two books on humanity's purpose and destiny in the context of the laws of physics and dimensions of the universe: *Why the Universe Is the Way It Is* (Grand Rapids: Baker, 2008) and *Beyond the Cosmos: What Recent Discoveries in Astrophysics Reveal about the Glory and Love of God*, 3rd ed. (Orlando: Signalman, 2010).

2. Carl Sagan, *Cosmos* (New York: Ballantine Books, 1985), 1.

### Chapter 2  The Way the World *Is*

1. John C. Armstrong, "Distribution of Impact Locations and Velocities of Earth Meteorites on the Moon," *Earth, Moon, and Planets* 107 (December 2010): 43–54; John C. Armstrong, Llyd E. Wells, and Guillermo Gonzalez, "Rummaging through Earth's Attic for Remains of Ancient Life," *Icarus* 160 (November 2002): 183–96.

2. J. William Schopf, "The Oldest Known Records of Life: Early Archean Stromatolites, Microfossils, and Organic Matter," in *Early Life on Earth, Nobel Symposium No. 84*, ed. Stefan Bengston (New York: Columbia University Press, 1994): 193–206; Elizabeth Pennisi, "World's Oldest Fossils Found in Ancient Australian Beach," *Science*, August 21, 2011, http://news.sciencemag.org/2011/08/worlds-oldest-fossils-found-ancient-australian-beach.

3. Kevin D. McKeegan, Anatoliy B. Kudryavtsev, and J. William Schopf, "Raman and Ion Microscopic Imagery of Graphitic Inclusions in Apatite from Older Than 3830 Ma Akilia Supracrustal Rocks, West Greenland," *Geology* 35 (July 2007): 591–94; Craig E. Manning, Stephen J. Mojzsis, and T. Mark Harrison, "Geology, Age, and Origin of Supracrustal Rocks at Akilia, West Greenland," *American Journal of Science* 306 (May 2006): 303–66; Allen P. Nutman et al., "Raman and Ion Microscopic Imagery of Graphitic Inclusions in Apatite from Older Than 3830 Ma Akilia Supracrustal Rocks, West Greenland: Comment and Reply," *Geology* 35 (January 2007): e169–e170, doi: 10.1130/G24384C.1.

4. There is some evidence that Earth might have suffered impact events by interplanetary bodies exceeding 50 kilometers in diameter between 3.5 and 3.85 billion years ago. See Donald R. Lowe, Gary R. Byerly, and Frank T. Kyte, "Recently Discovered 3.42–3.23 Ga Impact Layers, Barberton Belt, South Africa: 3.8 Ga Detrital Zircons, Archean Impact History, and Tectonic Implications," *Geology* 42 (September 2014): 747–50. Such impacts possibly could have wiped out all life on Earth.

5. Camilo Mora et al., "How Many Species Are There on Earth and in the Ocean?," *PLoS Biology* 9 (August 2011): e1001127, doi:10.1371/journal.pbio.1001127.

6. P. M. Hammond, "International Biodiversity Initiatives and the Global," in *Microbial Diversity and Ecosystem Function: Proceedings of the IUBS/IUMS Workshop Held at Egham, UK, 10–13 August 1993 in Support of the IUBS/UNESCO/SCOPE "DIVERSITAS" Programme*, ed. D. Allsopp, R. R. Colwell, and D. L. Hawksworth (Wallingford, Oxon, UK: CAB International, 1995), 29–71.

7. Valeria Souza et al., "Travel, Sex, and Food: What's Speciation Got to Do with It?," *Astrobiology* 12 (July 2012): 634.

8. Charles Darwin, *The Origin of Species* (1859) in *From So Simple a Beginning: The Four Great Books of Charles Darwin*, ed. Edward O. Wilson (New York: W. W. Norton, 2006), 648–54.

9. Niles Eldredge and Stephen Jay Gould, "Punctuated Equilibria: An Alternative to Phyletic Gradualism," in *Models in Paleobiology*, ed. T. J. M. Schopf (San Francisco: Freeman Cooper, 1972), 82–115; Stephen Jay Gould and Niles Eldredge, "Punctuated Equilibria: The Tempo and Mode of Evolution Reconsidered," *Paleobiology* 3 (April 1977): 115–51. The previous paper is available at http://www.blackwellpublishing.com/ridley/classictexts/eldredge.pdf.

10. George Gaylord Simpson, *Tempo and Mode in Evolution* (New York: Columbia University Press, 1944); George Gaylord Simpson, *The Major Features of Evolution* (New York: Columbia University Press, 1953).

11. Marcelo Gleiser, "Drake Equation for the Multiverse: From the String Landscape to Complex Life," *International Journal of Modern Physics D: Gravitation; Astrophysics and Cosmology* 19 (August 2010): 1299.

12. Duncan H. Forgan and Ken Rice, "Numerical Testing of the Rare Earth Hypothesis Using Monte Carlo Realization Techniques," *International Journal of Astrobiology* 9 (April 2010): 73–80; Paolo Musso, "On the Last Terms of Drake Equation: The Problem of Energy Sources and the 'Rare Earth Hypothesis,'" in *Exo-/astro-biology: Proceedings of the First European Workshop, 21–23 May, 2001, ESRIN, Frascati, Italy*, ed. P. Ehrenfreund, O. Angerer, and B. Battrick (Noordwijk, Netherlands: ESA Publications, 2001), 379–82.

13. Peter D. Ward and Donald Brownlee, *Rare Earth: Why Complex Life Is Uncommon in the Universe* (New York: Copernicus, 2000).

## Chapter 3 Essential Construction Materials

1. I describe how astronomers determined these values in my book *Why the Universe Is the Way It Is* (Grand Rapids: Baker, 2008), 30–41.

2. Stephen Hawking, *A Brief History of Time* (New York: Bantam Books, 1988), 126.

## Chapter 4 The Right Neighborhood

1. V. Petropoulou, J. Vílchez, and J. Iglesias-Páramo, "Environmental Effects on the Metal Enrichment of Low-Mass Galaxies in Nearby Clusters," *Astrophysical Journal* 749 (April 2012): id. 133, doi:10.1088/0004-637X/749/2/133.

2. Jacob P. Crossett et al., "Environments and Morphologies of Red Sequence Galaxies with Residual Star Formation in Massive Clusters," *Monthly Notices of the Royal Astronomical Society* 437 (January 2014): 2521–30; C. F. Bretherton, C. Moss, and P. A. James, "Star-Forming Galaxies in Low-Redshift Clusters: Effects of Environment on the Concentration of Star Formation," *Astronomy and Astrophysics* 553 (May 2013): id. A67; Yannick M. Bahé et al., "Why Does the Environmental Influence on Group and Cluster Galaxies Extend

beyond the Virial Radius?," *Monthly Notices of the Royal Astronomical Society* 430 (April 2013): 3017–31; Petropoulou, Vílchez, and Iglesias-Páramo, "Environmental Effects on the Metal Enrichment," id. 133; V. Petropoulou et al., "Spatially Resolved Spectroscopy and Chemical History of Star-Forming Galaxies in the Hercules Cluster: The Effects of the Environment," *Astrophysical Journal* 734 (June 2011): id. 32, doi:10.1088/0004-637X/734/1/32.

3. Lihwai Lin et al., "The PANS-STARRS1 Medium-Deep Survey: The Role of Galaxy Group Environment in the Star Formation Rate Versus Stellar Mass Relation and Quiescent Fraction out to $z \sim 0.8$," *Astrophysical Journal* 782 (February 2014): id. 33, doi:10.1088/0004 -637X/782/1/33; A. G. Noble et al., "A Kinematic Approach to Assessing Environmental Effects: Star-Forming Galaxies in a $z \sim 0.9$ SpARCS Cluster Using *Spitzer* 24 $\mu$m Observations," *Astrophysical Journal* 768 (May 2013): id. 118, doi:10.1088/0004-637X/768/2/118; Bretheron, Moss, and James, "Star-Forming Galaxies," A67; Bahé et al., "Environmental Influence?," 3017–31; Petropoulou et al., "Spatially Resolved Spectroscopy," 32; B. Cervantes-Sodi et al., "Quantifying Galactic Morphological Transformations in the Cluster Environment," *Monthly Notices of the Royal Astronomical Society* 414 (June 2011): 587–95; M. Huertas-Company et al., "The Role of Environment in the Morphological Transformation of Galaxies in 9 Rich Intermediate Redshift Clusters," *Astronomy and Astrophysics* 505 (October 2009): 83–96.

4. Igor D. Karachentsev et al., "Infall of Nearby Galaxies into the Virgo Cluster as Traced with Hubble Space Telescope," *Astrophysical Journal* 782 (February 2014): id. 4.

5. A. S. G. Robotham et al., "Galaxy and Mass Assembly (GAMA): In Search of Milky Way Magellanic Cloud Analogues," *Monthly Notices of the Royal Astronomical Society* 424 (August 2012): 1448–53; D. Crnojević et al., "How Unique Is the Local Group? A Comparison to the Nearby Centaurus A Group," in *Galactic Archeology: Near-Field Cosmology and the Formation of the Milky Way*, ed. Wako Aoki et al., ASP Conference Series, vol. 458 (San Francisco: Astronomical Society of the Pacific, 2012), 321; Dmitry Makarov and Igor D. Karachentsev, "Galaxy Groups and Clouds in the Local ($z \sim 0.01$) Universe," *Monthly Notices of the Royal Astronomical Society* 412 (April 2011): 2498–520; Peter Creasey et al., "The Effect of Environment on Milky-Way-Mass Galaxies in a Constrained Simulation of the Local Group," *Astrophysical Journal Letters* 800 (February 2015): L4.

6. F. Hammer et al., "The Milky Way, an Exceptionally Quiet Galaxy: Implications for the Formation of Spiral Galaxies," *Astrophysical Journal* 662 (June 2007): 322–34.

7. D. L. Block et al., "An Almost Head-On Collision as the Origin of Two Off-Centre Rings in the Andromeda Galaxy," *Nature* 443 (October 2006): 832–34.

8. Hugh Ross, *Why the Universe Is the Way It Is* (Grand Rapids: Baker, 2008), 43–48.

9. Rahul Shetty and E. C. Ostriker, "Formation and Destruction of Clouds and Spurs in Spiral Galaxies," in *Triggered Star Formation in a Turbulent ISM*, ed. B. G. Elmegreen and J. Palouš, Proceedings of the International Astronomical Union, vol. 2, Symposium S237 (August 2006): 474; Rahul Shetty and Eve C. Ostriker, "Global Modeling of Spur Formation in Spiral Galaxies," *Astrophysical Journal* 647 (August 2006): 997–1017; Woong-Tae Kim and Eve C. Ostriker, "Formation of Spiral-Arm Spurs and Bound Clouds in Vertically Stratified Galactic Gas Disks," *Astrophysical Journal* 646 (July 2006): 213–31; C. L. Dobbs and I. A. Bonnell, "Spurs and Feathering in Spiral Galaxies," *Monthly Notices of the Royal Astronomical Society* 367 (April 2006): 873–78; S. Chakrabarti, G. Laughlin, and F. H. Shu, "Branch, Spur, and Feather Formation in Spiral Galaxies," *Astrophysical Journal* 596 (October 2003): 220–39; Woong-Tae Kim and Eve C. Ostriker, "Formation and Fragmentation of Gaseous Spurs in Spiral Galaxies," *Astrophysical Journal* 570 (May 2002): 132–51.

10. Shetty and Ostriker, "Formation and Destruction," 474.

11. Misty A. La Vigne, Stuart N. Vogel, and Eve C. Ostriker, "A *Hubble Space Telescope* Archival Survey of Feathers in Spiral Galaxies," *Astrophysical Journal* 650 (October 2006): 818–34; J. H. Knapen and S. Stedman, "An Imaging Survey of Nearby Spiral Galaxies," in *Disks of Galaxies: Kinematics, Dynamics, and Perturbations*, ed. E. Athanassoula, A. Bosma, and R. Mujica, ASP Conference Series, vol. 275 (San Francisco: Astronomical Society of the Pacific, 2002), 319–22; M. Mouhcine, R. Ibata, and M. Rejkuba, "A Panoramic View of the Milky Way Analog NGC 891," *Astrophysical Journal Letters* 714 (May 2010): L12–L15; R. Rejkuba, M. Mouhcine, and R. Ibata, "The Stellar Population Content of the Thick Disk and Halo of the Milky Way Analogue NGC 891," *Monthly Notices of the Royal Astronomical Society* 396 (July 2009): 1231–46.

12. Erik Zackrisson et al., "Extragalactic SETI: The Tully-Fisher Relation as a Probe of Dysonian Astroengineering in Disk Galaxies," *Astrophysical Journal* 810 (August 2015): id. 23, doi: 10.1088/0004-637X/810/1/23; Hugh Ross, "Our Only Hope? A New Search for Extraterrestrial Intelligent Life," *Today's New Reason to Believe* (blog), December 3, 2015, http ://www.reasons.org/articles/our-only-hope-a-new-search-for-extraterrestrial-intelligent-life.

13. David Charbonneau et al., "A Super-Earth Transiting a Nearby Low-Mass Star," *Nature* 462 (December 2009): 891–94; Linda T. Elkins-Tanton and Sara Seager, "Ranges of Atmospheric Mass and Composition of Super-Earth Exoplanets," *Astrophysical Journal* 685 (October 2008): 1237–46; J. D. Gilmour and C. A. Middleton, "Anthropic Selection of a Solar System with a High $^{26}$Al/$^{27}$Al Ratio: Implications and a Possible Mechanism," *Icarus* 201 (June 2009): 821–23; J. Farihi et al., "Possible Signs of Water and Differentiation in a Rocky Exoplanetary Body," *Astrophysical Journal Letters* 728 (February 2011): L8.

14. Carbonneau et al., "Super-Earth Transiting," 891–94; Geoffrey Marcy, "Extrasolar Planets: Water World Larger Than Earth," *Nature* 462 (December 2009): 853–54.

15. Fred C. Adams, "The Birth Environment of the Solar System," *Annual Review of Astronomy and Astrophysics* 48 (September 2010): 69–72; Donald Dukes and Mark R. Krumholz, "Was the Sun Born in a Massive Cluster?," *Astrophysical Journal* 754 (July 2012): id. 56, doi:10.1088/0004-637X/754/1/56; Hugh Ross, "Sun's Rare Birth," *Today's New Reason to Believe* (blog), September 3, 2012, http://www.reasons.org/articles/suns-rare-birth.

16. Yu. N. Mishurov, Jacques R. D. Lépine, and I. A. Acharova, "Corotation: Its Influence on the Chemical Abundance Pattern of the Galaxy," *Astrophysical Journal Letters* 571 (June 2002): L113–L115; Sergio Scarano Jr. and Jacques R. D. Lépine, "The Effect of Corotation on the Radial Gradient of Metallicity of Spiral Galaxies," in *Chemical Abundances in the Universe: Connecting First Stars to Planets*, ed. K. Cunha, M. Spite, and B. Barbuy, Proceedings of the International Astronomical Union, vol. 5, Symposium S265 (March 2010): 251–52; Sergio Scarano Jr. and Jacques R. D. Lépine, "Radial Metallicity Distribution Breaks at Corotation Radius in Spiral Galaxies," *Monthly Notices of the Royal Astronomical Society* 428 (January 2013): 625–40; D. A. Barros, Jacques R. D. Lépine, and T. C. Junqueira, "A Galactic Ring of Minimum Stellar Density near the Solar Orbit Radius," *Monthly Notices of the Royal Astronomical Society* 435 (November 2013): 2299–321.

17. Mishurov, Lépine, and Acharova, "Corotation: Its Influence," L113–L115; Scarano and Lépine, "The Effect of Corotation," 251–52; Scarano and Lépine, "Radial Metallicity Distribution Breaks," 625–40.

18. A. Takigawa et al., "Injection of Short-Lived Radionuclides into the Early Solar System from a Faint Supernova with Mixing Fallback," *Astrophysical Journal* 688 (December 2008): 1382–87; T. Hayakawa et al., "Supernova Neutrino Nucleosynthesis of the Radioactive $^{92}$Nb Observed in Primitive Meteorites," *Astrophysical Journal Letters* 779 (December 2013): L9.

19. Richard J. Parker and James E. Dale, "Did the Solar System Form in a Sequential Triggered Star Formation Event?," *Monthly Notices of the Royal Astronomical Society* 456 (February 11, 2016): 1066–72.

20. Ibid., 1066.

21. Ibid.

22. Gilmour and Middleton, "Anthropic Selection," 821–23.

23. Exoplanet Team, *The Extrasolar Planets Encyclopaedia*, http://exoplanet.eu/.

24. Liubin Pan et al., "Mixing of Clumpy Supernova Ejecta into Molecular Clouds," *Astrophysical Journal* 756 (September 2012): id. 102, doi:10.1088/0004-637X/756/1/102.

25. Fred C. Adams et al., "Photoevaporation of Circumstellar Disks Due to External Far-Ultraviolet Radiation in Stellar Aggregates," *Astrophysical Journal* 611 (August 2004): 360–79.

26. Barros, Lépine, and Junqueira, "Galactic Ring," 2299–321.

27. John J. Matese et al., "Why We Study the Geological Record for Evidence of the Solar Oscillation about the Galactic Midplane," *Earth, Moon, and Planets* 72 (February 1996): 7–12; John J. Matese et al., "Periodic Modulation of the Oort Cloud Comet Flux by the Adiabatically Changing Galactic Tide," *Icarus* 116 (August 1995): 255–68.

28. Michael R. Rampino, "Disc Dark Matter in the Galaxy and Potential Cycles of Extraterrestrial Impacts, Mass Extinctions, and Geological Events," *Monthly Notices of the Royal Astronomical Society* 448 (April 2015): 1816–20.

29. Ross, *Why the Universe Is*, 79–93.

30. Freeman J. Dyson, *Disturbing the Universe* (New York: Basic, 1979), 250.

## Chapter 5  Site Preparations

1. Harold F. Levison and Craig Agnor, "The Role of Giant Planets in Terrestrial Planet Formation," *Astronomical Journal* 125 (May 2003): 2692–713; Harold F. Levison et al., "The Role of Giant Planets in Terrestrial Planet Formation," *Bulletin of the American Astronomical Society* 33, DDA 32nd Meeting, abstract 13.02 (November 2011): 1198.

2. George W. Wetherill, "Possible Consequences of Absence of 'Jupiters' in Planetary Systems," *Astrophysics and Space Science* 212 (February 1994): 23–32; J. Horner, B. W. Jones, and J. Chambers, "Jupiter—Friend or Foe? III. The Oort Cloud Comets," *International Journal of Astrobiology* 9 (January 2010): 1–10.

3. "Catalog," *The Extrasolar Planets Encyclopaedia*, accessed September 27, 2014, http://exoplanet.eu/catalog/?f=mass%3Amjup+%3E+0.0315+AND+axis%3Aau+%3C+3.23.

4. Hiroshi Kobayashi, Chris W. Ormel, and Shigeru Ida, "Rapid Formation of Saturn after Jupiter Completion," *Astrophysical Journal* 756 (September 2012): id. 70, doi: 10.1088/0004-637X/756/1/70.

5. G. M. Kennedy and M. C. Wyatt, "Confusion Limited Surveys: Using *WISE* to Quantify the Rarity of Warm Dust around *Kepler* Stars," *Monthly Notices of the Royal Astronomical Society* 426 (October 2012): 91–107; Joseph H. Rhee, Inseok Song, and B. Zuckerman, "Warm Dust in the Terrestrial Planet Zone of a Sun-Like Pleiades Star: Collisions between Planetary Embryos?," *Astrophysical Journal* 675 (March 2008): 777–83.

6. Farisa Y. Morales et al., "Common Warm Dust Temperatures around Main-Sequence Stars," *Astrophysical Journal Letters* 730 (April 2011): L29; R. Smith and M. C. Wyatt, "Warm Dusty Discs: Exploring the A Star 24 $\mu$m Debris Population," *Astronomy and Astrophysics* 515 (June 2010): id. A95; Rhee, Song, and Zuckerman, "Warm Dust?," 777–83; Inseok Song et al., "Extreme Collisions between Planetesimals as the Origin of Warm Dust around a Sun-Like Star," *Nature* 436 (July 2005): 363–65.

7. Even with the solar system's tiny asteroid belt, "a major impact sufficient to cripple human civilization will occur on time scales of one million years." R. A. F. Grieve and L. J. Pesonen, "The Terrestrial Impact Cratering Record," *Tectonophysics* 216 (December 1992): 1.

8. Kevin J. Walsh et al., "Populating the Asteroid Belt from Two Parent Source Regions Due to the Migration of Giant Planets—'The Grand Tack,'" *Meteoritics and Planetary Science* 47 (December 2012): 1941–47; Kevin J. Walsh et al., "A Low Mass for Mars from Jupiter's Early Gas-Driven Migration," *Nature* 475 (July 2011): 206–9.

9. Arnaud Pierens et al., "Outward Migration of Jupiter and Saturn in 3:2 or 2:1 Resonance in Radiative Disks: Implications for the Grand Tack and Nice Models," *Astrophysical Journal Letters* 795 (November 2014): L11.

10. Alessandro Morbidelli et al., "The Grand Tack Scenario: Reconstructing the Migration History of Jupiter and Saturn in the Disk of Gas," *American Astronomical Society*, ESS 2nd Meeting (September 2011): abstract 8.02.

11. Seth A. Jacobson et al., "'Getting Down to Brass Tacks' in the Grand Tack Scenario: Matching Important Accretion and Timing Constraints," *Bulletin of the American Astronomical Society* 45, DPS 45th Meeting (October 2013): abstract 503.02.

12. Ibid.

13. A. Pierens and S. N. Raymond, "Two Phase, Inward-Then-Outward Migration of Jupiter and Saturn in the Gaseous Solar Nebula," *Astronomy and Astrophysics* 533 (September 2011): id. A131.

14. "Catalog," *The Extrasolar Planet Encyclopaedia*, accessed September 27, 2014, http://exoplanet.eu/catalog/.

15. Morbidelli et al., "Grand Tack Scenario."

16. Nathan A. Kaib and John E. Chambers, "The Fragility of the Terrestrial Planets during a Giant-Planet Instability," *Monthly Notices of the Royal Astronomical Society* 455 (February 2016): 3561–69.

17. A. G. W. Cameron and W. R. Ward, "The Origin of the Moon," *7th Lunar and Planetary Science Conference* (1976): 120; W. Benz, W. L. Slattery, and A. G. W. Cameron, "The Origin of the Moon and the Single-Impact Hypothesis. I," *Icarus* 66 (June 1986): 515–35.

18. Keiichi Wada, Eiichiro Kokubo, and Junichiro Makino, "High-Resolution Simulations of a Moon-Forming Impact and Postimpact Evolution," *Astrophysical Journal* 638 (February 2006): 1180–86.

19. William R. Ward and Robin M. Canup, "Origin of the Moon's Orbital Inclination from Resonant Disk Interactions," *Nature* 403 (February 2000): 741–43.

20. Paul G. Lucey, G. Jeffrey Taylor, and Erick Malaret, "Abundance and Distribution of Iron on the Moon," *Science* 268 (May 1995): 1150–53.

21. Robin M. Canup and Erik Asphaug, "Origin of the Moon in a Giant Impact near the End of the Earth's Formation," *Nature* 412 (August 2001): 708–12.

22. Robin M. Canup, "Simulations of a Late Lunar-Forming Impact," *Icarus* 168 (April 2004): 433–56.

23. Robin M. Canup, "Lunar-Forming Collisions with Pre-Impact Rotation," *Icarus* 196 (August 2008): 518–38.

24. Randal C. Paniello, James M. D. Day, and Frédéric Moynier, "Zinc Isotopic Evidence for the Origin of the Moon," *Nature* 490 (October 2012): 376–79.

25. Daniel Herwartz et al., "Identification of the Giant Impactor Theia in Lunar Rocks," *Science* 344 (June 2014): 1146–50.

26. Hidenori Genda and Yutaka Abe, "Enhanced Atmospheric Loss on Protoplanets at the Giant Impact Phase in the Presence of Oceans," *Nature* 433 (February 2005): 842–44; Kevin Zahnle, "Planetary Science: Being There," *Nature* 433 (February 2005): 814–15.

27. Ibid.

28. Eugenio Jose Rivera, "Dynamical Evolution of the Earth-Moon Progenitors" (PhD thesis, State University of New York at Stony Brook, 2002).

29. U. Wiechert et al., "Oxygen Isotopes and the Moon-Forming Giant Impact," *Science* 294 (October 2001): 345–48.

30. JunJun Zhang et al., "The Proto-Earth as a Significant Source of Lunar Material," *Nature Geoscience* 5 (April 2012): 251–55.

31. Christine K. Gessmann and David C. Rubie, "The Origin of the Depletions of V, Cr, and Mn in the Mantles of the Earth and the Moon," *Earth and Planetary Science Letters* 184 (December 2000): 95–107.

32. Alex N. Halliday and Der-Chuen Lee, "Tungsten Isotopes and the Early Development of the Earth and Moon," *Geochimica et Cosmochimica Acta* 63 (December 1999): 4157–79; F. Nimmo, D. P. O'Brien, and T. Kleine, "Tungsten Isotopic Evolution during Late-Stage Accretion: Constraints on Earth-Moon Equilibration," *Earth and Planetary Science Letters* 292 (April 2010): 363–70; M. Touboul et al., "Late Formation and Prolonged Differentiation of the Moon Inferred from W Isotopes in Lunar Metals," *Nature* 450 (December 2007): 1206–9.

33. R. M. G. Armytage et al., "Silicon Isotopes in Lunar Rocks: Implications for the Moon's Formation and the Early History of the Earth," *Geochimica et Cosmochimica Acta* 77 (January 2012): 504–14.

34. Edward Belbruno and J. Richard Gott III, "Where Did the Moon Come From?," *Astronomical Journal* 129 (March 2005): 1724–45.

35. André Amarante, O. Winter, and M. Tsuchida, "Coorbital Formation with Earth and Theia's Origin," *American Astronomical Society*, DDA 44th Meeting (May 2013): abstract 204.26.

36. Robin M. Canup, "Planetary Science: Lunar Conspiracies," *Nature* 504 (December 2013): 27.

37. Robin M. Canup, "Forming a Moon with an Earth-Like Composition via a Giant Impact," *Science* 338 (November 2012): 1052–55.

38. Matija Ćuk and Sarah T. Stewart, "Making the Moon from a Fast-Spinning Earth: A Giant Impact Followed by Resonant Despinning," *Science* 338 (November 2012): 1047–52.

39. Tim Elliott and Sarah T. Stewart, "Planetary Science: Shadows Cast on Moon's Origin," *Nature* 504 (December 2013): 91.

40. Ibid.

41. Ibid., 90.

42. Seth A. Jacobson et al., "Highly Siderophile Elements in Earth's Mantle as a Clock for the Moon-Forming Impact," *Nature* 508 (April 2014): 84–87.

43. Ibid., 84.

44. W. F. Bottke et al., "Dating the Moon-Forming Impact Event with Asteroidal Meteorites," *Science* 348 (April 2015): 321–23.

45. A mechanism akin to lungs is required for high metabolic activity by large land animals, and that mechanism requires a surface air pressure within a factor of three of Earth's. See Michael J. Denton, *Nature's Destiny: How the Laws of Biology Reveal Purpose in the Universe* (New York: Free Press, 1998), 127–31, 251–52.

46. Louis A. Codispoti, "The Limits to Growth," *Nature* 387 (May 1997): 237; Kenneth H. Coale et al., "A Massive Phytoplankton Bloom Induced by an Ecosystem-Scale Iron Fertilization Experiment in the Equatorial Pacific Ocean," *Nature* 383 (October 1996): 495–99.

47. Peter D. Ward and Donald Brownlee, *Rare Earth: Why Complex Life Is Uncommon in the Universe* (New York: Copernicus, 2000), 191–234.

48. Jacobson et al., "Highly Siderophile Elements," 84–87.

49. William R. Ward, "Comments on the Long-Term Stability of the Earth's Obliquity," *Icarus* 50 (May–June 1982): 444–48; Carl D. Murray, "Seasoned Travellers," *Nature* 361 (February 1993): 586–87; Jacques Laskar and P. Robutel, "The Chaotic Obliquity of the Planets," *Nature* 361 (February 1993): 608–12; Jacques Laskar, F. Joutel, and P. Robutel, "Stabilization of the Earth's Obliquity by the Moon," *Nature* 361 (February 1993): 615–17.

50. Hugh Ross, *More Than a Theory: Revealing a Testable Model for Creation* (Grand Rapids: Baker, 2009), 137.

51. For a partial list see Neil F. Comins, *What If the Moon Didn't Exist? Voyages to Earths That Might Have Been* (New York: HarperCollins, 1993).

52. Dave Waltham, "Anthropic Selection for the Moon's Mass," *Astrobiology* 4 (Winter 2004): 460–68.

53. Hilke E. Schlichting, Paul H. Warren, and Qing-Zhu Yin, "The Last Stages of Terrestrial Planet Formation: Dynamical Friction and the Late Veneer," *Astrophysical Journal* 752 (June 2012): id. 8, doi:10.1088/0004-637X/752/1/8, p. 1; Jacobson et al., "Highly Siderophile Elements," 84–87.

54. Francis Albarède, "Volatile Accretion History of the Terrestrial Planets and Dynamic Implications," *Nature* 461 (October 2009): 1227–33. Additional evidence for the late veneer timing comes from Hadean zircon analyses from the Narryer Gneiss Complex in Western Australia. These analyses reveal that the first continental crust solidified 90–160 million years after the giant impact event. Thus, these two events place temporal bounds on when the late veneer occurred.

55. Schlichting, Warren, and Yin, "Last Stages," id. 8; Jacobson et al., "Highly Siderophile Elements," 84–87.

56. C. F. Chyba, "Impact Delivery and Erosion of Planetary Oceans in the Early Inner Solar System," *Nature* 343 (January 1990): 129–33.

57. Jacobson et al., "Highly Siderophile Elements," 84–87; Nicolas Dauphas and Bernard Marty, "Inference on the Nature and the Mass of Earth's Late Veneer from Noble Metals and Gases," *Journal of Geophysical Research: Planets* 107 (December 2002): id. 5129.

## Chapter 6  Not Quite Ready

1. Sylvaine Turck-Chièze, Laurent Piau, and Sébastien Couvidat, "The Solar Energetic Balance Revisited by Young Solar Analogs, Helioseismology, and Neutrinos," *Astrophysical Journal Letters* 731 (April 2011): L29; Ilídio Lopes and Joseph Silk, "Planetary Influence on the Young Sun's Evolution: The Solar Neutrino Probe," *Monthly Notices of the Royal Astronomical Society* 435 (November 2013): 2109–15; K. Olah et al., "Young Solar Type Active Stars: The TYC 2627-638-1 System," *Astronomy and Astrophysics* 515 (June 2010): id. A81; G. F. Gahm et al., "Activity on Young Stars," *Astronomy and Astrophysics* 301 (September 1995): 89–104.

2. Turck-Chièze, Piau, and Couvidat, "Solar Energetic Balance," L29; Joyce Ann Guzik and Katie Mussack, "Exploring Mass Loss, Low-Z Accretion, and Convective Overshoot in Solar Models to Mitigate the Solar Abundance Problem," *Astrophysical Journal* 713 (April 2010): 1108–19, doi:10.1088/0004-637X/713/2/1108; R. Mundt, "Mass Loss in T. Tauri Stars: Observational Studies of the Cool Parts of Their Stellar Winds and Expanding Shells," *Astrophysical Journal* 280 (May 1984): 749–70.

3. K. Tsiganis et al., "Origin of the Orbital Architecture of the Giant Planets of the Solar System," *Nature* 435 (May 2005): 459–61, doi:10.1038/nature03539.

4. Ibid., 459.

Notes

5. Alessandro Morbidelli et al., "Chaotic Capture of Jupiter's Trojan Asteroids in the Early Solar System," *Nature* 435 (May 2005): 462–65.

6. R. Gomes et al., "Origin of the Cataclysmic Late Heavy Bombardment Period of the Terrestrial Planets," *Nature* 435 (May 2005): 466–69.

7. Ronny Schoenberg et al., "Tungsten Isotope Evidence from ~3.8-Gyr Metamorphosed Sediments for Early Meteorite Bombardment of the Earth," *Nature* 418 (July 2002): 403; Ariel D. Anbar et al., "Extraterrestrial Iridium, Sediment Accumulation and the Habitability of the Early Earth's Surface," *Journal of Geophysical Research: Planets* 106 (February 2001): 3219–36.

8. Fouad Tera, D. A. Papanastassiou, and G. J. Wasserburg, "Isotopic Evidence for a Terminal Lunar Cataclysm," *Earth and Planetary Science Letters* 22 (April 1974): 1–21; Johannes Geiss and Angelo Pio Rossi, "On the Chronology of Lunar Origin and Evolution: Implications for Earth, Mars, and the Solar System as a Whole," *Astronomy and Astrophysics Review* 21 (November 2013): id. 68; Christian Koeberl, "The Late Heavy Bombardment in the Inner Solar System: Is There Any Connection to Kuiper Belt Objects?," *Earth, Moon, and Planets* 92 (June 2003): 79–87; T. Niihara et al., "Evidence for Multiple Impact Events from Centimeter-Sized Impact Melt Clasts in Apollo 16 Ancient Regolith Breccias: Support for Late Stage Heavy Bombardment of the Moon," *44th Lunar and Planetary Science Conference* (2013): abstract 2083.

9. Margarita M. Marinova, Oded Aharonson, and Erik Asphaug, "Geophysical Consequences of Planetary-Scale Impacts into a Mars-Like Planet," *Icarus* 211 (February 2011): 960–85; H. Frey, "Very Large Impacts in the Pre-Noachian on Mars: Conditioning the Noachian Environment," *EoS, Transactions American Geophysical Union* 89, Fall Meeting Supplemental (2008): abstract P53B-1455; Teresa L. Segura, Christopher P. McKay, and Owen B. Toon, "An Impact-Induced, Stable, Runaway Climate on Mars," *Icarus* 220 (July 2012): 144–48; S. C. Werner, "The Early Martian Evolution—Constraints from Basin Formation Ages," *Icarus* 195 (May 2008): 45–60.

10. Hervé Martin et al., "Building of a Habitable Planet," in *From Suns to Life: A Chronological Approach to the History of Life on Earth*, ed. Muriel Gargaud et al. (New York: Springer-Verlag, 2006), 97–151; Koeberl, "Late Heavy Bombardment," 79–87; Segura, McKay, and Toon, "An Impact-Induced," 144–48; Werner, "Early Martian Evolution," 45–60.

11. Simone Marchi et al., "The Onset of the Lunar Cataclysm as Recorded in Its Ancient Crater Populations," *Earth and Planetary Science Letters* 325 (April 2012): 27–38.

12. Ibid.

13. Gomes et al., "Origin of the Cataclysmic," 466–69.

14. Harold F. Levison et al., "Origin of the Structure of the Kuiper Belt during a Dynamical Instability in the Orbits of Uranus and Neptune," *Icarus* 196 (July 2008): 258–73.

15. Alessandro Morbidelli et al., "Origin of the Structure of the Kuiper Belt during a Giant Planets Orbital Instability," *Bulletin of the American Astronomical Society* 38, American Astronomical Society, DPS 38th meeting, abstract 54.03 (September 2006): 583; Alessandro Morbidelli et al., "Chaotic Capture of Planetesimals into Regular Regions of the Solar System. I: The Kuiper Belt," *Bulletin of the American Astronomical Society* 39, DDA 39th Meeting (May 2008): abstract 12.04.

16. Sébastien Charnoz et al., "Did Saturn's Rings Form during the Late Heavy Bombardment?," *Icarus* 199 (February 2009): 413–28.

17. William F. Bottke et al., "The E-Belt: A Possible Missing Link in the Late Heavy Bombardment," *41st Lunar and Planetary Science Conference* (2010): abstract 1269.

18. A. Matter, T. Guillot, and Alessandro Morbidelli, "Calculation of the Enrichment of the Giant Planet Envelopes during the 'Late Heavy Bombardment,'" *Planetary and Space Science* 57 (June 2009): 816–21.

19. Harold F. Levison et al., "Contamination of the Asteroid Belt by Primordial Trans-Neptunian Objects," *Nature* 460 (July 2009): 364–66.

20. Alessandro Morbidelli et al., "Are Some Asteroid Families from the Time of the Late Heavy Bombardment?," *Bulletin of the American Astronomical Society* 42, DPS 42nd meeting, abstract 4.08 (October 2010): 949.

21. William F. Bottke et al., "Stochastic Late Accretion to Earth, the Moon, and Mars," *Science* 330 (December 2010): 1527–30.

22. Ibid.

23. M. R. Kilburn and B. J. Wood, "Metal-Silicate Partitioning and the Incompatibility of S and Si during Core Formation," *Earth and Planetary Science Letters* 152 (November 1997): 139–48; Gerlind Dreibus and Herbert Palme, "Cosmochemical Constraints on the Sulfur Content in the Earth's Core," *Geochimica et Cosmochimica Acta* 60 (April 1996): 1125–30; Fabrice Gaillard and Bruno Scaillet, "The Sulfur Content of Volcanic Gases on Mars," *Earth and Planetary Science Letters* 279 (March 2009): 34–43; G. Fiquet, J. Badro, and F. Guyot, "New Constraints on the Earth's Core Chemical Composition," *EoS, Transactions American Geophysical Union* 85, Fall Meeting Supplemental (2004): abstract MR41A-01; Doris Breuer, Stephane Labrosse, and Tilman Spohn, "Thermal Evolution and Magnetic Field Generation in Terrestrial Planets and Satellites," *Space Science Reviews* 152 (May 2010): 449–500; David Gubbins et al., "Gross Thermodynamics of Two-Component Core Convection," *Geophysical Journal International* 157 (June 2004): 1407–14; G. F. Davies, "Geophysically Constrained Mantle Mass Flows and the $^{40}$Ar Budget: A Degassed Lower Mantle?," *Earth and Planetary Science Letters* 166 (March 1999): 149–62; Benton Clark, "Death by Sulfur: Consequences of Ubiquitous S before and after the Biotic Transition, for Mars and Other S-Rich Planets," *Astrobiology* 8 [Astrobiology Science Conference 2008, Santa Clara, CA] (April 14–17, 2008): 433; David C. Rubie, Christine K. Gessmann, and Daniel J. Frost, "Partitioning of Oxygen during Core Formation on the Earth and Mars," *Nature* 429 (May 2004): 58–61; Carl B. Agee, "Earth Science: Hot Metal," *Nature* 429 (May 2004): 33–35.

24. Z. D. Sharp and D. S. Draper, "The Chlorine Abundance of Earth: Evidence for Early Atmospheric Loss and Creation of a Life-Supporting Planet," *EoS, Transactions American Geophysical Union* 90, Fall Meeting Supplemental (2009): abstract V13H-05.

25. Kevin J. Walsh and Alessandro Morbidelli, "The Effect of an Early Planetesimal-Driven Migration of the Giant Planets on Terrestrial Planet Formation," *Astronomy and Astrophysics* 526 (February 2011): id. A126.

26. Alessandro Morbidelli et al., "Constructing the Secular Architecture of the Solar System. I. The Giant Planets," *Astronomy and Astrophysics* 507 (November 2009): 1041–52.

27. Alessandro Morbidelli et al., "Evidence from the Asteroid Belt for a Violent Past Evolution of Jupiter's Orbit," *Astronomical Journal* 140 (November 2010): 1391–401.

28. David Nesvorný, "Young Solar System's Fifth Giant Planet?," *Astrophysical Journal Letters* 742 (December 2011): L22.

29. David Nesvorný and Alessandro Morbidelli, "Statistical Study of the Early Solar System's Instability with Four, Five, and Six Giant Planets," *Astronomical Journal* 144 (October 2012): id. 117, doi:10.1088/0004-6256/144/4/117.

30. Nesvorný, "Young Solar System's Fifth?," L22; Nesvorný and Morbidelli, "Statistical Study," id. 117; R. Brasser, K. J. Walsh, and D. Nesvorný, "Constraining the Primordial Orbits of the Terrestrial Planets," *Monthly Notices of the Royal Astronomical Society* 433 (August 2013): 3417–27.

31. Konstantin Batygin, Michael E. Brown, and Hayden Betts, "Instability-Driven Dynamical Evolution Model of a Primordially Five-Planet Outer Solar System," *Astrophysical Journal Letters* 744 (January 2012): L3.

32. Rogerio Deienno et al., "Orbital Perturbations of the Galilean Satellites during Planetary Encounters," *Astronomical Journal* 148 (August 2014): id. 25, doi:10.1088/0004-62 56/148/2/25.

33. Konstantin Batygin and Michael E. Brown, "Evidence for a Distant Giant Planet in the Solar System," *Astronomical Journal* 151 (February 2016): id. 22; Benjamin C. Bromley and Scott J. Kenyon, "The Fate of Scattered Planets," *Astrophysical Journal* 795 (November 2014): id. 141.

34. Walsh and Morbidelli, "Early Planetesimal-Driven Migration," id. A126; Morbidelli et al., "Constructing the Secular Architecture," 1041–52; Alessandro Morbidelli et al., "Asteroid Belt Constraints on Giant Planets Evolution," *Bulletin of the American Astronomical Society* 41, American Astronomical Society, DPS 41st meeting, abstract 55.03 (September 2009); R. Brasser et al., "Constructing the Secular Architecture of the Solar System. II: The Terrestrial Planets," *Astronomy and Astrophysics* 507 (November 2009): 1053–65; M. Brož et al., "Did the Hilda Collisional Family Form during the Late Heavy Bombardment?," *Monthly Notices of the Royal Astronomical Society* 414 (July 2011): 2716–27.

35. Harold F. Levison and Alessandro Morbidelli, "The Formation of the Kuiper Belt by the Outward Transport of Bodies during Neptune's Migration," *Nature* 426 (November 2003): 419–21.

36. Morbidelli et al., "Asteroid Belt Constraints," abstract 55.03.

37. Ibid.; Bottke et al., "E-Belt," 1269.

38. David Nesvorný, David Vokrouhlický, and Alessandro Morbidelli, "Capture of Trojans by Jumping Jupiter," *Astrophysical Journal* 768 (May 2013): id. 45, doi:10.1088/0004 -637X/768/1/45.

39. Ibid.

40. Brasser et al., "Constructing the Secular Architecture," 1053–65.

41. M. Booth et al., "How Common Are Extrasolar, Late Heavy Bombardments?," in *Pathways Toward Habitable Planets*, ed. Vincent Coudé du Foresto, Dawn M. Gelino, and Ignasi Ribas, ASP Conference Series, vol. 430 (San Francisco: Astronomical Society of the Pacific, 2010), 407.

42. A. S. Libert and K. Tsiganis, "Trapping in High-Order Orbital Resonances and Inclination Excitation in Extrasolar Systems," *Monthly Notices of the Royal Astronomical Society* 400 (December 2009): 1373–82.

43. Exoplanet Team, *The Extrasolar Planets Encyclopaedia*, http://exoplanet.eu/.

44. Ravit Helled and Peter Bodenheimer, "The Formation of Uranus and Neptune: Challenges and Implications for Intermediate-Mass Exoplanets," *Astrophysical Journal* 789 (July 2014): id. 69, doi:10.1088/0004-637X/789/1/69.

45. Ibid., id. 69, p. 1.

46. Rebecca G. Martin and Mario Livio, "On the Evolution of the Snow Line in Protoplanetary Disks," *Monthly Notices of the Royal Astronomical Society Letters* 425 (September 2012): L6–L9; Rebecca G. Martin and Mario Livio, "On the Evolution of the Snow Line in Protoplanetary Disks—II. Analytic Approximations," *Monthly Notices of the Royal Astronomical Society* 434 (September 2013): 633–38; Rebecca G. Martin and Mario Livio, "On the Evolution of the CO Snow Line in Protoplanetary Disks," *Astrophysical Journal Letters* 783 (March 2014): L28.

47. Sean N. Raymond et al., "Building the Terrestrial Planets: Constrained Accretion in the Inner Solar System," *Icarus* 203 (October 2009): 644–62.

48. Rebecca G. Martin and Mario Livio, "On the Formation and Evolution of Asteroid Belts and Their Potential Significance for Life," *Monthly Notices of the Royal Astronomical Society Letters* 428 (January 2013): L12.

49. M. J. Mumma et al., "Remote Infrared Observations of Parent Volatiles in Comets: A Window on the Early Solar System," *Advances in Space Research* 31 (June 2003): 2563–75.

50. Martin and Livio, "On the Formation," L13.

51. Ibid., L14.

52. Philip J. Armitage et al., "Predictions for the Frequency and Orbital Radii of Massive Extrasolar Planets," *Monthly Notices of the Royal Astronomical Society* 334 (July 2002): 248–56.

53. Laura Vican and Adam Schneider, "The Evolution of Dusty Debris Disks around Solar Type Stars," *Astrophysical Journal* 780 (January 2014): id. 154, doi:10.1088/0004 -637X/780/2/154.

54. Martin and Livio, "On the Formation," L11–L15.

55. Ibid., L14.

56. T. A. Michtchenko and S. Ferraz-Mello, "Resonant Structure of the Outer Solar System in the Neighborhood of the Planets," *Astronomical Journal* 122 (July 2001): 474–81.

57. Kimmo Innanen, Seppo Mikkola, and Paul Wiegert, "The Earth-Moon System and the Dynamical Stability of the Inner Solar System," *Astronomical Journal* 116 (October 1998): 2055–57.

58. F. Varadi, B. Runnegar, and M. Ghil, "Successive Refinements in Long-Term Integrations of Planetary Orbits," *Astrophysical Journal* 592 (July 1993): 620–30.

59. Ibid., 629.

## Chapter 7 Ready for the Foundation

1. Thomas Curwen, "Behind the Grand Pour: Building L.A.'s New Tallest Tower," *Los Angeles Times*, April 26, 2014. The article also is available at http://graphics.latimes.com /wilshire-grand-the-big-pour.

2. Ibid.

3. Fazale Rana and Hugh Ross, *Origins of Life: Biblical and Evolutionary Models Face Off*, 2nd ed. (Covina, CA: RTB Press, 2014), 63–92; Allen P. Nutman et al., "≥3700 Ma Pre-Metamorphic Dolomite Formed by Microbial Mediation in the Isua Supracrustal Belt (W. Greenland): Simple Evidence for Early Life?," *Precambrian Research* 183 (December 2010): 725–37.

4. Rana and Ross, *Origins of Life*, 65–78; Yanan Shen, Roger Buick, and Donald E. Canfield, "Isotopic Evidence for Microbial Sulphate Reduction in the Early Archaean Era," *Nature* 410 (March 2001): 77–81; Minik T. Rosing and Robert Frei, "U-Rich Archaean Sea-Floor Sediments from Greenland—Indications of >3700 Ma Oxygenic Photosynthesis," *Earth and Planetary Science Letters* 217 (January 2004): 237–44.

5. "Alien Planet Looks 'Just Right' for Life," *NBC News*, September 29, 2010, http ://cosmiclog.nbcnews.com/_news/2010/09/29/5202633-alien-planet-looks-just-right-for-life.

6. Steven Vogt, quoted in University of California, Santa Cruz, "Newly Discovered Planet May Be First Truly Habitable Exoplanet," EurekaAlert!, news release, September 29, 2010, http://www.eurekalert.org/pub_releases/2010-09/uoc—ndp092810.php.

7. Amir D. Aczel, *Probability 1: The Book That Proves There Is Life in Outer Space* (New York: Mariner Books, 2000).

8. Jianpo Guo et al., "Probability Distribution of Terrestrial Planets in Habitable Zones around Host Stars," *Astrophysics and Space Science* 323 (October 2009): 367–73.

9. Erik A. Petigura, Andrew W. Howard, and Geoffrey W. Marcy, "Prevalence of Earth-Size Planets Orbiting Sun-Like Stars," *Proceedings of the National Academy of Sciences, USA* 110 (November 2013): 19273–78; Dennis Overbye, "Far-Off Planets Like the Earth Dot the Galaxy," *New York Times*, November 4, 2013, http://www.nytimes.com/2013/11/05/science/cosmic-census-finds-billions-of-planets-that-could-be-like-earth.html?pagewanted=all&_r=0.

10. See http://www.exoplanet.eu/catalog/.

11. Daniel Foreman-Mackey, David W. Hogg, and Timothy D. Morton, "Exoplanet Population Inference and the Abundance of Earth Analogs from Noisy, Incomplete Catalogs," *Astrophysical Journal* 795 (November 2014): id. 64, doi:10.1088/0004-637X/795/1/64.

12. Steven S. Vogt et al., "The Lick-Carnegie Exoplanet Survey: A 3.1 $M_\oplus$ Planet in the Habitable Zone of the Nearby M3V Star Gliese 581," *Astrophysical Journal* 723 (November 2010): 954–65, doi:10.1088/0004-637X/723/1/954.

13. A. P. Hatzes, "An Investigation into the Radial Velocity Variability of GJ 581: On the Significance of GJ 581g," *Astronomische Nachrichten* 334 (August 2013): 616; Roman V. Baluev, "The Impact of Red Noise in Radial Velocity Planet Searches: Only Three Planets Orbiting GJ 581?," *Monthly Notices of the Royal Astronomical Society* 429 (March 2013): 2052–68.

14. Paul Robertson et al., "Stellar Activity Masquerading as Planets in the Habitable Zone of the M Dwarf Gliese 581," *Science* 345 (July 2014): 440–44; Zs. Tóth and I. Nagy, "Dynamical Stability of the Gliese 581 Exoplanetary System," *Monthly Notices of the Royal Astronomical Society* 442 (July 2014): 454–61.

15. Documentation may be found in these two books: Rana and Ross, *Origins of Life*; Fazale Rana, *Creating Life in the Lab: How New Discoveries in Synthetic Biology Make a Case for the Creator* (Grand Rapids: Baker, 2011) with updates maintained at http://www.reasons.org/origins-of-life-updates.

16. James F. Kasting, Daniel P. Whitmire, and Ray T. Reynolds, "Habitable Zones around Main Sequence Stars," *Icarus* 101 (January 1993): 108–28.

17. Ravi Kumar Kopparapu et al., "Habitable Zones around Main-Sequence Stars: New Estimates," *Astrophysical Journal* 765 (March 2013): id. 131, doi:10.1088/0004-637X/765/2/131; Ravi Kumar Kopparapu et al., "Erratum: 'Habitable Zones around Main-Sequence Stars: New Estimates,'" *Astrophysical Journal* 770 (June 2013): id. 82, doi:10.1088/0004-637X/770/1/82.

18. Yutaka Abe et al., "Habitable Zone Limits for Dry Planets," *Astrobiology* 11 (June 2011): 443–60; Jérémy Leconte et al., "Increased Insolation Threshold for Runaway Greenhouse Processes on Earth-Like Planets," *Nature* 504 (December 2013): 268–71.

19. Andras Zsom et al., "Toward the Minimum Inner Edge Distance of the Habitable Zone," *Astrophysical Journal* 778 (December 2013): id. 109, doi:10.1088/0004-637X/778/2/109.

20. D. S. Abbot et al., "Effect of Land Fraction on Weathering and Tenure in the Habitable Zone of Terrestrial Planets around Main-Sequence Stars," American Geophysical Union, Fall Meeting 2011 (December 2011): abstract P21C-1673; Dorian S. Abbot, Nicolas B. Cowan, and Fred J. Ciesla, "Indication of Insensitivity of Planetary Weathering Behavior and Habitable Zone to Surface-Land Fraction," *Astrophysical Journal* 756 (September 2012): id. 178, doi:10.1088/0004-637X/756/2/178.

21. S. Ueta and T. Sasaki, "The Structure of Surface $H_2O$ Layers of Ice-Covered Planets with High-Pressure Ice," *Astrophysical Journal* 775 (October 2013): id. 96, doi:10.1088/0004-637X/775/2/96.

22. Jianpo Guo et al., "Habitable Zones and UV Habitable Zones around Host Stars," *Astrophysics and Space Science* 325 (January 2010): 25–30.

23. Ibid.

24. Ibid.

25. Charles H. Lineweaver, Yeshe Fenner, and Brad K. Gibson, "The Galactic Habitable Zone and the Age Distribution of Complex Life in the Milky Way," *Science* 303 (January 2004): 59–62.

26. Frederick S. Colwell and Steven D'Hondt, "Nature and Extent of the Deep Biosphere," *Reviews in Mineralogy and Geochemistry* 75 (January 2013): 547–74; Steven D'Hondt, Scott Rutherford, and Arthur J. Spivack, "Metabolic Activity of Subsurface Life in Deep-Sea Sediments," *Science* 295 (March 2002): 2067–70.

27. Ingrid Cnossen et al., "Habitat of Early Life: Solar X-Ray and UV Radiation at Earth's Surface 4–3.5 Billion Years Ago," *Journal of Geophysical Research: Planets* 112 (February 2007): id. E02008.

28. Jun Yang et al., "Strong Dependence of the Inner Edge of the Habitable Zone on Planetary Rotation Rate," *Astrophysical Journal Letters* 787 (May 2014): L2.

29. Gregory S. Jenkins, "Global Climate Model High-Obliquity Solutions to the Ancient Climate Puzzles of the Faint-Young Sun Paradox and Low-Altitude Proterozoic Glaciation," *Journal of Geophysical Research: Atmospheres* 105 (March 2000): 7357–70.

30. Kristen Menou, "Water-Trapped Worlds," *Astrophysical Journal* 774 (September 2013): id. 51, doi:10.1088/0004-637X/774/1/51.

31. W. Zhang, "Daily and Lunar Growth Features in Fossil Corals from Xinjiang and Guangxi: Information about Ancient Earth's Rotation and Huge Impacts," *Astrobiology Science Conference 2010* (2010): abstract 5198; John W. Wells, "Coral Growth and Geochronology," *Nature* 197 (March 1963): 948–50.

32. R. Heller, J. Leconte, and R. Barnes, "Tidal Obliquity Evolution of Potentially Habitable Planets," *Astronomy and Astrophysics* 528 (April 2011): id. A27.

33. David S. Smith and John M. Scalo, "Habitable Zones Exposed: Astrosphere Collapse Frequency as a Function of Stellar Mass," *Astrobiology* 9 (September 2009): 673–81.

34. Ibid.

35. Adrian L. Melott and Richard K. Bambach, "Do Periodicities in Extinction—With Possible Astronomical Connections—Survive a Revision of the Geological Timescale?," *Astrophysical Journal* 773 (August 2013): id. 6, doi:10.1088/0004-637X/773/1/6; Adrian L. Melott and Richard K. Bambach, "Nemesis Reconsidered," *Monthly Notices of the Royal Astronomical Society Letters* 407 (September 2010): L99–L102.

36. C. Tachinami, H. Senshu, and S. Ida, "Thermal Evolution and Lifetime of Intrinsic Magnetic Fields of Super-Earths in Habitable Zones," *Astrophysical Journal* 726 (January 2011): id. 70, doi:10.1088/0004-637X/726/2/70; Jorge I. Zuluaga et al., "The Influence of Thermal Evolution in the Magnetic Protection of Terrestrial Planets," *Astrophysical Journal* 770 (June 2013): id. 23, doi:10.1088/0004-637X/770/1/23.

37. Tachinami, Senshu, and Ida, "Thermal Evolution," id. 70.

38. Ibid.; C. Tachinami, H. Senshu, and S. Ida, "Life-Time of Intrinsic Magnetic Field of Terrestrial Planets in Habitable Zone," *39th Lunar and Planetary Science Conference* (2008): abstract 1546.

39. Zuluaga et al., "Influence of Thermal Evolution," id. 23.

40. David S. Spiegel and Edwin L. Turner, "Bayesian Analysis of the Astrobiological Implications of Life's Early Emergence on Earth," *Proceedings of the National Academy of Sciences, USA* 109 (January 2012): 395.

41. Ibid.

## Chapter 8 Construction Begins below Ground

1. Fazale Rana, *Creating Life in the Lab: How New Discoveries in Synthetic Biology Make a Case for the Creator* (Grand Rapids: Baker, 2011).

Notes

2. Aude Picard et al., "Experimental Diagenesis of Organo-Mineral Structures Formed by Microaerophilic Fe(II)-Oxidizing Bacteria," *Nature Communications* 6 (February 2015): id. 6277, doi:10.1038/ncomms7277.

3. Ibid.

4. John C. Armstrong, "Distribution of Impact Locations and Velocities of Earth Meteorites on the Moon," *Earth, Moon, and Planets* 107 (December 2010): 43–54.

5. Hubert P. Yockey, *Information Theory and Molecular Biology* (Cambridge, UK: Cambridge University Press, 1992), 233–41; Minik T. Rosing, "$^{13}$C-Depleted Carbon Microparticles in >3700-Ma Sea-Floor Sedimentary Rocks from West Greenland," *Science* 283 (January 1999): 674–76; Daniele L. Pinti, Ko Hashizume, and Jun-ichi Matsuda, "Nitrogen and Argon Signatures in 3.8 to 2.8 Ga Metasediments: Clues on the Chemical State of the Archean Ocean and the Deep Biosphere," *Geochimica et Cosmochimica Acta* 65 (July 2001): 2301–15.

6. Rosing, "$^{13}$C-Depleted Carbon Microparticles," 674–76; M. Schidlowski, "A 3,800-Million-Year Isotopic Record of Life from Carbon in Sedimentary Rocks," *Nature* 333 (May 1988): 313–18; N. V. Grassineau et al., "Distinguishing Biological from Hydrothermal Signatures via Sulphur and Carbon Isotopes in Archaean Mineralizations at 3.8 and 2.7 Ga," *Geological Society of London, Special Publications* 248 (2005): 195–212; Kevin D. McKeegan, Anatoliy B. Kudryavtsev, and J. William Schopf, "Raman and Ion Microscopic Imagery of Graphitic Inclusions in Apatite from Older Than 3830 Ma Akilia Supracrustal Rocks, West Greenland," *Geology* 35 (July 2007): 591–94.

7. S. Fox and K. Dose, *Molecular Evolution and the Origin of Life* (San Francisco: Freeman, 1972), 44–45; I. S. Shklovskii and Carl Sagan, *Intelligent Life in the Universe* (San Francisco: Holden-Day, 1966), 231.

8. These studies are described and cited in our book, Fazale Rana and Hugh Ross, *Origins of Life: Biblical and Evolutionary Models Face Off*, 2nd ed. (Covina, CA: RTB Press, 2014), 70–75.

9. Niles Eldredge, *The Triumph of Evolution and the Failure of Creationism* (New York: W. H. Freeman, 2000), 35–36.

10. Martin J. Whitehouse, Balz S. Kamber, and Stephen Moorbath, "Age Significance of U-Th-Pb Zircon Data from Early Archaean Rocks of West Greenland—A Reassessment Based on Combined Ion-Microprobe and Imaging Studies," *Chemical Geology* 160 (August 1999): 201–24; Christopher M. Fedo and Martin J. Whitehouse, "Metasomatic Origin of Quartz-Pyroxene Rock, Akilia, Greenland, and Implications for Earth's Earliest Life," *Science* 296 (May 2002): 1448–52; Aivo Lepland et al., "Questioning the Evidence for Earth's Earliest Life—Akilia Revisited," *Geology* 33 (January 2005): 77; Martin J. Whitehouse et al., "Integrated Pb- and S-Isotope Investigation of Sulphide Minerals from the Early Archaean of Southwest Greenland," *Chemical Geology* 222 (October 2005): 112–31; Martin J. Whitehouse, John S. Myers, and Christopher M. Fedo, "The Akilia Controversy: Field, Structural and Geochronological Evidence Questions Interpretations of >3.8 Ga Life in SW Greenland," *Journal of the Geological Society* 166 (March 2009): 335–48.

11. Oleg Abramov and Stephen J. Mojzsis, "Microbial Habitability of the Hadean Earth during the Late Heavy Bombardment," *Nature* 459 (May 2009): 419–22; Oleg Abramov, David A. Kring, and Stephen J. Mojzsis, "The Impact Environment of the Hadean Earth," *Chemie der Erde - Geochemistry* 73 (October 2013): 227–48.

12. John M. Hayes, "The Earliest Memories of Life on Earth," *Nature* 384 (November 1996): 21–22; S. J. Mojzsis et al., "Evidence for Life on Earth before 3,800 Million Years Ago," *Nature* 384 (November 1996): 55–59; Heinrich D. Holland, "Evidence for Life on Earth More Than 3850 Million Years Ago," *Science* 275 (January 1997): 38–39.

13. Whitehouse, Kamber, and Moorbath, "Age Significance," 201–24; John M. Eiler, "The Oldest Fossil or Just Another Rock?," *Science* 317 (August 2007): 1046–47.

14. Craig E. Manning, Stephen J. Mojzsis, and T. Mark Harrison, "Geology, Age and Origin of Supracrustal Rocks at Akilia, West Greenland," *American Journal of Science* 306 (May 2006): 303–66.

15. Ibid.

16. Ibid.; Eiler, "Oldest Fossil?," 1046–47.

17. McKeegan, Kudryavtsev, and Schopf, "Raman and Ion," 591.

18. Ibid., 591–94.

19. Ibid.; Allen P. Nutman and Clark R. L. Friend, "Raman and Ion Microscopic Imagery of Graphitic Inclusions in Apatite from Older Than 3830 Ma Akilia Supracrustal Rocks, West Greenland: COMMENT," *Geology* 35 (January 2007): e169, doi: 10.1130 /G24384C.1; Kevin D. McKeegan, Anatoliy B. Kudryavtsev, and J. William Schopf, "Raman and Ion Microscopic Imagery of Graphitic Inclusions in Apatite from Older Than 3830 Ma Akilia Supracrustal Rocks, West Greenland: REPLY," *Geology* 35 (January 2007): e170, doi:10.1130/G24987Y.1.

20. McKeegan, Kudryavtsev, and Schopf, "Raman and Ion," 593.

21. Minik T. Rosing and Robert Frei, "U-Rich Archaean Sea-Floor Sediments from Greenland—Indications of >3700 Ma Oxygenic Photosynthesis," *Earth and Planetary Science Letters* 217 (January 2004): 237–44.

22. Yoko Ohtomo et al., "Evidence for Biogenic Graphite in Early Archaean Isua Metasedimentary Rocks," *Nature Geoscience* 7 (January 2014): 25–28.

23. Ibid., 25.

24. Norman H. Sleep, Emily Pope, and Dennis K. Bird, "Two-Way Feedback between Biology and Deep Earth Processes," American Geophysical Union, Fall Meeting 2012 (December 2012): abstract P14A-07; Norman H. Sleep, "Tectonics and the Photosynthetic Habitable Zone," *EoS, Transactions American Geophysical Union* 90, Fall Meeting Supplemental (2009): abstract B11E-03; Norman H. Sleep and Dennis K. Bird, "Biological Modulation of Tectonics," *EoS, Transactions American Geophysical Union* 89, Fall Meeting Supplemental (2008): abstract U42B-04.

25. Sleep, Pope, and Bird, "Two-Way Feedback," abstract P14A-07.

26. Minik T. Rosing et al., "The Rise of Continents—An Essay on the Geologic Consequences of Photosynthesis," *Palaeogeography, Palaeoclimatology, Palaeoecology* 232 (March 2006): 99–113.

27. Ibid.

28. Ibid.

29. Brent G. Dalrymple and Graham Ryder, "Argon-40/Argon-39 Age Spectra of Apollo 17 Highlands Breccia Samples by Laser Step Heating and the Age of the Serenitatis Basin," *Journal of Geophysical Research: Planets* 101 (November 1996): 26069–84; Fouad Tera, D. A. Papanastassiou, and G. J. Wasserburg, "Isotopic Evidence for a Terminal Lunar Cataclysm," *Earth and Planetary Science Letters* 22 (April 1974): 1–21.

30. B. A. Cohen, T. D. Swindle, and D. A. Kring, "Support for the Lunar Cataclysm Hypothesis from Lunar Meteorite Impact Melt Ages," *Science* 290 (December 2000): 1754–56; B. A. Cohen, T. D. Swindle, and D. A. Kring, "Geochemistry and 40Ar-39Ar Geochronology of Impact-Melt Clasts in Feldspathic Lunar Meteorites: Implications for Lunar Bombardment History," *Meteoritics and Planetary Science* 40 (May 2005): 755.

31. Teresa L. Segura, Christopher P. McKay, and Owen B. Toon, "An Impact-Induced, Stable, Runaway Climate on Mars," *Icarus* 220 (July 2012): 144–48.

32. Ronny Schoenberg et al., "Tungsten Isotope Evidence from ~3.8-Gyr Metamorphosed Sediments for Early Meteorite Bombardment of the Earth," *Nature* 418 (July 2002): 403.

33. Abramov and Mojzsis, "Microbial Habitability," 419–22; Abramov, Kring, and Mojzsis, "Impact Environment," 227–48.

34. Stephen J. Mojzsis, "Lithosphere-Hydrosphere Interactions on the Hadean (>4 Ga) Earth," *EoS, Transactions American Geophysical Union* 82, Fall Meeting Supplemental (2001): abstract U52A-0009; Stephen J. Mojzsis and Graham Ryder, "Accretion to Earth and Moon ~3.85 Ga," in *Accretion of Extraterrestrial Matter throughout Earth's History*, ed. Bernhard Peucker-Ehrenbrink and Birger Schmitz (New York: Kluwer Academic / Plenum Publishers, 2001), 423–26; Stephen J. Mojzsis and T. Mark Harrison, "Establishment of a 3.83-Ga Magmatic Age for the Akilia Tonalite (Southern West Greenland)," *Earth and Planetary Science Letters* 202 (September 2002): 563–76; Schoenberg et al., "Tungsten Isotope Evidence," 403–5.

35. Ariel D. Anbar et al., "Extraterrestrial Iridium, Sediment Accumulation and the Habitability of the Early Earth's Surface," *Journal of Geophysical Research: Planets* 106 (February 2001): 3219–36; Schoenberg et al., "Tungsten Isotope Evidence," 403–5.

36. B. A. Cohen, "The Violent Early Solar System, as Told by Lunar Sample Geochronology," American Geophysical Union, Fall Meeting 2012 (December 2012): abstract P42A-10.

37. Ibid.

38. Simone Marchi et al., "Reconciling HED Collisional Ages with the Lunar Late Heavy Bombardment," *American Astronomical Society*, DPS 44th meeting (October 2012): abstract 207.12.

39. Ibid.

40. Uffe Gråe Jørgensen et al., "The Earth-Moon System during the Late Heavy Bombardment Period—Geochemical Support for Impacts Dominated by Comets," *Icarus* 204 (December 2009): 368–80.

41. Ibid.

42. Ibid.

43. Elizabeth A. Bell and T. Mark Harrison, "Post-Hadean Transitions in Jack Hills Zircon Provenance: A Signal of the Late Heavy Bombardment?," *Earth and Planetary Science Letters* 364 (February 2013): 1–11.

44. Abramov and Mojzsis, "Microbial Habitability," 419–22.

45. Simon A. Wilde et al., "Evidence from Detrital Zircons for the Existence of Continental Crust and Oceans on the Earth 4.4 Gyr Ago," *Nature* 409 (January 2001): 175–78; Stephen J. Mojzsis, T. Mark Harrison, and Robert T. Pidgeon, "Oxygen-Isotope Evidence from Ancient Zircons for Liquid Water at the Earth's Surface 4,300 Myr Ago," *Nature* 409 (January 2001): 178–81.

46. Samuel A. Bowring and Ian S. Williams, "Priscoan (4.00–4.03 Ga) Orthogneisses from Northwestern Canada," *Contributions to Mineralogy and Petrology* 134 (January 1999): 3–16.

47. S. Marchi et al., "Widespread Mixing and Burial of Earth's Hadean Crust by Asteroid Impacts," *Nature* 511 (July 2014): 578–82.

48. H. James Cleaves II and John H. Chalmers, "Extremophiles May Be Irrelevant to the Origin of Life," *Astrobiology* 4 (March 2004): 1–9.

49. Rosa Larralde, Michael P. Robertson, and Stanley L. Miller, "Rates of Decomposition of Ribose and Other Sugars: Implications for Chemical Evolution," *Proceedings of the National Academy of Sciences, USA* 92 (August 1995): 8158–60.

50. Abramov and Mojzsis, "Microbial Habitability," 420.

51. Charles S. Cockell et al., "Impact Disruption and Recovery of the Deep Subsurface Biosphere," *Astrobiology* 12 (March 2012): 231–46.

52. William B. Whitman, David C. Coleman, and William J. Wiebe, "Prokaryotes: The Unseen Majority," *Proceedings of the National Academy of Sciences, USA* 95 (June 1998): 6578–83.

53. Jens Kallmeyer et al., "Global Distribution of Microbial Abundance and Biomass in Subseafloor Sediment," *Proceedings of the National Academy of Sciences, USA* 109 (October 2012): 16213–16.

54. Takayuki Ushikubo et al., "Lithium in Jack Hills Zircons: Evidence for Extensive Weathering of Earth's Earliest Crust," *Earth and Planetary Science Letters* 272 (August 2008): 666–76.

55. Rana and Ross, *Origins of Life*, 125–36; Fazale Rana, "Explanation for Origin-of-Life's Molecular Handedness Is Insoluble," *Today's New Reason to Believe* (blog), May 8, 2008, http://www.reasons.org/articles/explanation-for-origin-of-lifes-molecular-handedness-is-insoluble; Fazale Rana, "One More Crack in the Mirror: Misplaced Hope in the Latest Model for the Origin of Life," *Today's New Reason to Believe* (blog), October 10, 2011, http://www.reasons.org/articles/one-more-crack-in-the-mirror-misplaced-hope-in-the-latest-model-for-the-origin-of-life; Hugh Ross, "Homochirality and the Origin of Life," *Today's New Reason to Believe* (blog), November 7, 2011, http://www.reasons.org/articles/homochirality-and-the-origin-of-life.

56. Hugh Ross, "Natural Sugar Synthesis?," *Today's New Reason to Believe* (blog), August 5, 2007, http://www.reasons.org/articles/natural-sugar-synthesis; Abraham F. Jalbout et al., "Sugar Synthesis from a Gas-Phase Formose Reaction," *Astrobiology* 7 (June 2007): 433–34; D. T. Halfen et al., "A Systematic Study of Glycolaldehyde in Sagittarius B2(N) at 2 and 3 mm: Criteria for Detecting Large Interstellar Molecules," *Astrophysical Journal* 639 (March 2006): 237–45.

57. Gene D. McDonald and Michael C. Storrie-Lombardi, "Biochemical Constraints in a Protobiotic Earth Devoid of Basic Amino Acids: The 'BAA(-) World,'" *Astrobiology* 10 (December 2010): 989–1000; Hugh Ross, "Rare Amino Acid Challenge to the Origin of Life," *Today's New Reason to Believe* (blog), April 11, 2011, http://www.reasons.org/articles/rare-amino-acid-challenge-to-the-origin-of-life.

## Chapter 9 Up to Ground Level

1. Stephen J. Giovannoni et al., "Genome Streamlining in a Cosmopolitan Oceanic Bacterium," *Science* 309 (August 2005): 1242–45.

2. Ibid.

3. Brandon Carter, "The Anthropic Principle and Its Implications for Biological Evolution," *Philosophical Transactions of the Royal Society of London A* 310 (December 1983): 347–60; John D. Barrow and Frank J. Tipler, *The Anthropic Cosmological Principle* (New York: Oxford University Press, 1986), 510–73.

4. Alexis Dufresne et al., "Genome Sequence of the Cyanobacterium *Prochlorococcus marinus* SS120, a Nearly Minimal Oxyphototrophic Genome," *Proceedings of the National Academy of Sciences, USA* 100 (August 2003): 10020–25.

5. Yasukazu Nakamura et al., "Complete Genome Structure of the Thermophilic Cyanobacterium *Thermosynechococcus elongatus* BP-1," *DNA Research* 9 (August 2002): 123–30.

6. Qiao Jiang, Song Qin, and Qing-Yu Wu, "Genome-Wide Comparative Analysis of Metacaspases in Unicellular and Filamentous Cyanobacteria," *BMC Genomics* 11 (March 2010): id. 198, doi:10.1186/1471-2164-11-198.

7. Minik T. Rosing et al., "Earliest Part of Earth's Stratigraphic Record: A Reappraisal of the >3.7 Ga Isua (Greenland) Supracrustal Sequence," *Geology* 24 (January 1996): 43–46;

Martin J. Whitehouse and Christopher M. Fedo, "Microscale Heterogeneity of Fe Isotopes in >3.71 Ga Banded Iron Formation from the Isua Greenstone Belt, Southwest Greenland," *Geology* 35 (August 2007): 719–22.

8. Hiroshi Ohmoto et al., "Chemical and Biological Evolution of Early Earth: Constraints from Banded Iron Formations," *Geological Society of America Memoirs* 198 (2006): 291–331.

9. Ibid., 291.

10. Minik T. Rosing et al., "The Rise of Continents—An Essay on the Geologic Consequences of Photosynthesis," *Palaeogeography, Palaeoclimatology, Palaeoecology* 232 (March 2006): 99–113.

11. Ibid., 99.

12. Eugene G. Grosch and Robert M. Hazen, "Microbes, Mineral Evolution, and the Rise of Microcontinents—Origin and Coevolution of Life with Early Earth," *Astrobiology* 15 (October 2015): 922–39.

13. Guy Simpson, "Influence of Erosion and Deposition on Deformation in Fold Belts," *Geological Society of America, Special Papers* 398 (2006): 267–81. The quotes are from page 267.

14. Tatsuhiko Kawamoto et al., "Mantle Wedge Infiltrated with Saline Fluids from Dehydration and Decarbonation of Subducting Slab," *Proceedings of the National Academy of Sciences, USA* 110 (June 2013): 9663–68; Simon M. Peacock and Kelin Wang, "Seismic Consequences of Warm versus Cool Subduction Metamorphism: Examples from Southwest and Northeast Japan," *Science* 286 (October 1999): 937–39; Simon M. Peacock and Roy D. Hyndman, "Hydrous Minerals in the Mantle Wedge and the Maximum Depth of Subduction Thrust Earthquakes," *Geophysical Research Letters* 26 (August 1999): 2517–20.

15. Craig O'Neill, "A Window of Opportunity for Plate Tectonics in Evolution of Earth-Like Planets?," American Geophysical Union, Fall Meeting 2011 (December 2011): abstract P24B-05.

16. Craig O'Neill and A. Lenardic, "Geological Consequences of Super-Sized Earths," *Geophysical Research Letters* 34 (October 2007): L19204.

17. Ibid., L19204, p. 1.

18. A. Lenardic, C. M. Cooper, and L. Moresi, "A Note on Continents and the Earth's Urey Ratio," *Physics of the Earth and Planetary Interiors* 188 (September 2011): 127–30; Tobias Rolf and Paul J. Tackley, "Focussing of Stress by Continents in 3D Spherical Mantle Convection with Self-Consistent Plate Tectonics," *Geophysical Research Letters* 38 (September 2011): L18301; Tobias Rolf, Nicolas Coltice, and Paul J. Tackley, "Linking Continental Drift, Plate Tectonics and the Thermal State of the Earth's Mantle," *Earth and Planetary Science Letters* 351–352 (October 2012): 134–46; Nicolas Coltice et al., "Dynamic Causes of the Relation between Area and Age of the Ocean Floor," *Science* 336 (April 2012): 335–38.

19. A. Lenardic and J. W. Crowley, "On the Notion of Well-Defined Tectonic Regimes for Terrestrial Planets in this Solar System and Others," *Astrophysical Journal* 755 (August 2012): id. 132, doi:10.1088/0004-637X/755/2/132; Craig O'Neill, A. M. Jellinek, and A. Lenardic, "Conditions for the Onset of Plate Tectonics on Terrestrial Planets and Moons," *Earth and Planetary Science Letters* 261 (September 2007): 20–32.

20. A. Lenardic, A. M. Jellinek, and L. Moresi, "A Climate Induced Transition in the Tectonic Style of a Terrestrial Planet," *Earth and Planetary Science Letters* 271 (July 2008): 34–42.

21. Kent C. Condie, Craig O'Neill, and Richard C. Aster, "Evidence and Implications for a Widespread Magmatic Shutdown for 250 My on Earth," *Earth and Planetary Science Letters* 282 (May 2009): 294–98.

22. Ibid.

23. J. Parnell, "Plate Tectonics, Surface Mineralogy, and the Early Evolution of Life," *International Journal of Astrobiology* 3 (April 2004): 131–37; Norman H. Sleep, Dennis K. Bird, and Emily Pope, "Paleontology of Earth's Mantle," *Annual Review of Earth and Planetary Sciences* 40 (May 2012): 277–300.

24. Joost van Summeren, Clinton P. Conrad, and Carolina Lithgow-Bertelloni, "The Importance of Slab Pull and a Global Asthenosphere to Plate Motions," *Geochemistry, Geophysics, Geosystems* 13 (February 2012): id. Q0AK03, doi:10.1029/2011GC003873; W. P. Schellart, "Quantifying the Net Slab Pull Force as a Driving Mechanism for Plate Tectonics," *Geophysical Research Letters* 31 (April 2004): L07611.

25. Clinton P. Conrad and Carolina Lithgow-Bertelloni, "The Temporal Evolution of Plate Driving Forces: Importance of 'Slab Suction' versus 'Slab Pull' during the Cenozoic," *Journal of Geophysical Research: Solid Earth* 109 (October 2004): id. B10407; Clinton P. Conrad and Carolina Lithgow-Bertelloni, "The Relative Importance of Asymmetrical Slab-Pull and Symmetrical Slab-Suction in Driving Plate Motions," American Geophysical Union, Spring Meeting 2002 (May 2002): abstract S32A-05.

26. C. Grigné, S. Labrosse, and Paul J. Tackley, "Convective Heat Transfer as a Function of Wavelength: Implications for the Cooling of the Earth," *Journal of Geophysical Research: Solid Earth* 110 (March 2005): id. B03409; Shunxing Xie and Paul J. Tackley, "Evolution of U-Pb and Sm-Nd Systems in Numerical Models of Mantle Convection and Plate Tectonics," *Journal of Geophysical Research: Solid Earth* 109 (November 2004): id. B11204; Russell N. Pysklywec and Christopher Beaumont, "Intraplate Tectonics: Feedback between Radioactive Thermal Weakening and Crustal Deformation Driven by Mantle Lithosphere Instabilities," *Earth and Planetary Science Letters* 221 (April 2004): 275–92.

27. Sleep, Bird, and Pope, "Paleontology of Earth's Mantle," 277–300; Rosing et al., "Rise of Continents," 99–113; Tilman Spohn, "Thermal History of Planetary Objects: From Asteroids to Super-Earths, from Plate Tectonics to Life," *Geophysical Research Abstracts* 15, EGU General Assembly (April 2013): abstract 13537.

28. Peter D. Ward and Donald Brownlee, *Rare Earth: Why Complex Life Is Uncommon in the Universe* (New York: Copernicus, 2000), 191–220.

29. A. M. Jellinek and M. G. Jackson, "Connections between the Bulk Composition, Geodynamics, and Habitability of Earth," *Nature Geoscience* 8 (August 2015): 587–93.

30. O'Neill, Jellinek, and Lenardic, "Conditions for the Onset," 20–32.

31. Jeroen van Hunen and Arie P. van den Berg, "Plate Tectonics on the Early Earth: Limitations Imposed by Strength and Buoyancy of Subducted Lithosphere," *Lithos* 103 (June 2008): 217–35.

32. William F. Bottke et al., "An Archaean Heavy Bombardment from a Destabilized Extension of the Asteroid Belt," *Nature* 485 (May 2012): 78–81; B. C. Johnson and H. J. Melosh, "Impact Spherules as a Record of an Ancient Heavy Bombardment of Earth," *Nature* 485 (May 2012): 75–77; Donald R. Lowe et al., "Spherule Beds 3.47–3.24 Billion Years Old in the Barberton Greenstone Belt, South Africa: A Record of Large Meteorite Impacts and Their Influence on Early Crustal and Biological Evolution," *Astrobiology* 3 (January 2003): 7–48; Gary R. Byerly et al., "An Archean Impact Layer from the Pilbara and Kaapvaal Cratons," *Science* 297 (August 2002): 1325–27.

33. Javier Ruiz, "Giant Impacts and the Initiation of Plate Tectonics on Terrestrial Planets," *Planetary and Space Science* 59 (June 2011): 749–53.

34. J. Korenaga, "Thermal Evolution with a Hydrating Mantle and the Initiation of Plate Tectonics in the Early Earth," *Journal of Geophysical Research: Solid Earth* 116 (December 2011): id. B12403.

35. L. Saha, A. Hofmann, and H. Xie, "Style of Palaeoarchaean Tectonics from the SE Kaapvaal and Singhbhum Cratons: Constraints from Metamorphic Studies and Zircon Geochronology," *Geophysical Research Abstracts* 15, EGU General Assembly (April 2012): abstract 3549; Svetlana G. Tessalina et al., "Influence of Hadean Crust Evident in Basalts and Cherts from the Pilbara Craton," *Nature Geoscience* 3 (March 2010): 214–17; Byerly et al, "Archean Impact Layer," 1325–27.

36. Stephen B. Shirey and Stephen H. Richardson, "Start of the Wilson Cycle at 3 Ga Shown by Diamonds from Subcontinental Mantle," *Science* 333 (July 2011): 434–36.

37. Vinciane Debaille et al., "Stagnant-Lid Tectonics in Early Earth Revealed by $^{142}$Nd Variations in Late Archean Rocks," *Earth and Planetary Science Letters* 373 (July 2013): 83–92.

38. C. J. Hale and D. J. Dunlop, "Evidence for an Early Archean Geomagnetic Field: A Paleomagnetic Study of the Komati Formation, Barberton Greenstone Belt, South Africa," *Geophysical Research Letters* 11 (February 1984): 97–100; N. W. McElhinny and W. E. Senanayake, "Paleomagnetic Evidence for the Existence of the Geomagnetic Field 3.5 Ga Ago," *Journal of Geophysical Research: Solid Earth* 85 (July 1980): 3523–28; Yoichi Usui et al., "Evidence for a 3.45-Billion-Year-Old Magnetic Remanence: Hints of an Ancient Geodynamo from Conglomerates of South Africa," *Geochemistry, Geophysics, Geosystems* 10 (September 2009): id. Q09Z07, doi:10.1029/2009GC002496; John A. Tarduno et al., "Geodynamo, Solar Wind, and Magnetopause 3.4 to 3.45 Billion Years Ago," *Science* 327 (March 2010): 1238–40.

39. M. Ozima et al., "Terrestrial Nitrogen and Noble Gases in Lunar Soils," *Nature* 436 (August 2005): 655–59; Bernard Marty, "Geochemistry: On the Moon as It Was on Earth," *Nature* 436 (August 2005): 631–32; J. Arkani-Hamed, "Geodynamo in Hadean," American Geophysical Union, Fall Meeting 2013 (December 2013): abstract V33D-2801.

40. Stephen B. Shirey et al., "A Review of the Isotopic and Trace Element Evidence for Mantle and Crustal Processes in the Hadean and Archean: Implications for the Onset of Plate Tectonic Subduction," *Geological Society of America, Special Papers* 440 (2008): 1–29; David Bercovici and Yanick Ricard, "Plate Tectonics, Damage and Inheritance," *Nature* 508 (April 2014): 513–16.

41. Shirey et al., "Review of the Isotopic," 1–29; Bercovici and Ricard, "Plate Tectonics," 513–16; Ali Polat, W. U. Appel, and Brian J. Fryer, "An Overview of the Geochemistry of Eoarchean to Mesoarchean Ultramafic to Mafic Volcanic Rocks, SW Greenland: Implications for Mantle Depletion and Petrogenetic Processes at Subduction Zones in the Early Earth," *Gondwana Research* 20 (September 2011): 255–83.

42. C. Grigne and Paul J. Tackley, "The Effect of Continents on the Initiation and Configuration of Plate Tectonics," *EoS, Transactions American Geophysical Union* 87, Fall Meeting Supplemental (2006): abstract T52D-02.

43. Lenardic, Jellinek, and Moresi, "Climate Induced Transition," 34–42.

44. Rosing et al., "Rise of Continents," 99–113; Sleep, Bird, and Pope, "Paleontology of Earth's Mantle," 277–300; Parnell, "Plate Tectonics," 131–37.

45. Dennis Höning, Hendrik Hansen-Goos, and Tilman Spohn, "Subducted Sediments and Mantle Regassing—How Life Impacts the Earth's Geodynamics," *Geophysical Research Abstracts* 15, EGU General Assembly (April 2013): abstract 13531; Spohn, "Thermal History," 13537.

## Chapter 10 Air-Conditioning

1. Lee R. Kump, "The Rise of Atmospheric Oxygen," *Nature* 451 (January 2008): 277–78; Alexander A. Pavlov and J. F. Kasting, "Mass-Independent Fractionation of Sulfur Isotopes

in Archean Sediments: Strong Evidence for an Anoxic Archean Atmosphere," *Astrobiology* 2 (March 2002): 27–41.

2. Jacob R. Waldbauer, Dianne K. Newman, and Roger E. Summons, "Microaerobic Steroid Biosynthesis and the Molecular Fossil Record of Archean Life," *Proceedings of the National Academy of Sciences, USA* 108 (August 2011): 13409–14; Minik T. Rosing and Richard Frei, "U-Rich Archaean Sea-Floor Sediments from Greenland—Indications of >3700 Ma Oxygenic Photosynthesis," *Earth and Planetary Science Letters* 217 (January 2004): 237–44; Jochen J. Brocks et al., "Archean Molecular Fossils and the Early Rise of Eukaryotes," *Science* 285 (August 1999): 1033–36; Timothy W. Lyons, Christopher T. Reinhard, and Noah J. Planavsky, "The Rise of Oxygen in Earth's Early Ocean and Atmosphere," *Nature* 506 (February 2014): 307–15.

3. A. Bekker et al., "Dating the Rise of Atmospheric Oxygen," *Nature* 427 (January 2004): 117–20; Kump, "Rise of Atmospheric Oxygen," 277–78; Lyons, Reinhard, and Planavsky, "Rise of Oxygen," 307–15.

4. C. Brenhin Keller and Blair Schoene, "Statistical Geochemistry Reveals Disruption in Secular Lithospheric Evolution about 2.5 Gyr Ago," *Nature* 485 (May 2012): 490–93; John W. Grula, "Rethinking the Paleoproterozoic Great Oxidation Event: A Biological Perspective," ArXiv.org (March 2013): eprint arXiv:1203.6701.

5. Lyons, Reinhard, and Planavsky, "Rise of Oxygen," 307–15.

6. Kevin J. Zahnle, M. Claire, and David C. Catling, "The Loss of Mass-Independent Fractionation in Sulfur Due to a Palaeoproterozoic Collapse of Atmospheric Methane," *Geobiology* 4 (December 2006): 271–83; David C. Catling, Kevin J. Zahnle, and Christopher P. McKay, "Biogenic Methane, Hydrogen Escape, and the Irreversible Oxidation of Early Earth," *Science* 293 (August 2001): 839–43; Alexander A. Pavlov et al., "Greenhouse Warming by $CH_4$ in the Atmosphere of Early Earth," *Journal of Geophysical Research: Planets* 105 (May 2000): 11981–90.

7. Emily C. Pope, Dennis K. Bird, and Minik T. Rosing, "Isotope Composition and Volume of Earth's Early Oceans," *Proceedings of the National Academy of Sciences, USA* 109 (March 2012): 4371–76.

8. Heinrich D. Holland, "Volcanic Gases, Black Smokers, and the Great Oxidation Event," *Geochimica et Cosmochimica Acta* 66 (November 2002): 3811–25.

9. Lee R. Kump and Mark E. Barley, "Increased Subaerial Volcanism and the Rise of Atmospheric Oxygen 2.5 Billion Years Ago," *Nature* 448 (August 2007): 1033–36; Lee R. Kump, James F. Kasting, and Mark E. Barley, "Rise of Atmospheric Oxygen and the 'Upside-Down' Archean Mantle," *Geochemistry, Geophysics, Geosystems* 2 (January 2001): 1025, doi:10.1029/2000GC000114.

10. Kurt O. Konhauser et al., "Oceanic Nickel Depletion and a Methanogen Famine before the Great Oxidation Event," *Nature* 438 (April 2009): 750–53.

11. P. G. Eriksson and Kent C. Condie, "Cratonic Sedimentation Regimes in the Ca. 2450–2000 Ma Period: Relationship to a Possible Widespread Magmatic Slowdown on Earth?," *Gondwana Research* 25 (January 2014): 30–47; Kent C. Condie, Craig O'Neill, and Richard C. Aster, "Evidence and Implications for a Widespread Magmatic Shutdown for 250 My on Earth," *Earth and Planetary Science Letters* 282 (May 2009): 294–98; Kent C. Condie and Craig O'Neill, "The Archean-Proterozoic Boundary: 500 My of Tectonic Transition in Earth History," *American Journal of Science* 310 (November 2010): 775–90. Evidence that the tectonic lull was not ubiquitous is presented in C. A. Partin et al., "Filling in the Juvenile Magmatic Gap: Evidence for Uninterrupted Paleoproterozoic Plate Tectonics," *Earth and Planetary Science Letters* 388 (February 2014): 123–33.

12. Kurt O. Konhauser et al., "The Archean Nickel Famine Revisited," *Astrobiology* 15 (October 2015): 804.

13. Grant M. Young et al., "Earth's Oldest Reported Glaciation: Physical and Chemical Evidence from the Archean Mozaan Group (~2.9 Ga) of South Africa," *Journal of Geology* 106 (September 1998): 523–38; Robert E. Kopp et al., "The Paleoproterozoic Snowball Earth: A Climate Disaster Triggered by the Evolution of Oxygenic Photosynthesis," *Proceedings of the National Academy of Sciences, USA* 102 (August 2005): 11131–36.

14. Kopp et al., "Paleoproterozoic Snowball Earth," 11131–36.

15. V. Harcouët et al., "Pre-Mineralization Thermal Evolution of the Palaeoproterozoic Gold-Rich Ashanti Belt, Ghana," *Geological Society of London, Special Publications* 248 (January 2005): 103–18; David J. Groves and Frank P. Bierlein, "Geodynamic Settings of Mineral Deposit Systems," *Journal of the Geological Society, London* 164 (January 2007): 19–30.

16. Dimitri A. Sverjensky and Namhey Lee, "The Great Oxidation Event and Mineral Diversification," *Elements* 6 (February 2010): 31–36.

17. V. Beaumont and F. Robert, "Nitrogen Isotope Ratios of Kerogens in Precambrian Cherts: A Record of the Evolution of Atmosphere Chemistry?," *Precambrian Research* 96 (June 1999): 63–82; S. S. Brake et al., "Eukaryotic Stromatolite Builders in Acid Mine Drainage: Implications for Precambrian Iron Formations and Oxygenation of the Atmosphere?," *Geology* 30 (July 2002): 599; James Farquhar, Huiming Bao, and Mark Thiemens, "Atmospheric Influence of Earth's Earliest Sulfur Cycle," *Science* 289 (August 2000): 756–58; Ariel D. Anbar et al., "A Whiff of Oxygen before the Great Oxidation Event?," *Science* 317 (September 2007): 1903–6; K. T. Goto et al., "Geochemistry of the Nsuta Mn Deposit in Ghana: Implications for the Paleoproterozoic Atmosphere and Ocean Chemistry," American Geophysical Union, Fall Meeting 2013 (December 2013): abstract PP51B-1947.

18. Joseph L. Kirschvink et al., "Paleoproterozoic Snowball Earth: Extreme Climatic and Geochemical Global Change and Its Biological Consequences," *Proceedings of the National Academy of Sciences, USA* 97 (February 2000): 1400–1405; Joseph L. Kirschvink, "The Paleoproterozoic Snowball as the Trigger for Atmospheric Oxygen and the Evolution of Eukaryotes," American Geophysical Union, Spring Meeting 2001 (May 2001): abstract U22A-01.

19. E. Blaurock-Busch, "The Clinical Effects of Manganese," Townsend Letter for Doctors and Patients, July 1998, 92, http://www.tldp.com/issue/180/Clinical%20Effects%20of%20Mn.html.

20. Ibid.

21. Yasuhito Sekine et al., "Anomalous Negative Excursion of Carbon Isotope in Organic Carbon after the Last Paleoproterozoic Glaciation in North America," *Geochemistry, Geophysics, Geosystems* 11 (August 2010): id. Q08019, doi:10.1029/2010GC003210; Lee R. Kump et al., "Isotopic Evidence for Massive Oxidation of Organic Matter following the Great Oxidation Event," *Science* 334 (December 2011): 1694–96; Victor A. Melezhik et al., "Petroleum Surface Oil Seeps from Palaeoproterozoic Petrified Giant Oilfield," *Geophysical Research Abstracts* 11, EGU General Assembly (April 2009): abstract 4888.

22. Hugh Ross, *Why the Universe Is the Way It Is* (Grand Rapids: Baker, 2008), 44–56, 108–15; Hugh Ross, *More Than a Theory: Revealing a Testable Model for Creation* (Grand Rapids: Baker, 2009), 160–64, 192–93.

23. Robert M. Hazen et al., "Mineral Evolution," *American Minerologist* 93 (November–December 2008): 1693–720.

24. Dimitri A. Sverjensky and Namhey Lee, "The Great Oxidation Event and Mineral Diversification," *Elements* 6 (February 2010): 31–36.

25. Robert Frei et al., "Fluctuations in Precambrian Atmospheric Oxygenation Recorded by Chromium Isotopes," *Nature* 461 (September 2009): 250–53.

26. H. D. Holland and A. Bekker, "Oxygen Overshoot and Recovery during the Paleoproterozoic," American Geophysical Union, Fall Meeting 2010 (December 2010): abstract U32A-07.

27. Clint Scott et al., "Pyrite Multiple-Sulfur Isotope Evidence for Rapid Expansion and Contraction of the Early Paleoproterozoic Seawater Sulfate Reservoir," *Earth and Planetary Science Letters* 389 (March 2014): 95–104; Noah J. Planavsky et al., "Sulfur Record of Rising and Falling Marine Oxygen and Sulfate Levels during the Lomagundi Event," *Proceedings of the National Academy of Sciences, USA* 109 (November 2012): 18300–18305.

28. C. A. Partin et al., "Large-Scale Fluctuations in Precambrian Atmospheric and Oceanic Oxygen Levels from the Record of U in Shales," *Earth and Planetary Science Letters* 369–370 (May 2013): 284–93.

29. C. K. Junium et al., "Nitrogen Cycling Following the Great Oxidation Event, Evidence from the Paleoproterozoic of Fennoscandia," American Geophysical Union, Fall Meeting 2011 (December 2011): abstract B331-02.

30. Donald E. Canfield et al., "Oxygen Dynamics in the Aftermath of the Great Oxidation of Earth's Atmosphere," *Proceedings of the National Academy of Sciences, USA* 110 (October 2013): 16736–41.

31. M. Harada et al., "Rise of Oxygen Induced by Paleoproterozoic Snowball Glaciation: Insights from Biogeochemical Cycle Modeling," American Geophysical Union, Fall Meeting 2012 (December 2012): abstract P11B-1825.

## Chapter 11  Invisible Progress

1. M. D. Brasier and J. F. Lindsay, "A Billion Years of Environmental Stability and the Emergence of Eukaryotes: New Data from Northern Australia," *Geology* 26 (June 1998): 555.

2. Gregory S. Jenkins, Christopher P. McKay, and Mark A. S. McMenamin, "Introduction: The Proterozoic," in *The Extreme Proterozoic: Geology, Geochemistry, and Climate* 146, ed. Gregory S. Jenkins et al. (Washington, DC: American Geophysical Union, 2004), 1.

3. C. Archer and D. Vance, "The Isotopic Signature of the Global Riverine Molybdenum Flux and Anoxia in the Ancient Oceans," *Nature Geoscience* 1 (September 2008): 597–600.

4. Linda C. Kah and Robert Riding, "Mesoproterozoic Carbon Dioxide Levels Inferred from Calcified Cyanobacteria," *Geology* 35 (September 2007): 799.

5. Ibid.; James F. Kasting, "Methane as a Climate Driver during the Precambrian Eon," American Geophysical Union, Fall Meeting 2013 (December 2013): abstract U33A-01.

6. Shamik Dasgupta et al., "Biosynthesis of Sterols and Wax Esters by *Euglena* of Acid Mine Drainage Biofilms: Implications for Eukaryotic Evolution and the Early Earth," *Chemical Geology* 306–307 (May 2012): 139–45.

7. David Halter et al., "Surface Properties and Intracellular Speciation Revealed an Original Adaptive Mechanism to Arsenic in the Acid Mine Drainage Bio-Indicator *Euglena mutabilis*," *Applied Microbiology and Biotechnology* 93 (February 2012): 1735–44.

8. S. S. Brake et al., "Eukaryotic Stromatolite Builders in Acid Mine Drainage: Implications for Precambrian Iron Formations and Oxygenation of the Atmosphere?," *Geology* 30 (July 2002): 599.

9. Graham A. Logan et al., "Terminal Proterozoic Reorganization of Biogeochemical Cycles," *Nature* 376 (July 1995): 53–56.

10. John Elmsley, *The Elements*, 3rd ed. (Oxford, UK: Clarendon Press, 1998), 26, 40, 56, 58, 60, 62, 78, 102, 106, 120, 122, 130, 138, 152, 160, 188, 194, 198, 214, 222, 230; A. Scott

McCall et al., "Bromine Is an Essential Trace Element for Assembly of Collagen IV Scaffolds in Tissue Development and Architecture," *Cell* 157 (June 2014): 1380–92.

11. James C. G. Walker, "Precambrian Evolution of the Climate System," *Palaeogeography, Palaeoclimatology, Palaeoecology* 82 (August 1990): 261–89.

12. Kirk S. Hansen, "Secular Effects of Oceanic Tidal Dissipation on the Moon's Orbit and the Earth's Rotation," *Reviews of Geophysics* 20 (August 1982): 457–80.

13. Tobias Rolf, Nicolas Coltice, and Paul J. Tackley, "Linking Continental Drift, Plate Tectonics and the Thermal State of the Earth's Mantle," *Earth and Planetary Science Letters* 351–352 (October 2012): 134–46.

14. I explain and document the brevity of the human civilization time window in my book *Why the Universe Is the Way It Is* (Grand Rapids: Baker, 2008), 43–56.

15. Joseph G. Meert and Bruce S. Lieberman, "The Neoproterozoic Assembly of Gondwana and Its Relationship to the Ediacaran-Cambrian Radiation," *Gondwana Research* 14 (August 2008): 5–21.

16. Lee R. Kump, James F. Kasting, and Mark E. Barley, "Rise of Atmospheric Oxygen and the 'Upside-Down' Archean Mantle," *Geochemistry, Geophysics, Geosystems* 2 (January 2001): 1025, doi:10.1029/2000GC000114; R. J. Stern et el., "Evidence for the Snowball Earth Hypothesis in the Arabian-Nubian Shield and the East African Orogen," *Journal of African Earth Sciences* 44 (January 2006): 1–20; V. Harcouët, A. Bonneville, and L. Guillou-Frottier, "Spatial and Temporal Distribution of Ore Deposits, in Relation with Thermal Anomalies," *Geophysical Research Abstracts* 5, EGS-AGU-EUG Joint Assembly (April 2003): abstract 10325.

17. Stefan G. Müller et al., "Giant Iron-Ore Deposits of the Hamersley Province Related to the Breakup of Paleoproterozoic Australia: New Insights from In Situ SHRIMP Dating of Baddeleyite from Mafic Intrusions," *Geology* 33 (July 2005): 577; and reply to comment, Stefan G. Müller et al., "Giant Iron-Ore Deposits of the Hamersley Province Related to the Breakup of Paleoproterozoic Australia: New Insights from In Situ SHRIMP Dating of Baddeleyite from Mafic Intrusions: Comment and Reply," *Geology* 34 (January 2006): e97, doi: 10.1130/G22654.1.

18. David L. Huston et al., "Lode-Gold Mineralization in the Tanami Region, Northern Australia," *Mineralium Deposita* 42 (January 2007): 175–204.

19. Xin-Fu Zhao et al., "Late Paleoproterozoic Sedimentary Rock-Hosted Stratiform Copper Deposits in South China: Their Possible Link to the Supercontinent Cycle," *Mineralium* 48 (January 2013): 129–36.

20. Denis Gapais et al., "Pop-Down Tectonics, Fluid Channelling and Ore Deposits within Ancient Hot Orogens," *Tectonophysics* 618 (March 2014): 102–6.

21. Marcel G. A. van der Heijen, Richard D. Bardgett, and Nico M. van Straalen, "The Unseen Majority: Soil Microbes as Drivers of Plant Diversity and Productivity in Terrestrial Ecosystems," *Ecology Letters* 11 (March 2008): 296–310.

22. Wolfgang Elbert et al., "Contribution of Cryptogamic Covers to the Global Cycles of Carbon and Nitrogen," *Nature Geoscience* 5 (July 2012): 459–62.

23. G. J. Michaelson, C. Ping, and D. A. Walker, "Biogeochemistry of Soils Associated with Cryptogamic Crusts on Frost Boils," *EoS, Transactions American Geophysical Union* 83, Fall Meeting Supplemental (2002): abstract B12A-0778.

24. Grant McTainsh and Craig Strong, "The Role of Aeolian Dust in Ecosystems," *Geomorphology* 89 (September 2007): 39–54; John F. Leys and David J. Eldridge, "Influence of Cryptogamic Crust Disturbance to Wind Erosion on Sand and Loam Rangeland Soils," *Earth Surface Processes and Landforms* 23 (November 1998): 963–74.

25. Jayne Belnap, "The World at Your Feet: Desert Biological Soil Crusts," *Frontiers in Ecology and the Environment* 1 (May 2003): 181–89.

26. Van der Heijen et al., "Unseen Majority," 296–310; Michaelson, Ping, and Walker, "Biogeochemistry of Soils," abstract B12A-0778.

27. Wendy J. Williams and David J. Eldridge, "Deposition of Sand over a Cyanobacterial Soil Crust Increases Nitrogen Bioavailability in a Semi-Arid Woodland," *Applied Soil Ecology* 49 (September 2011): 26–31.

## Chapter 12  Heating and Ventilation

1. Carl Sagan and George Mullen, "Earth and Mars: Evolution of Atmospheres and Surface Temperatures," *Science* 177 (July 1972): 52–56.

2. A brighter Sun with no compensating factor would generate a runaway evaporation of Earth's surface liquid water, turning it into vapor. As a greenhouse gas, the extra water vapor would trap more of the Sun's heat, causing yet more evaporation and so on until all the planet's surface liquid water would be converted into water vapor. On the other hand, a *dimmer* Sun without any compensating factor would generate a runaway freezing of surface water. A dimmer Sun would cause greater snowfalls. Snow is more reflective than soil, rock, or liquid water. Extra reflection of sunlight would cool Earth's surface. This extra cooling would cause more snow to fall and even more sunlight to be reflected away from Earth. Eventually, Earth's entire surface would be covered in snow or ice. The sensitivity of Earth's life to small changes in the Sun's luminosity was first explained and calculated by Michael Hart, "Habitable Zones about Main Sequence Stars," *Icarus* 37 (January 1979): 351–57.

3. James F. Kasting, "Stability of Ammonia in the Primitive Terrestrial Atmosphere," *Journal of Geophysical Research: Oceans* 87 (April 1982): 3091–98.

4. William R. Kuhn and James F. Kasting, "Effects of Increased $CO_2$ Concentrations on Surface Temperature of the Early Earth," *Nature* 301 (January 1983): 53–55; James F. Kasting, James B. Pollack, and David Crisp, "Effects of High $CO_2$ Levels on Surface Temperature and Atmospheric Oxidation State of the Early Earth," *Journal of Atmospheric Chemistry* 1 (1984): 403–28; James F. Kasting, "Earth's Early Atmosphere," *Science* 259 (February 1993): 920–26.

5. Alexander A. Pavlov et al., "High Methane Abundance throughout Precambrian," *EoS, Transactions American Geophysical Union* 85, Spring Meeting Supplemental (May 2004): abstract U22A-04; Alexander A. Pavlov et al., "High Methane Abundance in the Archean and Proterozoic Atmosphere: Why $CO_2$ Is Not Enough," *EoS, Transactions American Geophysical Union* 84, Fall Meeting Supplemental (2003): abstract PP21B-1168.

6. Pavlov et al., "High Methane Abundance in the Archean and Proterozoic Atmosphere," abstract PP21B-1168.

7. Michael T. Mellon, "Limits on the $CO_2$ Content of the Martian Polar Deposits," *Icarus* 124 (November 1996): 268–79.

8. Rob Rye, Phillip H. Kuo, and Heinrich D. Holland, "Atmospheric Carbon Dioxide Concentrations before 2.2 Billion Years Ago," *Nature* 378 (December 1995): 603–5.

9. Alexander A. Pavlov et al., "Methane-Rich Proterozoic Atmosphere?," *Geology* 31 (January 2003): 87; Pavlov et al., "High Methane Abundance in the Archean and Proterozoic Atmosphere," abstract PP21B-1168; Pavlov et al., "High Methane Abundance throughout Precambrian," abstract U22A-04.

10. Minik T. Rosing et al., "No Climate Paradox under the Faint Early Sun," *Nature* 464 (April 2010): 744.

11. Ibid.

12. Colin Goldblatt et al., "Nitrogen-Enhanced Greenhouse Warming on Early Earth," *Nature Geoscience* 2 (December 2009): 891–96.

13. Sanjoy M. Som et al., "Air Density 2.7 Billion Years Ago Limited to Less Than Twice Modern Levels by Fossil Raindrop Imprints," *Nature* 484 (April 2012): 359–62.

14. S. Kadoya and E. Tajika, "Conditions for Oceans on Earth-Like Planets Orbiting within the Habitable Zone: Importance of Volcanic $CO_2$ Degassing," *Astrophysical Journal* 790 (August 2014): id. 107, doi:10.1088/0004-637X/790/2/107.

15. Rosing et al., "No Climate Paradox," 744–47.

16. Colin Goldblatt and Kevin J. Zahnle, "Faint Young Sun Paradox Remains," *Nature* 474 (June 2011): E1, doi:10.1038/nature09961.

17. C. Goldblatt and Kevin J. Zahnle, "Clouds and the Faint Young Sun Paradox," *Climate of the Past* 7 (March 2011): 203–20.

18. Christopher T. Reinhard and Noah J. Planavsky, "Mineralogical Constraints on Precambrian $pCO_2$," *Nature* 474 (June 2011): E1, doi:10.1038/nature09959; N. Dauphas and James F. Kasting, "Low $pCO_2$ in the Pore Water, Not in the Archean Air," *Nature* 474 (June 2011): E1, doi:10.1038/nature09960.

19. Minik T. Rosing et al., "Rosing, Bird, Sleep and Bjerrum Reply," *Nature* 474 (June 2011): E1, doi:10.1038/nature09962.

20. G. Le Hir et al., "The Faint Young Sun Problem Revisited with a 3-D Climate-Carbon Model—Part 1," *Climate of the Past Discussions* 9 (March 2013): 1509–34; G. Le Hir et al., "The Faint Young Sun Problem Revisited with a 3-D Climate-Carbon Model—Part 2," *Climate of the Past* 10 (April 2014): 697–713; B. Charnay et al., "Exploring the Faint Young Sun Problem and the Possible Climates of the Archean Earth with a 3-D GCM," *Journal of Geophysical Research: Atmospheres* 118 (September 2013): 10414–31.

21. Ibid.

22. Ibid.

23. Alexander A. Pavlov et al., "Passing through a Giant Molecular Cloud: 'Snowball' Glaciations Produced by Interstellar Dust," *Geophysical Research Letters* 32 (February 2005): L03705.

24. George E. Williams, "History of the Earth's Obliquity," *Earth-Science Reviews* 34 (March 1993): 1–45.

25. Gregory S. Jenkins, "Global Climate Model High-Obliquity Solutions to the Ancient Climate Puzzles of the Faint-Young Sun Paradox and Low-Altitude Proterozoic Glaciation," *Journal of Geophysical Research: Atmospheres* 105 (March 2000): 7357–70.

26. Michael D. Rutter et al., "Towards Evaluating the Viscosity of the Earth's Outer Core: An Experimental High Pressure Study of Liquid Fe-S (8.5 wt.% S)," *Geophysical Research Letters* 29 (April 2002): 58-1–58-4; P. W. Livermore, R. Hollerbach, and A. Jackson, "Reconciling Westward Drift and Inner-Core Super-Rotation in Very Low Viscosity Models of the Geodynamo," *American Geophysical Union*, Fall Meeting 2012 (December 2012): abstract DI31A-2388; D. E. Smylie, Vadim V. Brazhkin, and Andrew Palmer, "Direct Observations of the Viscosity of Earth's Outer Core and Extrapolation of Measurements of the Viscosity of Liquid Iron," *Physics-Uspekhi* 52 (2009): 79.

27. Darren M. Williams, James F. Kasting, and Lawrence A. Frakes, "Low-Latitude Glaciation and Rapid Changes in the Earth's Obliquity Explained by Obliquity-Oblateness Feedback," *Nature* 396 (December 1998): 453–55.

28. Gongjie Li and Konstantin Batygin, "Pre-Late Heavy Bombardment Evolution of the Earth's Obliquity," *Astrophysical Journal* 795 (November 2014): id. 67.

29. Nir G. Shaviv, "Toward a Solution to the Early Faint Sun Paradox: A Lower Cosmic Ray Flux from a Stronger Solar Wind," *Journal of Geophysical Research: Space Physics* 108 (December 2003): id. 1437.

30. Vincent Chevrier, Francois Poulet, and Jean-Pierre Bibring, "Early Geochemical Environment of Mars as Determined from Thermodynamics of Phyllosilicates," *Nature* 448 (July 2007): 60–63; Takasumi Karahashi-Nakamura and Eiichi Tajika, "Atmospheric Collapse and Transport of Carbon Dioxide into the Subsurface on Early Mars," *Geophysical Research Letters* 33 (September 2006): id. L18205.

31. Daniel P. Whitmire et al., "A Slightly More Massive Young Sun as an Explanation for Warm Temperatures on Early Mars," *Journal of Geophysical Research: Planets* 100 (March 1995): 5457–64.

32. I.-Juliana Sackmann and Arnold I. Boothroyd, "Our Sun. v. A Bright Young Sun Consistent with Helioseismology and Warm Temperatures on Ancient Earth and Mars," *Astrophysical Journal* 583 (February 2003): 1024–39.

33. Eric J. Gaidos, Manuel Güdel, and Geoffrey A. Blake, "The Faint Young Sun Paradox: An Observational Test of an Alternative Solar Model," *Geophysical Research Letters* 27 (February 2000): 501–3.

34. A separate study, B. E. Wood et al., "New Mass-Loss Measurements from Astrospheric Lyα Absorption," *Astrophysical Journal Letters* 628 (August 2005): L143–L146, calls into question relevant mass-loss rates as high as $10^{-11}$ solar mass/year. Measurements of stellar wind mass loss rates of eleven Sun-like stars spanning in age from 0.36–6.5 billion years showed mass losses ranging from $3 \times 10^{-12}$ to $1 \times 10^{-14}$ solar mass/year. The measurement uncertainties, however, were high and the expected inverse correlation of mass loss rate with age was barely evident.

35. Christene R. Lynch, R. L. Mutel, and K. G. Gayley, "Is a High Mass Loss Rate for the Sun a Solution to the Faint Young Sun Paradox?," *Bulletin of the American Astronomical Society* 43, American Astronomical Society, AAS 217th Meeting (January 2011): abstract 319.04; Bibiana Fichtinger et al., "Analysis of Stellar Winds of Solar-Like Stars with the JVLA and ALMA to Define Mass Loss Rates for the Young Sun" (poster presented at Protostars and Planets VI, Heidelberg July 15–20, 2013, poster 1K098).

36. Alicia N. Aarnio, Sean P. Matt, and Keivan G. Stassun, "Mass Loss in Pre-Main-Sequence Stars via Coronal Mass Ejections and Implications for Angular Momentum Loss," *Astrophysical Journal* 760 (November 2012): id. 9, doi:10.1088/0004-637X/760/1/9.

37. Joyce Ann Guzik and Katie Mussack, "Exploring Mass Loss, Low-Z Accretion, and Convective Overshoot in Solar Models to Mitigate the Solar Abundance Problem," *Astrophysical Journal* 713 (April 2010): 1108–19, doi:10.1088/0004-637X/713/2/1108.

38. Sylvaine Turck-Chièze, Laurent Piau, and Sébastian Couvidat, "The Solar Energetic Balance Revisited by Young Solar Analogs, Helioseismology, and Neutrinos," *Astrophysical Journal Letters* 731 (April 2011): L29.

39. O. Cohen and J. J. Drake, "A Grid of MHD Models for Stellar Mass Loss and Spin-Down Rates of Solar Analogs," *Astrophysical Journal* 783 (March 2014): id. 55, doi:10.1088/0004-637X/783/1/55.

40. Ibid., id. 55, 1.

41. Courtney R. Epstein and Marc H. Pinsonneault, "How Good a Clock Is Rotation? The Stellar Rotation-Mass-Age Relationship for Old Field Stars," *Astrophysical Journal* 780 (January 2014): id. 159, doi:10.1088/0004-637X/780/2/159; D. J. A. Brown et al., "Are Falling Planets Spinning Up Their Host Stars?," *Monthly Notices of the Royal Astronomical Society* 415 (July 2011): 605–18; J.-D. do Nascimento Jr. et al., "Rotation Periods and Ages

for Solar Analogs and Solar Twins Revealed by the *Kepler* Mission," *Astrophysical Journal Letters* 790 (August 2014): L23.

42. N. V. Erkaev et al., "Escape of the Martian Protoastmosphere and Initial Water Inventory," *Planetary and Space Science* 98 (August 2014): 106–19.

43. The coverage of Earth's surface by continents and islands is still increasing, albeit at a slower rate than in the past: Kent C. Condie and C. Storey, "Growth of Continental Crust: A Balance between Preservation and Recycling," *Mineralogical Magazine* 78 (June 2014): 623–37; Nicolas Coltice, Tobias Rolf, and Paul J. Tackley, "Seafloor Spreading Evolution in Response to Continental Growth," *Geology* 42 (March 2014): 235–38; Bruno Dhuime et al., "A Change in the Geodynamics of Continental Growth 3 Billion Years Ago," *Science* 335 (March 2012): 1334–36.

## Chapter 13 The Structure Rises

1. Linda T. Elkins-Tanton and Sara Seager, "Ranges of Atmospheric Mass and Composition of Super-Earth Exoplanets," *Astrophysical Journal* 685 (October 2008): 1237–46; Hugh Ross, "Planet Formation: Problems with Water, Carbon, and Air," *Today's New Reason to Believe* (blog), January 12, 2009, http://www.reasons.org/rtbs-creation-model/cosmic -design/planet-formation-problems-too-much-water-too-much-carbon-and-too-much-air.

2. Elkins-Tanton and Seager, "Ranges of Atmospheric Mass," 1237–46; Ross, "Planet Formation," http://www.reasons.org/rtbs-creation-model/cosmic-design/planet-formation -problems-too-much-water-too-much-carbon-and-too-much-air.

3. Matthew Pasek, Dominic Papineau, and Jelte Harnmeijer, "Session 15. The Evolution of the Biogeochemical Cycling of Phosphorus and Other Bioessential Elements," *Astrobiology* 8 (April 2008): 356–61, see specifically M. S. Sisodia, "15-17-P. Evidences Support an Extraordinary Event, Possibly an Impact during the Proterozoic for Phosphorus Abundance on the Earth," 360; Hugh Ross, "Where Did Earth Get Its Phosphorus?," *Reasons to Believe*, October 13, 2008, http://www.reasons.org/where-did-earth-get-its-phosphorus.

4. Fabrice Gaillard and Bruno Scaillet, "The Sulfur Content of Volcanic Gases on Mars," *Earth and Planetary Science Letters* 279 (March 2009): 34–43; Hugh Ross, "Sulfur-Poor Earth Conducive to Life," *Today's New Reason to Believe* (blog), May 4, 2009, http://www .reasons.org/articles/sulfur-poor-earth-conducive-to-life; Jack Farmer and David Des Marais, "Session 29. The New Mars: Habitability of a Neighbor World," *Astrobiology* 8 (April 2008): 431–36, see specifically, Benton Clark, "29-08-O. Death By Sulfur: Consequences of Ubiquitous S before and after the Biotic Transition, for Mars and Other S-Rich Planets," *Astrobiology* 8 (April 2008): 433.

5. Michael J. Benton, *When Life Nearly Died: The Greatest Mass Extinction of All Time* (London: Thames and Hudson, 2003); Zhong-Qiang Chen and Michael J. Benton, "The Timing and Pattern of Biotic Recovery following the End-Permian Mass Extinction," *Nature Geoscience* 5 (June 2012): 375–83; Bernadette C. Proemse et al., "Ocean Anoxia Did Not Cause the Latest Permian Extinction," *Geophysical Research Abstracts* 16, EGU General Assembly (May 2014): abstract 9089. I describe the sources of these biodeposits and provide extensive citations in chapter 17 of my book, *Navigating Genesis: A Scientist's Journey through Genesis 1–11* (Covina, CA: RTB Press, 2014).

6. Gennady G. Kochemasov, "On the Uniqueness of Earth as a Harbor of Steady Life: A Comparative Planetology Approach," *Astrobiology* 7 (June 2007): 518.

7. D. M. Raup and J. John Sepkoski Jr., "Periodicity of Extinctions in the Geologic Past," *Proceedings of the National Academy of Sciences, USA* 81 (February 1984): 801–5.

8. Adrian L. Melott and Richard K. Bambach, "Nemesis Reconsidered," *Monthly Notices of the Royal Astronomical Society Letters* 407 (September 2010): L99–L102.

9. Felix M. Gradstein et al., eds., *The Geologic Time Scale* (Amsterdam: Elsevier, 2012).

10. Adrian L. Melott and Richard K. Bambach, "Do Periodicities in Extinction—With Possible Astronomical Connections—Survive a Revision of the Geological Timescale?," *Astrophysical Journal* 773 (August 2013): id. 6, doi:10.1088/0004-637X/773/1/6.

11. Ibid.

12. W. M. Napier, "Evidence for Cometary Bombardment Episodes," *Monthly Notices of the Royal Astronomical Society* 366 (March 2006): 977–82; John J. Maltese et al., "Why We Study the Geological Record for Evidence of the Solar Oscillation about the Galactic Midplane," *Earth, Moon, and Planets* 72 (February 1996): 7–12; John J. Matese et al., "Periodic Modulation of the Oort Cloud Flux by the Adiabatically Changing Galactic Tide," *Icarus* 116 (August 1995): 255–68.

13. Richard B. Stothers, "The Period Dichotomy in Terrestrial Impact Crater Ages," *Monthly Notices of the Royal Astronomical Society* 365 (January 2006): 178–80.

14. Michael R. Rampino, "Disc Dark Matter in the Galaxy and Potential Cycles of Extraterrestrial Impacts, Mass Extinctions, and Geological Events," *Monthly Notices of the Royal Astronomical Society* 448 (April 2015): 1816–20.

15. Ibid., 1816.

16. Y. Goddéris et al., "The Sturtian 'Snowball' Glaciation: Fire and Ice," *Earth and Planetary Science Letters* 211 (June 2003): 1–12; Paul F. Hoffman et al., "A Neoproterozoic Snowball Earth," *Science* 281 (August 1998): 1342–46.

17. Francis A. Macdonald et al., "Calibrating the Cryogenian," *Science* 327 (March 2010): 1241–43.

18. Graham Anthony Shields, "Palaeoclimate: Marinoan Meltdown," *Nature Geoscience* 1 (June 2008): 351–53; Ian J. Fairchild and Martin J. Kennedy, "Neoproterozoic Glaciation in the Earth System," *Journal of the Geological Society of London* 164 (September 2007): 895–921.

19. Gradstein et al., *Geologic Time Scale*, 428.

20. Zheng-Xiang Li, David A. D. Evans, and Galen P. Halverson, "Neoproterozoic Glaciations in a Revised Global Palaeogeography from the Breakup of Rodinia to the Assembly of Gondwanaland," *Sedimentary Geology* 294 (August 2013): 219–32; Goddéris et al., "Sturtian 'Snowball' Glaciation," 1–12.

21. Goddéris et al., "Sturtian 'Snowball' Glaciation," 1–12.

22. Alan D. Rooney et al., "A Cryogenian Chronology: Two Long-Lasting Synchronous Neoproterozoic Glaciations," *Geology* 43 (May 2015): 459–62; Qin Ye et al., "The Survival of Benthic Macroscopic Phototrophs on a Neoproterozoic Snowball Earth," *Geology* 43 (June 2015): 507–10.

23. Ye et al., ibid.

24. Benjamin Mills et al., "Timing of Neoproterozoic Glaciations Linked to Transport-Limited Global Weathering," *Nature Geoscience* 4 (December 2011): 861–64.

25. Fairchild and Kennedy, "Neoproterozoic Glaciation," 895–921.

26. Graham Shields, "Possible Connections between the Precambrian Carbonate Record, the Faint Young Sun Paradox and Neoproterozoic Glaciation," *EGS-AGU-EUG Joint Assembly* (April 2003): abstract 10825; Alexander A. Pavlov et al., "A Methane-Rich Proterozoic Atmosphere: Possible Link to the Neoproterozoic Snowball Earth Glaciations," *EoS, Transactions American Geophysical Union* 82, Fall Meeting Supplemental (2001): abstract PP42B-0522.

27. Fairchild and Kennedy, "Neoproterozoic Glaciation," 895–921.

28. N. Butterfield, "The Eukaryotic Fossil Record in Deep Time," *American Geophysical Union*, Fall Meeting (2011): abstract B33L-04.

29. Don E. Canfield, Simon W. Poulton, and Guy M. Narbonne, "Late-Neoproterozoic Deep-Ocean Oxygenation and the Rise of Animal Life," *Science* 315 (January 2007): 92–95; D. T. Johnston et al., "Late Ediacaran Redox Stability and Metazoan Evolution," *Earth and Planetary Science Letters* 335–336 (June 2012): 25–35.

30. Canfield, Poulton, and Narbonne, "Late-Neoproterozoic Deep-Ocean Oxygenation," 92–95; Guy M. Narbonne and James G. Gehling, "Life after Snowball: The Oldest Complex Ediacaran Fossils," *Geology* 31 (January 2003): 27–30; Guy M. Narbonne, "The Ediacara Biota: Neoproterozoic Origin of Animals and Their Ecosystems," *Annual Review of Earth and Planetary Sciences* 33 (May 2005): 421–42.

31. Narbonne and Gehling, "Life after Snowball," 27–30; Narbonne, "Ediacara Biota," 421–42.

32. Narbonne, "Ediacara Biota," 421–42.

33. A. A. Venn, J. E. Loram, and A. E. Douglas, "Photosynthetic Symbioses in Animals," *Journal of Experimental Botany* 59 (March 2008): 1069–80.

34. Narbonne, "Ediacara Biota," 421–42.

35. Johnson et al., "Late Ediacaran Redox Stability," 25–35.

36. Mikhail A. Fedonkin and Benjamin M. Waggoner, "The Late Precambrian Fossil *Kimberella* Is a Mollusc-Like Bilaterian Organism," *Nature* 388 (August 1997): 868–71.

37. Narbonne, "Ediacara Biota," 421–42.

38. Ibid., 436.

39. Hiroto Kimura and Yoshio Watanabe, "Oceanic Anoxia at the Precambrian-Cambrian Boundary," *Geology* 29 (November 2001): 995–98.

40. R. D. K. Thomas, Rebecca M. Shearman, and Graham W. Stewart, "Evolutionary Exploitation of Design Options by the First Animals with Hard Skeletons," *Science* 288 (May 2000): 1239–42.

41. Artem Kouchinsky et al., "Chronology of Early Cambrian Biomineralization," *Geological Magazine* 149 (March 2012): 221–51; Shanan E. Peters and Robert R. Gaines, "Formation of the 'Great Unconformity' as a Trigger for the Cambrian Explosion," *Nature* 484 (April 2012): 363–66.

42. Tomoko Ishikawa et al., "Carbon Isotope Chemostratigraphy of a Precambrian/ Cambrian Boundary Section in the Three Gorges Area, South China: Prominent Global-Scale Isotope Excursions Just before the Cambrian Explosion," *Gondwana Research* 14 (August 2008): 193–208.

43. J. Han, Z.-F. Zhang, and J.-N. Liu, "A Preliminary Note on the Dispersal of the Cambrian Burgess Shale-Type Faunas," *Gondwana Research* 14 (August 2008): 269–76.

44. D.-G. Shu et al., "Lower Cambrian Vertebrates from South China," *Nature* 402 (November 1999): 42–46.

45. Simon Conway Morris and Jean-Bernard Caron, "A Primitive Fish from the Cambrian of North America," *Nature* 512 (August 2014): 419–22.

46. Jun-Yuan Chen, Di-Ying Huang, and Chia-Wei Li, "An Early Cambrian Craniate-Like Chordate," *Nature* 402 (December 1999): 518–22.

47. Xiaoya Ma et al., "Complex Brain and Optic Lobes in an Early Cambrian Arthropod," *Nature* 490 (October 2012): 258–61.

48. Xiaoya Ma et al., "An Exceptionally Preserved Arthropod Cardiovascular System from the Early Cambrian," *Nature Communications* 5 (April 2014): id. 3560, doi:10.1038 /ncomms4560.

49. D.-G. Shu et al., "Primitive Deuterostomes from the Chengjiang Lagerstätte (Lower Cambrian, China)," *Nature* 414 (November 2001): 424.

50. Andrew R. Parker et al., "An Unusual Cornea from a Well Preserved ('Orsten') Cambrian Compound Eye," *Paleontological Research* 17 (August 2013): 251–61; Andrew R. Parker, "On the Origin of Optics," *Optics and Laser Technology* 43 (March 2011): 323–29.

51. Xi-Guang Zhang and Brian R. Pratt, "The First Stalk-Eyed Phosphatocopine Crustacean from the Lower Cambrian of China," *Current Biology* 22 (November 2012): 2149–54; Christopher Castellani et al., "Exceptionally Well-Preserved Isolated Eyes from Cambrian 'Orsten' Fossil Assemblages of Sweden," *Paleontology* 55 (May 2012): 553–66.

52. Martin Stein et al., "*Isoxys* (Arthropoda) with Preserved Soft Anatomy from the Sirius Passet Lagerstätte, Lower Cambrian of North Greenland," *Lethaia* 43 (June 2010): 258–65; Jean Vannier and Jun-Yuan Chen, "The Early Cambrian Colonization of Pelagic Niches Exemplified by *Isoxys* (Arthropoda)," *Lethaia* 33 (December 2000): 295–311.

53. Simon Conway Morris, "The Community Structure of the Middle Cambrian Phyllopod Bed (Burgess Shale)," *Paleontology* 29 (1986): 423–67.

54. Parker, "Origin of Optics," 323.

55. Richard Dawkins, *The Blind Watchmaker: Why the Evidence of Evolution Reveals a Universe without Design* (New York: W. W. Norton, 1987), 229.

56. Jeffrey S. Levinton, "The Cambrian Explosion: How Do We Use the Evidence," *BioScience* 58 (October 2008): 855.

57. Gregory A. Wray, "Rates of Evolution in Developmental Processes," *American Zoologist* 32 (January–February 1992): 131.

58. Kevin J. Peterson, Michael R. Dietrich, and Mark A. McPeek, "MicroRNAs and Metazoan Macroevolution: Insights into Canalization, Complexity, and the Cambrian Explosion," *BioEssays* 31 (July 2009): 737.

59. Jaime E. Blair and S. Blair Hedges, "Molecular Clocks Do Not Support the Cambrian Explosion," *Molecular Biology and Evolution* 22 (March 2005): 387–90.

60. L. D. Bromham and M. D. Hendy, "Can Fast Early Rates Reconcile Molecular Dates with the Cambrian Explosion?," *Proceedings of the Royal Society B* 267 (May 2000): 1041–47.

61. Levinton, "Cambrian Explosion," 858.

62. Thomas Cavalier-Smith, "Cell Evolution and Earth History: Stasis and Revolution," *Philosophical Transactions of the Royal Society B* 361 (June 2006): 969–1006.

## Chapter 14 Finishing Touches

1. Seth A. Young et al., "Did Changes in Atmospheric $CO_2$ Coincide with Latest Ordovician Glacial-Interglacial Cycles?," *Palaeogeography, Palaeoclimatology, Palaeoecology* 296 (October 2010): 376–88.

2. Peter M. Sheehan, "The Late Ordovician Mass Extinction," *Annual Review of Earth and Planetary Sciences* 29 (May 2001): 331–64.

3. Ibid.

4. Axel Munnecke et al., "Ordovician and Silurian Sea-Water Chemistry, Sea Level, and Climate: A Synopsis," *Palaeogeography, Palaeoclimatology, Palaeoecology* 296 (October 2010): 389–413.

5. Heather M. Wilson and Lyall I. Anderson, "Morphology and Taxonomy of Paleozoic Millipedes (Diplopoda: Chilognatha: Archipolypoda) from Scotland," *Journal of Paleontology* 78 (January 2004): 169–84.

6. Mats E. Eriksson, Eva K. Nilsson, and Lennart Jeppsson, "Vertebrate Extinctions and Reorganizations during the Late Silurian Lau Event," *Geology* 37 (August 2009): 739–42.

7. Mikael Calner, "A Late Silurian Extinction Event and Anachronistic Period," *Geology* 33 (April 2005): 305–8.

8. Mikael Calner and Mårten J. Eriksson, "Evidence for Rapid Environmental Changes in Low Latitudes during the Late Silurian Lau Event: The Burgen-1 Drillcore, Gotland, Sweden," *Geological Magazine* 143 (January 2006): 15–24.

9. Gregory J. Retallack, "Early Forest Soils and Their Role in Devonian Global Change," *Science* 276 (April 1997): 583–85; Walter L. Cressler III, "Evidence of Earliest Known Wildfires," *Palaios* 16 (April 2001): 171–74.

10. Robert A. Berner, "Atmospheric Oxygen over Phanerozoic Time," *Proceedings of the National Academy of Sciences, USA* 96 (September 1999): 10955–57; Andrew C. Scott and Ian J. Glasspool, "The Diversification of Paleozoic Fire Systems and Fluctuations in Atmospheric Oxygen Concentration," *Proceedings of the National Academy of Sciences, USA* 103 (July 2006): 10861–65; Claire M. Belcher et al., "Fuelling the Palaeoatmospheric Oxygen Debate: How Much Atmospheric Oxygen Is Required for Ignition and Propagation of Smoldering Fires?," *Geophysical Research Abstracts* 12, EGU General Assembly (May 2010): abstract 6364.

11. George R. McGhee, *The Late Devonian Mass Extinction: The Frasnian/Famennian Crisis* (New York: Columbia University Press 1996), 303.

12. Leszek Marynowski et al., "Deciphering the Upper Famennian Hangenberg Black Shale Depositional Environments Based On Multi-Proxy Record," *Palaeogeography, Palaeoclimatology, Palaeoecology* 346–347 (August 2012): 66–86.

13. Thomas J. Algeo and Stephen E. Scheckler, "Terrestrial-Marine Teleconnections in the Devonian: Links between the Evolution of Land Plants, Weathering Processes, and Marine Anoxic Events," *Philosophical Transactions of the Royal Society B* 353 (January 1998): 113–30.

14. Some researchers cite fossil evidence of very large insects as evidence for oxygen levels as high as 35 percent by volume. However, that much oxygen would cause virtually all of Earth's land vegetation to be consumed by wildfires. The persistence of forests throughout the Carboniferous and succeeding geological eras sets an upper limit of about 30 percent by volume. See Scott and Glasspool, "Diversification of Paleozoic Fire," 10861–65; T. M. Lenton, "Fires and the Rise and Regulation of Atmospheric Oxygen," *Geophysical Research Abstracts* 14, EGU General Assembly (April 2012): abstract 12930.

15. Shu-Zhong Shen et al., "Calibrating the End-Permian Mass Extinction," *Science* 334 (December 2011): 1367–72.

16. Bernadette C. Proemse et al., "Ocean Anoxia Did Not Cause the Latest Permian Extinction," *Geophysical Research Abstracts* 16, EGU General Assembly (May 2014): abstract 9089; Sarda Sahney and Michael J. Benton, "Recovery from the Most Profound Mass Extinction of All Time," *Proceedings of the Royal Society B* 275 (April 2008): 759–65.

17. Conrad C. Labandeira and J. John Sepkoski Jr., "Insect Diversity in the Fossil Record," *Science* 261 (July 1993): 310–15.

18. Ralph R. B. von Frese et al., "GRACE Gravity Evidence for an Impact Basin in Wilkes Land, Antarctica," *Geochemistry, Geophysics, Geosystems* 10 (February 2009): id. Q02014, doi:10.1029/2008GC002149.

19. Victoria A. Hudspith, Susan M. Rimmer, and Claire M. Belcher, "Latest Permian Chars May Derive from Wildfires, Not Coal Combustion," *Geology* 43 (May 2015): e363.

20. Yadong Sun et al., "Lethally Hot Temperatures during the Early Triassic Greenhouse," *Science* 338 (October 2012): 366–70.

21. Alexa R. C. Sedlacek et al., "87Sr/86Sr Stratigraphy from the Early Triassic of Zal, Iran: Linking Temperature to Weathering Rates and the Tempo of Ecosystem Recovery," *Geology* 42 (September 2014): 779–82.

22. Terrence J. Blackburn et al., "Zircon U-Pb Geochronology Links the End-Triassic Extinction with the Central Atlantic Magmatic Province," *Science* 340 (May 2013): 943.

23. Paul E. Olsen et al., "Continental Triassic-Jurassic Boundary in Central Pangea: Recent Progress and Discussion of an Ir Anomaly," in *Catastrophic Events and Mass Extinctions: Impacts and Beyond*, ed. Christian Koeberl and Kenneth G. MacLeod (Boulder, CO: Geological Society of America, 2002), 505–22.

24. Michael J. Benton, "Diversification and Extinction in the History of Life," *Science* 268 (April 1995): 52–58.

25. Blackburn et al., "Zircon U-Pb Geochronology," 941–45.

26. Ibid.

27. Morgan F. Schaller, James D. Wright, and Dennis V. Kent, "Atmospheric $p$CO$_2$ Perturbations Associated with the Central Atlantic Magmatic Province," *Science* 331 (March 2011): 1404–9.

28. Ibid.

29. Micha Ruhl et al., "Atmospheric Carbon Injection Linked to End-Triassic Mass Extinction," *Science* 333 (July 2011): 430–34; D. J. Beerling and R. A. Berner, "Biogeochemical Constraints on the Triassic-Jurassic Boundary Carbon Cycle Event," *Global Biogeochemical Cycles* 16 (September 2002): 10-1–10.13.

30. Caroline M. B. Jaraula et al., "Elevated $p$CO$_2$ Leading to Late Triassic Extinction, Persistent Photic Zone Euxinia, and Rising Sea Levels," *Geology* 41 (September 2013): 955–58.

31. Sarah E. Greene et al., "Recognizing Ocean Acidification in Deep Time: An Evaluation of the Evidence for Acidification across the Triassic-Jurassic Boundary," *Earth-Science Reviews* 113 (June 2012): 72–93; Sarah E. Greene et al., "A Subseafloor Carbonate Factory across the Triassic-Jurassic Transition," *Geology* 40 (November 2012): 1043–46.

32. R. C. Martindale et al., "The Evidence for Ocean Acidification across the Triassic-Jurassic Boundary," *American Geophysical Union*, Fall Meeting (December 2012): abstract PP21D-07.

33. Kenneth H. Williford et al., "An Organic Record of Terrestrial Ecosystem Collapse and Recovery at the Triassic-Jurassic Boundary in East Greenland," *Geochimica et Cosmochimica Acta* 127 (February 2014): 251–63; Claire M. Belcher et al., "Increased Fire Activity at the Triassic/Jurassic Boundary in Greenland Due to Climate-Driven Floral Change," *Nature Geoscience* 3 (June 2010): 426–29.

34. József Pálfy and Norbert Zajzon, "Environmental Changes across the Triassic-Jurassic Boundary and Coeval Volcanism Inferred from Elemental Geochemistry and Mineralogy in the Kendlbachgraben Section (Northern Calcareous Alps, Austria)," *Earth and Planetary Science Letters* 335–336 (June 2012): 121–34.

35. J. C. McElwain, D. J. Beerling, and F. I. Woodward, "Fossil Plants and Global Warming at the Triassic-Jurassic Boundary," *Science* 285 (August 1999): 1386–90.

36. P. E. Olsen et al., "Ascent of Dinosaurs Linked to an Iridium Anomaly at the Triassic-Jurassic Boundary," *Science* 296 (May 2002): 1305–7.

37. Ibid.

38. Schaller, Wright, and Kent, "Atmospheric $p$CO$_2$Perturbations," 1404–9.

39. Zachary D. Blount, Christina Z. Borland, and Richard E. Lenski, "Historical Contingency and the Evolution of a Key Innovation in an Experimental Population of *Escherichia coli*," *Proceedings of the National Academy of Sciences, USA* 105 (June 2008): 7899–906; Zachary D. Blount et al., "Genomic Analysis of a Key Innovation in an Experimental *Escherichia coli* Population," *Nature* 489 (September 2012): 513–18; Hugh Ross, *More Than a Theory: Revealing a Testable Model for Creation* (Grand Rapids: Baker, 2009), 167–71; Hsin-Hung Chou et al., "Diminishing Returns Epistasis among Beneficial Mutations Decelerates

Adaptation," *Science* 332 (June 2011): 1190–92; Aisha I. Khan et al., "Negative Epistasis between Beneficial Mutations in an Evolving Bacterial Population," *Science* 332 (June 2011): 1193–96; Maitreya J. Dunham et al., "Characteristic Genome Rearrangements in Experimental Evolution of *Saccharomycescerevisiae*," *Proceedings of the National Academy of Sciences, USA* 99 (December 2002): 16144–49.

40. Olsen et al., "Ascent of Dinosaurs," 1307.

41. Morgan W. Kelly, Eric Sanford, and Richard K. Grosberg, "Limited Potential for Adaptation to Climate Change in a Broadly Distributed Marine Crustacean," *Proceedings of the Royal Society B* 279 (January 2012): 349–56.

42. James Buckley and Jon R. Bridle, "Loss of Adaptive Variation during Evolutionary Responses to Climate Change," *Ecology Letters* 17 (October 2014): 1316–25.

43. Ben Collen et al., "Predicting How Populations Decline to Extinction," *Philosophical Transactions of the Royal Society B* 366 (September 2011): 2577–86; Andy Purvis et al., "Predicting Extinction Risk in Declining Species," *Proceedings of the Royal Society of London B* 267 (October 2000): 1947–52; John H. Lawton and Robert M. May, eds., *Extinction Rates* (New York: Oxford University Press, 1995); Marjorie L. Reaka-Kudla, Don E. Wilson, and Edward O. Wilson, eds., *Biodiversity II: Understanding and Protecting Our Biological Resources* (Washington, DC: Joseph Henry, 1997); David H. Reed, David A. Briscoe, and Richard Frankham, "Inbreeding and Extinction: The Effect of Environmental Stress and Lineage," *Conservation Genetics* 3 (September 2002): 301–7; Richard Frankham and Katherine Ralls, "Conservation Biology: Inbreeding Leads to Extinction," *Nature* 392 (April 1998): 441–42; Julie A. Jiménez et al., "An Experimental Study of Inbreeding Depression in a Natural Habitat," *Science* 266 (October 1994): 271–73.

44. Kevin J. Gaston and Tim M. Blackburn, "Birds, Body Size and the Threat of Extinction," *Philosophical Transactions of the Royal Society of London B* 347 (January 1995): 205–12; Marcel Cardillo et al., "Multiple Causes of High Extinction Risk in Large Mammal Species," *Science* 309 (August 2005): 1239–41; German Forero-Medina et al., "Body Size and Extinction Risk in Brazilian Carnivores," *Biota Neotropica* 9 (January–March 2009): 45–50.

45. Min Wang et al., "The Oldest Record of Ornithuromorpha from the Early Cretaceous of China," *Nature Communications* 6 (May 2015): id. 6987, doi:10.1038/ncomms7987; Yaoming Hu et al., "New Basal Eutherian Mammal from the Early Cretaceous Jehol Biota, Liaoning China," *Proceedings of the Royal Society B* 217 (January 2010): 229–36; Anjali Goswami et al., "A Radiation of Arboreal Basal Eutherian Mammals Beginning in the Late Cretaceous of India," *Proceedings of the National Academy of Sciences, USA* 108 (September 2011): 16333–38; Zhe-Xi Luo et al., "An Early Cretaceous Tribosphenic Mammal and Metatherian Evolution," *Science* 302 (December 2003): 1934–40.

46. Jianliang Jia et al., "Tectonic and Climate Control of Oil Shale Deposition in the Upper Cretaceous Qingshankou Formation (Songliao Basin, NE China)," *International Journal of Earth Sciences* 102 (September 2013): 1717–34; Uwe Langrock et al., "Late Jurassic to Early Cretaceous Black Shale Formation and Paleoenvironment in High Northern Latitudes: Examples from the Norwegian-Greenland Seaway," *Paleoceanography* 18 (September 2003): id. 1074; J. O. Idowu and E. I. Enu, "Petroleum Geochemistry of Some Late Cretaceous Shales from the Lokoja Sandstone of Middle Niger Basin, Nigeria," *Journal of African Earth Sciences* 14 (April 1992): 443–55.

47. Anne-Lise Chenet et al., "Determination of Rapid Deccan Eruptions across the Cretaceous-Tertiary Boundary Using Paleomagnetic Secular Variation: 2. Constraints from Analysis of Eight New Sections and Synthesis for a 3500-m-Thick Composite Section," *Journal of Geophysical Research: Solid Earth* 114 (June 2009): id. B06103.

48. Jane Qiu, "Dinosaur Climate Probes," *Science* 348 (June 12, 2015): 1185.

49. Paul R. Renne et al., "Time Scales of Critical Events around the Cretaceous-Paleogene Boundary," *Science* 339 (February 2013): 684–87.

50. Curt Covey et al., "Global Climatic Effects of Atmospheric Dust from an Asteroid or Comet Impact on Earth," *Global and Planetary Change* 9 (December 1994): 263–73.

51. Peter Schulte et al., "The Chicxulub Asteroid Impact and Mass Extinction at the Cretaceous-Paleogene Boundary," *Science* 327 (March 2010): 1214–18; Owen B. Toon et al., "Environmental Perturbations Caused by the Impacts of Asteroids and Comets," *Reviews of Geophysics* 35 (February 1997): 41–78.

52. Paul R. Renne et al., "State Shift in Deccan Volcanism at the Cretaceous-Paleogene Boundary, Possibly Induced by Impact," *Science* 350 (October 2015): 76–78.

53. Mark A. Richards et al., "Triggering of the Largest Deccan Eruptions by the Chicxulub Impact," *Geological Society of America Bulletin* 127 (November 2015): 1507–20.

54. Tvrtko Korbar et al., "Potential Cretaceous-Paleogene Boundary Tsunami Deposit in the Intra-Tethyan Adriatic Carbonate Platform Section of Hvar (Croatia)," *Geological Society of America Bulletin* 127 (November 2015): 1666–80.

55. Johan Vellekoop et al., "Rapid Short-Term Cooling Following the Chicxulub Impact at the Cretaceous-Paleogene Boundary," *Proceedings of the National Academy of Sciences, USA* 111 (May 27, 2014): 7537–41.

56. Nicholas R. Longrich, Bhart-Anjan S. Bhullar, and Jacques A. Gauthier, "Mass Extinction of Lizards and Snakes at the Cretaceous-Paleogene Boundary," *Proceedings of the National Academy of Sciences, USA* 109 (December 26, 2012): 21396–401.

57. Toby Tyrrell, Agnostino Merico, and David Ian Armstrong McKay, "Severity of Ocean Acidification Following the End-Cretaceous Asteroid Impact," *Proceedings of the National Academy of Sciences, USA* 112 (May 26, 2015): 6556–61.

58. Vivi Vajda and Stephen McLoughlin, "Fungal Proliferation at the Cretaceous-Tertiary Boundary," *Science* 303 (March 2004): 1489.

59. D. W. Jolley et al., "Climatic Oscillations Stall Vegetation Recovery from K/Pg Event Devastation," *Journal of the Geological Society* 170 (May 2013): 477–82.

60. David Jablonski and W. G. Chaloner, "Extinctions in the Fossil Record [and Discussion]," *Philosophical Transactions of the Royal Society of London B* 344 (April 1994): 11–17; Vellekoop et al., "Rapid Short-Term Cooling," 7537–41; Schulte et al., "The Chicxulub Asteroid Impact," 1214–18; Longrich, et al., "Mass Extinction of Lizards and Snakes at the Cretaceous-Paleogene Boundary."

61. Ronald I. Dorn, "Ants as a Powerful Biotic Agent of Olivine and Plagioclase Dissolution," *Geology* 42 (September 2014): 771–74.

62. Ibid., 771.

63. L. Augusto et al., "The Enigma of the Rise of Angiosperms: Can We Untie the Knot?," *Ecology Letters* 17 (October 2014): 1326–38.

64. Ibid.

65. Ibid.

66. I describe the critical role that certain advanced birds and mammals played in the launch of civilization in my book *Hidden Treasures in the Book of Job: How the Oldest Book in the Bible Answers Today's Scientific Questions* (Grand Rapids: Baker, 2011), 131–65.

67. Labandeira and Sepkoski, "Insect Diversity," 310–15.

## Chapter 15 Ready for Occupancy

1. Stella C. Woodard et al., "Antarctic Role in Northern Hemisphere Glaciation," *Science* 346 (November 2014): 847–51.

2. Ibid.

3. Bernhard Steinberger et al., "The Key Role of Global Solid-Earth Processes in Preconditioning Greenland's Glaciation Since the Pliocene," *Terra Nova* 27 (February 2015): 1–8.

4. Ibid., 1.

5. Prakash Kumar et al., "The Rapid Drift of the Indian Tectonic Plate," *Nature* 449 (October 2007): 894–97.

6. An Zhisheng et al., "Evolution of Asian Monsoons and Phased Uplift of the Himalaya-Tibetan Plateau since Late Miocene Times," *Nature* 411 (May 2001): 62–66; Warren L. Prell and John E. Kutzbach, "Sensitivity of the Indian Monsoon to Forcing Parameters and Implications for Its Evolution," *Nature* 360 (December 1992): 647–52.

7. Matthias Kuhle, "A Relief-Specific Model of the Ice Age on the Basis of Uplift-Controlled Glacier Areas in Tibet and the Corresponding Albedo Increase as Well as Their Positive Climatological Feedback by Means of the Global Radiation Geometry," *Climate Research* 20 (February 2002): 1–7.

8. Zhisheng et al., "Asian Monsoons," 62–66.

9. Nat Rutter and Z. Ding, "Paleoclimates and Moonsoon Variations Interpreted from Micromorphogenic Features of the Beoji Paleosols, China," *Quaternary Science Reviews* 12 (1993): 853–62.

10. Shih Ya-feng et al., "Distribution, Feature, and Variations of Glaciers in China," in *World Glacier Inventory, Proceedings of the Riederalp Workshop, September 1978*, IAHS-AISH Publication No. 126 (1980): 111–16; Rex Victor Cruz et al., "10.6.2. The Himalayan Glaciers," in *Climate Change 2007: Impacts, Adaptation and Vulnerability. Contribution of Working Group II to the Fourth Assessment Report of the Intergovernmental Panel on Climate Change*, ed. Martin Parry et al. (Cambridge, UK: Cambridge University Press, 2007), 493–94; J. Graham Cogley, "Present and Future States of Himalaya and Karakoram Glaciers," *Annals of Glaciology* 52 (December 2011): 69–73.

11. Kuhle, "Relief-Specific Model," 1–7; Zhisheng et al., "Asian Monsoons," 62–66; Lewis A. Owen and Jason M. Dortch, "Nature and Timing of Quaternary Glaciation in the Himalayan-Tibetan Orogen," *Quaternary Science Reviews* 88 (March 2014): 14–54.

12. Matthias Kuhle, "Reconstruction of the 2.4 Million $km^2$ Late Pleistocene Ice Sheet on the Tibetan Plateau and Its Impact on the Global Climate," *Quaternary International* 45–46 (1998): 71–108.

13. Leopoldo D. Pena and Steven L. Goldstein, "Thermohaline Circulation Crisis and Impacts during the Mid-Pleistocene Transition," *Science* 345 (July 2014): 318–22.

14. Joseph J. Morley and Beth A. Dworetzky, "Evolving Pliocene-Pleistocene Climate: A North Pacific Perspective," *Quaternary Science Reviews* 10 (1991): 225–37; Kuhle, "Relief-Specific Model," 1–7; Matthias Kuhle, "The Tibetan Ice Sheet, Its Impact on the Palaeomonsoon and Relation to the Earth's Orbital Variations," *Polarforschung* 71 (2001): 1–13.

15. Pena and Goldstein, "Thermohaline Circulation Crisis," 318–22.

16. Guocan Wang et al., "On the Geodynamic Mechanism of Episodic Uplift of the Tibetan Plateau during the Cenozoic Era," *Acta Geologica Sinica (English Edition)* 88 (April 2014): 699–716; Xiaomin Fang et al., "Oligocene Slow and Miocene–Quaternary Rapid Deformation and Uplift of the Yumu Shan and North Qilian Shan: Evidence from High-Resolution Magnetostratigraphy and Tectonosedimentology," *Geological Society of London, Special Publications* 373 (2013): 149–71.

17. Kuhle, "Tibetan Ice Sheet," 1–13; Kuhle, "Relief-Specific Model," 1–7.

18. Zaijun Li et al., "Chronology and Paleoenvironmental Records of a Drill Core in the Central Tengger Desert of China," *Quaternary Science Reviews* 85 (February 2014): 85–98; Zhengguo Shi et al., "Simulated Variations of Eolian Dust from Inner Asian Deserts

# Notes

at the Mid-Pliocene, Last Glacial Maximum, and Present Day: Contributions from the Regional Tectonic Uplift and Global Climate Change," *Climate Dynamics* 37 (December 2011): 2289–301.

19. Fang et al., "Oligocene Slow," 149–71.

20. Owen and Dortch, "Nature and Timing," 14–54; Kuhle, "Reconstruction," 71–108; Kuhle, "Relief-Specific Model," 1–7.

21. Fang et al., "Oligocene Slow," 149–71.

22. A. S. Dyke et al., "The Laurentide and Innuitian Ice Sheets during the Last Glacial Maximum," *Quaternary Science Reviews* 21 (January 2002): 9–31; Kuhle, "Tibetan Ice Sheet," 1–13; Kuhle, "Relief-Specific Model," 1–7.

23. Shaun A. Marcott et al., "Centennial-Scale Changes in the Global Carbon Cycle during the Last Deglaciation," *Nature* 514 (October 2014): 616–19; François Baudin, Nathalie Combourieu-Nebout, and Rainer Zahn, "Signatures of Rapid Climate Changes in Organic Matter Records in the Western Mediterranean Sea during the Last Glacial Period," *Bulletin de la Societe Geologique de France* 178 (January 2007): 3–13; Thomas Blunier and Edward J. Brook, "Timing of Millennial-Scale Climate Change in Antarctica and Greenland during the Last Glacial Period," *Science* 291 (January 2001): 109–12; Gerard C. Bond and Rusty Lotti, "Iceberg Discharges into the North Atlantic on Millennial Time Scales during the Last Glaciation," *Science* 267 (February 1995): 1005–10.

24. Peter J. Richardson, Robert Boyd, and Robert L. Bettinger, "Was Agriculture Impossible during the Pleistocene but Mandatory during the Holocene? A Climate Change Hypothesis," *American Antiquity* 66 (July 2001): 387–411.

25. David S. Heeszel, Fabian Walter, and Deborah L. Kilb, "Humming Glaciers," *Geology* 42 (December 2014): 1099–102.

26. Christopher T. Hayes et al., "A Stagnation Event in the Deep South Atlantic during the Last Interglacial Period," *Science* 346 (December 2014): 1514–17.

27. Gina E. Moseley et al., "Multi-Speleothem Record Reveals Tightly Coupled Climate between Central Europe and Greenland during Marine Isotope Stage 3," *Geology* 42 (December 2014): 1043–46.

28. Borexino Collaboration, "Neutrinos from the Primary Proton-Proton Fusion Process in the Sun," *Nature* 512 (August 2014): 383–86.

29. Q. R. Ahmad et al., "Measurement of the Rate of $v_e + d \rightarrow p + p + e^-$ Interactions Produced by $^8B$ Solar Neutrinos at the Sudbury Neutrino Observatory," *Physical Review Letters* 87 (July 2001): 71301–5; Hugh Ross and Eric Agol, "Missing Solar Neutrinos Found," *Facts for Faith*, no. 9 (Q2 2002), 11, http://www.reasons.org/articles/missing-solar-neutrinos-found.

30. Narciso Benitez, Jesús Maíz-Apellániz, and Matilde Canelles, "Evidence for Nearby Supernova Explosions," *Physical Review Letters* 88 (February 2002): id. 081101.

31. Ibid.

32. R. B. Firestone, "Observation of 23 Supernovae That Exploded <300 pc from Earth during the Past 300 kyr," *Astrophysical Journal* 789 (July 2014): id. 29, doi:10.1088/0004-637X/789/1/29.

33. Ibid., id. 29, 3–4.

34. Ibid., id. 29, 2.

35. Li Weidong et al., "Nearby Supernova Rates from the Lick Observatory Supernova Search—III. The Rate-Size Relation, and the Rates as a Function of Galaxy Hubble Type and Colour," *Monthly Notices of the Royal Astronomical Society* 412 (April 2011): 1473–507; Or Graur, Federica B. Bianco, and Maryam Modjaz, "A Unified Explanation for the Supernova Rate-Galaxy Mass Dependency Based on Supernovae Discovered in Sloan Galaxy Spectra," *Monthly Notices of the Royal Astronomical Society* (forthcoming), eprint arXiv:1412.7991.

36. Michael J. Benton, "Diversification and Extinction in the History of Life," *Science* 268 (April 1995): 52–58.

37. Ibid., 53.

38. Sandra Quijas, Bernhard Schmid, and Patricia Balvanera, "Plant Diversity Enhances Provision of Ecosystem Services: A New Synthesis," *Basic and Applied Ecology* 11 (November 2010): 582–93; Sarda Sahney, Michael J. Benton, and Paul A. Perry, "Links between Global Taxonomic Diversity, Ecological Diversity and the Expansion of Vertebrates on Land," *Biology Letters* 6 (August 2010): 544–47; Jurgis Sapijanskas et al., "Tropical Tree Diversity Enhances Light Capture through Crown Plasticity and Spatial and Temporal Niche Differences," *Ecology* 95 (September 2014): 2479–92; Jenny L. Chapman and Michael B. V. Roberts, *Biodiversity: The Abundance of Life* (Cambridge, UK: Cambridge University Press, 1997).

## Chapter 16 Why We're Here

1. Lawrence M. Krauss, "No, Astrobiology Has Not Made the Case for God," *New Yorker*, January 24, 2015, http://www.newyorker.com/tech/elements/astrobiology-made-case-god.

2. Ibid., second page of the article.

3. Kenneth R. Miller, *Only a Theory: Evolution and the Battle for America's Soul* (New York: Viking, 2008), 52.

4. I discuss the benefits and the optimization of so-called natural disasters in my book, *More Than a Theory: Revealing a Testable Model for Creation* (Grand Rapids: Baker, 2009), 204–7.

5. Christopher Stringer and Robin McKie, *African Exodus: The Origins of Modern Humanity* (New York: Henry Holt, 1997), 165–66; Paul S. Martin and Richard G. Klein, eds., *Quaternary Extinctions: A Prehistoric Revolution* (Tucson: University of Arizona Press, 1984); Hugh Ross, *Navigating Genesis: A Scientist's Journey through Genesis 1–11* (Covina, CA: RTB Press, 2014), 75–77.

6. Exodus 12:38.

7. 1 Kings 4:34; 10:1–9.

8. Daniel 2:48–49; 5:16, 29; 6:3, 25–28.

9. Esther 8:7–10:3.

10. Esther 10:2–3.

11. Ralph Winter, "The Diminishing Task: The Field and the Force," *Mission Frontiers*, January–February 1991, http://www.missionfrontiers.org/issue/article/the-diminishing-task.

## Appendix A Why Not Life on a Moon?

1. Lena Noack and Doris Breuer, "Plate Tectonics on Rocky Exoplanets: Influence of Initial Conditions and Mantle Rheology," *Planetary and Space Science* 98 (August 2014): 41–49; John D. A. Piper, "A Planetary Perspective on Earth Evolution: Lid Tectonics before Plate Tectonics," *Tectonophysics* 589 (March 2013): 44–56; Bradford J. Foley, David Bercovici, and William Landuyt, "The Conditions for Plate Tectonics on Super-Earths: Inferences from Convection Models with Damage," *Earth and Planetary Science Letters* 331–332 (May 2012): 281–90; Vlada Stamenković et al., "The Influence of Pressure-Dependent Viscosity on the Thermal Evolution of Super-Earths," *Astrophysical Journal* 748 (March 2012): id. 41, doi:10.1088/0004-637X/748/1/41; H. J. van Heck and Paul J. Tackley, "Plate Tectonics on Super-Earths: Equally or More Likely Than on Earth," *Earth and Planetary Science Letters* 310 (October 2011): 252–61; Craig O'Neill, "A Window of Opportunity for Plate Tectonics in Evolution of Earth-Like Planets?," American Geophysical Union, Fall Meeting 2011 (December 2011): abstract P24B-05.

2. High eccentricity here is defined as an orbit where the eccentricity measure is e ≥ 0.07, where the closest approach of the planet to its host star is a(1 − e) and the farthest distance of the planet from its host star is a(1 + e), where a = the semimajor axis of the planet's orbit. Of the 54 planets, 47 exhibit orbits where e ≥ 0.10. The data for gas giant planets was taken from the catalog section of *The Extrasolar Planets Encyclopaedia*, accessed October 30, 2014, http://exoplanet.eu/.

3. René Heller et al., "Formation, Habitability, and Detection of Extrasolar Moons," *Astrobiology* 14 (September 2014): 798–835.

### Appendix B  Are We Alone in the Universe?

1. Michel Mayor and Didier Queloz, "A Jupiter-Mass Companion to a Solar-Type Star," *Nature* 378 (November 1995): 355–59.

2. Jorge Meléndez et al., "The Peculiar Solar Composition and Its Possible Relation to Planet Formation," *Astrophysical Journal Letters* 704 (October 2009): L66–L70; G. F. Porto de Mello and L. da Silva, "HR 6060: The Closest Ever Solar Twin?," *Astrophysical Journal Letters* 482 (June 1997): L89–L92; Jorge Meléndez, Katie Dodds-Eden, and José A. Robles, "HD 98618: A Star Closely Resembling Our Sun," *Astrophysical Journal Letters* 641 (April 2006): L133–L136; Y. Takeda et al., "Behavior of Li Abundances in Solar Analog Stars: Evidence for Line-Width Dependence," *Astronomy and Astrophysics* 468 (June 2007): 663–77; Jorge Meléndez and Iván Ramírez, "HIP 56948: A Solar Twin with a Low Lithium Abundance," *Astrophysical Journal Letters* 669 (November 2007): L89; Hugh Ross, "Search for the Sun's Twin," *Today's New Reason To Believe* (blog), March 17, 2008, http://www .reasons.org/articles/search-for-the-suns-twin; Hugh Ross, "Rare Solar System, Rare Sun," *Today's New Reason To Believe* (blog), December 14, 2009, http://www.reasons.org/articles /rare-solar-system-rare-sun.

3. Matthew 28:20.

# Index

# Index

# Index

# Index

Index

**Hugh Ross** (PhD, University of Toronto) is founder and president of Reasons to Believe (www.reasons.org). He is the author of many books, including *More Than a Theory* and *Why the Universe Is the Way It Is*. An astronomer and a member of the pastoral staff of a church near Caltech, Ross has addressed students and faculty on over 300 campuses in the United States and abroad on a wide variety of science-faith topics. From science conferences to churches to government and private research labs, Ross presents powerful evidence for a purpose-filled universe. He lives in the Los Angeles area.

## ABOUT REASONS TO BELIEVE

Uniquely positioned within the science-faith discussion since 1986, Reasons to Believe (RTB) communicates that science and faith are, and always will be, allies, not enemies. Distinguished for integrating science and faith respectfully and with integrity, RTB welcomes dialogue with both skeptics and believers. Addressing topics such as the origin of the universe, the origin and history of life, and the origin, history, and destiny of humanity, RTB's website offers a vast array of helpful resources. Through their books, blogs, podcasts, and speaking events, RTB scholars present powerful reasons from science to trust in the reliability of the Bible and the message it conveys about creation and redemption.

*For more information, contact us via:*
www.reasons.org
818 S. Oak Park Rd. Covina, CA 91724
(855) REASONS

# CHECK OUT THESE OTHER
## **REASONS TO BELIEVE** RESOURCES . . .

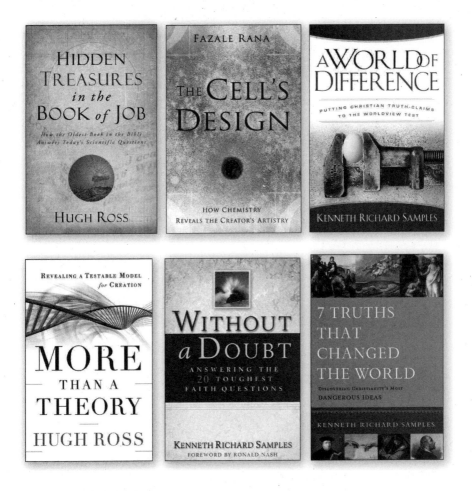

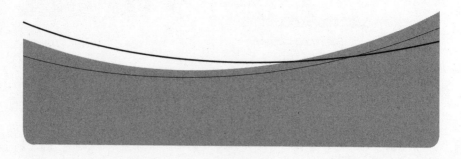